THE THEATRE OF D.H. LAWRENCE

James Moran is Professor of Modern Engl...
University of Nottingham, UK. Hi...
Seán O'Casey (Bloom... ...er
Rising (2005), and h ...egional
Modernisms (2013)

Also available in the Critical Companions series from Bloomsbury Methuen Drama:

BRITISH THEATRE AND PERFORMANCE 1900–1950
by Rebecca D'Monté

THE IRISH DRAMATIC REVIVAL 1899–1939
by Anthony Roche

MODERN ASIAN THEATRE AND PERFORMANCE 1900–2000
by Kevin J. Wetmore, Siyuan Liu and Erin B. Mee

THE PLAYS OF SAMUEL BECKETT
by Katherine Weiss

THE THEATRE OF JEZ BUTTERWORTH
by David Ian Rabey

THE THEATRE OF CARYL CHURCHILL
By R. Darren Gobert

THE THEATRE OF MARTIN CRIMP: SECOND EDITION
by Aleks Sierz

THE THEATRE OF BRIAN FRIEL: TRADITION AND MODERNITY
by Christopher Murray

THE THEATRE OF DAVID GREIG
by Clare Wallace

THE THEATRE AND FILMS OF MARTIN MCDONAGH
by Patrick Lonergan

THE THEATRE OF SEÁN O'CASEY
by James Moran

THE THEATRE OF HAROLD PINTER
by Mark Taylor-Batty

THE THEATRE OF TIMBERLAKE WERTENBAKER
by Sophie Bush

THE THEATRE OF TENNESSEE WILLIAMS
by Brenda Murphy

THE THEATRE OF D.H. LAWRENCE

DRAMATIC MODERNIST AND THEATRICAL INNOVATOR

James Moran

Series Editors: Patrick Lonergan and Kevin J. Wetmore, Jr.

Bloomsbury Methuen Drama
An imprint of Bloomsbury Publishing Plc

B L O O M S B U R Y
LONDON · NEW DELHI · NEW YORK · SYDNEY

Bloomsbury Methuen Drama

An imprint of Bloomsbury Publishing Plc

Imprint previously known as Methuen Drama

50 Bedford Square	1385 Broadway
London	New York
WC1B 3DP	NY 10018
UK	USA

www.bloomsbury.com

BLOOMSBURY, METHUEN DRAMA and the Diana logo are trademarks of Bloomsbury Publishing Plc

First published 2015

British Library Cataloguing-in-Publication Data
A catalogue record for this book is available from the British Library.

ISBN:	HB:	978-1-4725-7038-3
	PB:	978-1-4725-7037-6
	ePDF:	978-1-4725-7040-6
	ePub:	978-1-4725-7039-0

Library of Congress Cataloging-in-Publication Data
Moran, James, 1978–
The theatre of D. H. Lawrence : dramatic modernist and theatrical innovator / James Moran.
pages cm. — (Critical companions)
Includes bibliographical references and index.
ISBN 978-1-4725-7038-3 (hardback) — ISBN 978-1-4725-7037-6 (paperback)
1. Lawrence, D. H. (David Herbert), 1885–1930—Dramatic works. I. Title.
PR6023.A93Z6885 2015
822'.912—dc23
2015010417

Typeset by RefineCatch Limited, Bungay, Suffolk
Printed and bound in India

For Alana and Michael Moran

Just as I was getting over the last stages of flu, my agent called to say that one of Lawrence's plays was being performed, *The Widowing of Mrs Holroyd*. Did I want to go?

'When is it?' I said.

'Thursday night'.

'Oh, Thursday I'm going to see Nusrat'.

'Who?'

'Nusrat Fateh Ali Khan, the qawali singer. That's a shame. I would like to have come', I said, thinking how fortunate it was that they overlapped. I had not been to the theatre for twenty years and I had no intention of going again now. It was not even a question of liking or disliking the theatre. The important thing was the pleasure that came from not being interested in the theatre. I am interested in all sorts of things but it is lovely to not be interested in the theatre. Not being interested in the theatre means a whole area of life and culture means nothing to me: there are entire pages of the listing magazines that I don't need to consult, vast areas of conversation I don't need to take part in, great wads of cash that I don't need to consider parting with. It is bliss, not being interested in the theatre. Not being interested in the theatre provides me with more happiness than all the things I am interested in put together.[1]

---

[1] Geoff Dyer, *Out of Sheer Rage: In the Shadow of D.H. Lawrence* (London: Abacus, 1997), p.205.

CONTENTS

FOREWORD
Sir Richard Eyre

Like most of my generation – I'm now 70 – I grew up admiring Lawrence's novels for their sexual openness, their pictures of working-class life and their concern to embrace everything – passion, ideas, aspiration and desperation. 'There is no such thing as sin', he said, 'There is only life and anti-life'.[1] Reputations are fickle. Now Lawrence's poetry is admired, his novels neglected, his paintings scorned and his plays largely unperformed. What's more he is reviled for his priapism, his fascism and his sexism. I can't think of Lawrence as being bound by any 'ism'; I still think of him as a fine novelist, a brilliant poet and one of the very best (and least celebrated) of twentieth-century English playwrights.

The first thing to realize about Lawrence's best plays – *A Collier's Friday Night*, *The Widowing of Mrs Holroyd* and *The Daughter-in-Law* – is that they aren't novelist's offcuts: they're skilled and instinctive. He wrote them early in life convinced, not that he was joining a movement, but that he was starting one: 'We have to hate our immediate predecessors to get free from their authority'.[2] Most of all, he distanced himself from the elite at the Royal Court Theatre, then run by Harley Granville Barker and premiering plays by Shaw, Ibsen, Maeterlinck, Galsworthy, Masefield, Yeats and Hauptmann:

> I believe that, just as an audience was found in Russia for Tchekhov, so an audience might be found in England for some of my stuff, if there were a man to whip 'em in. It's the producer that is lacking, not the audience. I am sure we are sick of the rather bony, bloodless drama we get nowadays – it is time for a reaction against Shaw and Galsworthy and Barker and Irishy (except Synge) people – the rule and measure mathematical folk.[3]

So Lawrence wrote for a theatre that didn't exist – more national, more regional and less middle-class than even Barker or Shaw imagined. The grandness of the characters' emotions and the nuance of what happens between them is expressed in dialect. It's supple, strong and beautiful, authentic and an accurate delineation of class distinctions. But it meant that the plays fell foul of the first law of English aesthetics, which is that working-class life is a low form, art is a high one, and the two don't mix. It's a further reminder of how few English writers write with authority about the working class. 'Why don't you speak ordinary English?' says Lady Chatterley to Mellors. 'I thowt it *wor* ordinary', he replies.[4] So Lawrence had to wait until 1968 – nearly 40 years after his death – for his reputation as a playwright to be made, when a season of his plays was presented at the Royal Court, flawlessly directed by Peter Gill.

A Collier's Friday Night is a sensuous exploration of the themes that would evolve into *Sons and Lovers* – the way in which sexual and spiritual love is bound up inextricably with class and with society. Lawrence's plays are concerned with what it means to live in an industrial age, to hold on to your own self when everything conspires to obliterate it. His characters endure by enduring as Lawrence endured in the face of poverty, controversy, condemnation and illness. 'We've got to live', he wrote, 'no matter how many skies have fallen'.[5]

The Widowing of Mrs Holroyd is a short, packed tragedy of working life: it owes a lot to Synge's *Riders to the Sea* but has an added sexual ambiguity. 'I wish I could write such dialogue', said Shaw when he saw Lawrence's play. 'With mine I always hear the sound of the typewriter'.[6]

The Daughter-in-Law is Lawrence's masterpiece. Its themes (if you can describe anything as subtle and organic as 'themes') are sex, class, dependence and freedom – all couched in the language of a mining community, whose speech is both authentic and poetic: it's true playwrighting. But Lawrence has a concern that is rare in playwrights: a love of the physical, the way that men and women use their bodies to work, or wash, or eat, or touch, or avoid each other. Minnie, the daughter-in-law, has ideas above her station: a relic of her years 'i' service'.[7] But Lawrence never sneers at her pretensions in the way that a middle-class writer would: they're lovingly drawn. When it's revealed that her husband has made a local girl pregnant, neither Minnie nor anyone else pretends to be shocked: they're too grown-up.

What follows is a meditation on themes of sex, dependence and freedom. Minnie is affronted by what the episode reveals about her husband's moral laziness: only his mother (he feels) deserves the best of him, and that's the trouble. Joe, his brother, is the family joker: now he reveals a sense of tragic incompleteness. Brought up under his mother's wing, adored and dominated, he's doomed to eternal adolescence. The mother – a daughter, wife and mother of miners – is challenging, wily, articulate: so are they all. The test of

Foreword

any play is whether the characters exist outside it; with Lawrence, the blood of real humanity pulses through every word.

Sir Richard Eyre is a theatre, film, television and opera director. He acted as director of the National Theatre of Great Britain between 1988 and 1997, was a governor of the BBC from 1997 to 2003, and is a five-time Olivier award winner.

ACKNOWLEDGEMENTS

First and foremost, I am grateful to Soudabeh Ananisarab, Richard Eyre, Peter Gill, William Ivory and Stephen Lowe for producing their insightful contributions to this volume with such speed and good humour. Without their assistance this book would have been far less enjoyable to research and to write. I am also thankful to Kerry Mason and the wonderful year-ten drama students at Eastwood's Hall-Park Academy for tolerating my attempts at directing and helping me to see how Lawrence's texts might translate into performance. Martin Berry at the Lakeside Arts Theatre proved similarly kind in allowing me to intrude into his rehearsal room, whilst my colleagues at BBC Radio Nottingham, particularly Michaela Atkins and Verity Cowley, have been generous in allowing me to test my ideas about Lawrence on a wider audience. Claire Bates and her co-workers at the D.H. Lawrence Heritage Centre, the staff of Eastwood library and Nottingham University archives, and Annalise Grice at Nottingham's School of English, have all been sustained sources of assistance and good sense; and I remain deeply indebted to Joseph Anderton, Jo Guy, Vic Merriman, Lynda Pratt and Julie Sanders for helping me to secure the time and space that I needed in order to complete the research. Much of the theatrical thinking that underpins this volume also derives from invigorating conversations and co-teaching with Janette Dillon, Sarah Grandage, Sam Haddow, Brean Hammond, Peter Kirwan, Gordon Ramsay, Jo Robinson and Lucie Sutherland.

This book is made possible by the British Academy's support via the Mid-Career Fellowship scheme. I am grateful to the British Academy for this help, and to the University of Nottingham for allowing me to take up the fellowship. I am also thankful to Lionel Pilkington and the directors of the Moore Institute for the award of a visiting fellowship that allowed me to write part of this book in the congenial environment of NUI Galway. At Bloomsbury, I have been greatly helped by Mark Dudgeon, Emily Hockley and Patrick Lonergan, and the two anonymous readers whose suggestions vastly improved my original motley proposal. Most of all, I would like to thank two of 'the black-gowned priests of knowledge' at Nottingham University: my colleagues Andrew Harrison and John Worthen, who have been the very model of scholarly

Acknowledgements

generosity and personal kindness during this project. Without their advice, encouragement and friendship this book could never have been written. Finally, as always, I'd like to thank Maria, Thomas and Joseph for their forbearance and love.

Various poems and quotations from both published and unpublished works by D.H. Lawrence reprinted by permission of Pollinger Limited (www.pollingerltd.com) on behalf of the estate of Frieda Lawrence Ravagli. Extracts from unpublished letters by Frieda Lawrence Ravagli reprinted by permission of Pollinger Limited (www.pollingerltd.com) on behalf of the Estate of Frieda Lawrence Ravagli. I am grateful for permission to reprint unpublished material from Manuscripts and Special Collections, The University of Nottingham. The interview with Peter Gill is by kind permission of Peter Gill care of Casarotto Ramsay & Associates Ltd., 7–12 Noel Street, London W1F 8GQ (info@casarotto.co.uk). United Artists have been generous in allowing me to quote from unpublished material by Sir Peter Hall. For the UK and Commonwealth, I am grateful to quote from *Out of Sheer Rage: In the Shadow of D.H. Lawrence* by Geoff Dyer, published in Great Britain by Canongate Books Ltd, 14 High Street, Edinburgh, EH1 1TE. For all other territories, excerpt from *Out of Sheer Rage: In the Shadow of D.H. Lawrence* by Geoff Dyer. Copyright © 1997 by Geoff Dyer. Reprinted by permission of Farrar, Straus and Giroux, LLC.

OVERVIEW

D.H. Lawrence wrote eight full-length plays during his lifetime, as well as two incomplete dramatic works. Yet only two of these scripts were performed whilst he was alive, and he never personally saw any of his writing produced in the playhouse. The influential critic F.R. Leavis later praised the author simply as *D.H. Lawrence: Novelist*, and today Lawrence's reputation still largely rests on his novels. It would be easy to see the plays as something interesting but inessential, to be placed alongside Lawrence's idiosyncratic studies of the unconscious, or the derivative school history-book that he wrote. The plays might be important for Lawrence devotees, but are scarcely likely to trouble the great tradition of twentieth-century literature. After all, as Lawrence himself declared in a letter of November 1912 to his friend Edward Garnett, 'I don't know much about plays'.[1]

However, this book makes the argument that Lawrence remained deeply concerned with performed drama throughout his career, proved himself a skilled if somewhat undeveloped playwright, and that the theatrical element of his work is key to understanding Lawrence's development and his overall achievement as a writer. Although the reputation of Lawrence's plays has fluctuated, they have nonetheless impressed and influenced a range of important theatrical thinkers, from Seán O'Casey and G.B. Shaw, to Raymond Williams and Richard Eyre.

Lawrence's talent as a playwright was to speak about day-to-day personal relationships, particularly those of the overlooked mining communities in the English East Midlands, yet do so through a sophisticated set of theatrical techniques, which he discovered by reading and watching an impressive range of drama. From an early age Lawrence proved a keen playgoer, and this interest continued into his mature period when he studied and described various kinds of performance, from puppet theatre in Italy to Native-American ritual in the USA. Lawrence's plays, then, may often appear to describe his hometown of Eastwood, but some of the most innovative moments in those scripts rely upon an eclectic and international theatrical palette.

However, a combination of bad luck and poor judgement led to Lawrence's ambitions being stymied in playhouse production, and so, instead, he ploughed his theatrical interests into essays, novels and short fiction. Paradoxically, then, some of his most original dramatic ideas appear in writings that were never intended for actors, and an awareness of theatrical innovation suffuses some of his best-known novels. *The Theatre of D.H. Lawrence* highlights the fact that many of the novels' familiar concerns with sexual experience were, in fact, derived from ideas that he associated with drama, and this volume also examines the way that Lawrence repeatedly engaged with the theatrically experimental throughout his career.

However, in recent years, much of Lawrence's work has been neglected, and parts of his oeuvre have generated hostility for expressing regressive social, racial and sexual attitudes. With the decline of Leavisite criticism in the latter part of the twentieth century, and following the 1970 publication of Kate Millett's important feminist text, *Sexual Politics*, Lawrence's work vanished from many undergraduate reading lists. By 1991, the critic Jonathan Dollimore had characterized Lawrence as, 'This increasingly disregarded and often despised writer.'[2] Yet in the final four chapters of this book, the director Peter Gill, the playwright Stephen Lowe, the screenwriter William Ivory and the theatre historian Soudabeh Ananisarab show how a theatrical consideration of Lawrence reveals him as an enduring and artistically inspiring figure. Fiona Becket may have observed in 2004 that, 'Critical interest in Lawrence's plays has been relatively slight', and Ian Clarke may have noted in 2001 that, 'No other generic body of Lawrence's work has suffered such extensive obscurity', but the four new interventions at the end of this volume raise the suggestive idea that, in performances from the Royal Court to *Coronation Street*, Lawrence's dramatic thinking has continued to exert an influence.[3]

Furthermore, despite the criticisms that have been made of Lawrence, his drama has the potential to emphasize the structures of injustice that still exist in the twenty-first century. Jeremy Seabrook has argued that modern Britain – with all of its elevation of the rich – has simply institutionalized the unfairness of the industrial age, since when material comforts have always been acquired 'at the costs of others, largely invisible to the modest beneficiaries of the violence done to them.'[4]

As I tap away at my laptop computer, for example, I generally avoid thinking about those in the Congo who mine the coltan that allows such devices to run. But, as the introductory chapter of this study will show, Lawrence used playwriting to point back, insistently, to the lives of the poor, to the graft of industrial communities and to the daily toil of female work in particular. He wanted spectators to visualize the individual human faces of labourers and mining families, and to see these lives in full seriousness and complexity. Of course, the daily business of such life has changed enormously within Britain during the last century, and there is no longer a mining community in Lawrence's hometown. But the condescension that Lawrence battled against still remains. As Owen Jones has argued, British popular and political discourses in the early twenty-first century have often seen the poor being marginalized and dismissed as cartoonish and feckless.[5] By contrast, in Lawrence's dramatic work, we find an attempt to represent the detailed nuances of working-class life, and to make an unsentimental version of that life central to the public forum of the theatre stage.

INTRODUCTION
THE SIGNIFICANCE OF LAWRENCE'S PLAYS: SHIFTS IN REPUTATION FROM 1930 TO 2014

The dead playwright

In March 1930 D.H. Lawrence died of pleurisy and tuberculosis at the age of 44. During his life, he had written eight complete plays as well as two unfinished dramatic sketches. Yet only three of those scripts had actually been published. The first play, *The Widowing of Mrs Holroyd*, had appeared in 1914; *Touch and Go* in 1920; and *David* in 1926. Accordingly, when Martin Secker published the posthumous volume *The Plays of D.H. Lawrence* in 1933, the volume contained just this incongruous trio of pieces. For many years afterwards, Lawrence's reputation as a dramatist relied on a partial assessment of his oeuvre, and it would take until the mid-1960s for all of Lawrence's full-length plays to appear in print.[1]

Some of Lawrence's obituarists did gamely attempt to highlight his playwriting, but an accurate critical overview proved difficult, as readers could only access three examples of his plays, written in contrasting styles at very different moments from Lawrence's career. He had, after all, penned *David* a decade and a half after, and nearly five thousand miles away, from first composing *The Widowing of Mrs Holroyd*. Nonetheless, the *Manchester Guardian* pointed to *David* as 'the best of his plays', although this work was unlikely to win a permanent place in the theatrical repertoire, featuring, as it does, at least fifty-eight onstage characters, and revolving around a mode of epic storytelling that would not be embraced by the Anglophone stage until well into the second half of the century.[2] The obituary in *The Times* described *The Widowing of Mrs Holroyd* as 'so far biographical as to tell the world that his father was a coalminer and his mother a woman of finer grain', a reductive summary that raised the question of why such a text would appeal to the theatregoer who cared little about the details of Lawrence's life.[3] Meanwhile, that year also saw the publication of Amy Lowell's posthumous volume *Poetry and Poets* (1930), which reprised her decade-old praise of *Touch and Go*. Lowell pointed out that Lawrence's play concerned itself with the clash between Capital and Labour, and wrote that 'Mr. Lawrence has courageously uttered a truth which will be popular with neither side, largely because it is the stark truth'.[4] Lowell approved of the script, but her idea that *Touch and Go* risked unpopularity was again scarcely likely to cause a stampede towards Lawrence by theatre producers.

Lowell had been one of Lawrence's friends and correspondents, yet even such acquaintances could be dismissive of his dramatic writing. Richard Aldington, for example, had known Lawrence well, but in 1950 wrote: 'Except for *David* I am bound to say I think Lawrence's plays almost negligible. I don't think he had any real "theatre" in him. The play was not his form'.[5] In fact, Aldington had a personal reason for bearing a grudge with Lawrence over the theatre, as Lawrence had declined to give a public endorsement to some of Aldington's own playwriting in the 1920s.[6] Additionally, like almost everyone else during this period, Aldington never knew the play that Richard Eyre hails as 'Lawrence's masterpiece'. Although written in 1913, *The Daughter-in-Law* had to wait for more than half a century before being published in 1965, and even then appeared in a highly corrupt version that garbled many of Lawrence's lines. Readers were left trying to decipher misprints such as 'he's *never* up to the cratch'.[7] Indeed, when the play first premiered, at the Traverse Theatre in 1967, the reviewer for *The Times* even got the title wrong and applauded a piece called 'The *Mother*-in-Law'.[8] Only with the publication of the Cambridge edition of Lawrence's plays in 1999 did an authoritative version of *The Daughter-in-Law* emerge, with the volume's editors lamenting that 'actors, directors, and audiences have been struggling to make sense of words and phrases for which no obvious meaning exists'.[9]

Crucially, at the time of Lawrence's death, *The Daughter-in-Law* and another of his most accomplished scripts, *A Collier's Friday Night*, remained unknown. *A Collier's Friday Night* went unprinted until 1934, although when it finally appeared it won praise from the dramatist Seán O'Casey. O'Casey argued that, 'Had Lawrence got the encouragement the play called for and deserved, England might have had a great dramatist'.[10] At this time O'Casey had tried and failed to establish himself in the British theatrical world, and felt riled by the critical and commercial success of rivals such as Noël Coward, so the Irishman sympathized with Lawrence as another outsiderly writer who had sought to depict working-class life. Admittedly, O'Casey's version of working-class dialogue veers towards a more heightened alliterative effect than the poetry of day-to-day speech that is found in most of Lawrence's plays, but there nevertheless existed a sufficient affinity between their writings for the Dubliner to laud *A Collier's Friday Night* for giving 'an acute scene of a clash between woman and man, and woman and woman. Not as a cocktail-nourished dramatist gives them gives he them unto us [. . .] neither is there in it the sound of silken garments moving, but there is the sweat of life in it'.[11]

O'Casey's friend, George Bernard Shaw, expressed similarly positive sentiments. Shaw had seen *The Widowing of Mrs Holroyd* in 1926, and reportedly declared, 'Compared to that, my prose is machine-made lace', before publishing an article that praised the 'vividly effective' speech in the play.[12] Indeed, Lawrence's ability to script effective dialogue was one of the features of his work that was most admired by modernist poet-playwrights. T.S. Eliot may not have seen Lawrence's plays, but read the novel *Aaron's Rod* and pronounced that 'there is one scene in this book – a dialogue between an Italian and several Englishmen, in which one feels that the whole is governed by a creator who is purely creator, with the terrifying disinterestedness of the true creator'.[13] Similarly, when W.B. Yeats read *Lady Chatterley's Lover* he expressed admiration for the way that, when Mellors and Connie talk, 'the coarse language of the one, accepted by both, becomes a forlorn poetry uniting their solitudes, something ancient, humble and terrible'.[14]

Yet despite such positive verdicts on Lawrence's ability to craft dialogue, for most of the twentieth century his reputation as a dramatist remained undistinguished. Martin Secker planned, but then abandoned, a project to publish a volume of Lawrence's plays in 1934.[15] Subsequently, in 1936–1938, there appeared a brief flurry of British and Swedish productions of 'An Unrevised Play by D.H. Lawrence', entitled *My Son's My Son*. But that drama turned out to be a version of *The Daughter-in-Law* that had been altered and adapted by the novelist Walter Greenwood.[16] Much as Nahum Tate had rewritten Shakespeare's *King Lear* in the late seventeenth century, so Greenwood sought to bring a more resolved conclusion to Lawrence's unknown work, and, ultimately, Greenwood's new script generated better reviews for himself than for Lawrence. Critics tended to concur with the view of the *Evening Standard*, that Greenwood was 'well qualified' to finish the drama, but that Lawrence's script 'rambled too much from one theme to another'.[17] Meanwhile, Lawrence's original plays remained rarely seen in performance. Audiences watched a smattering of isolated productions during the 1920s and 1930s, and then almost nothing during the 1940s and 1950s.[18]

Mid-century reassessments

In 1955, Lawrence's critical reputation was boosted by the publication of F.R. Leavis's *D.H. Lawrence: Novelist*, which argues that Lawrence is 'our last great writer; he is still the great writer of our own phase of civilization'.[19] But Leavis had little time for Lawrence the dramatist and avoided mentioning the plays. As Richard Storer points out, for Leavis, 'Theatrical performance was just an opportunity for actors and directors to get in the way of the essential critical process. "How I hate actors" Leavis once wrote, "being myself histrionic"'.[20] Nonetheless, Leavis did at times reach for the language of playhouse in order to describe what he found most admirable about Lawrence. For example, in *D.H. Lawrence: Novelist*, when Leavis begins his discussion of *Women in Love*, he praises both the way that the fiction presents 'a self-dramatization of Lawrence' and how parts of the novel work 'by dramatic and poetic means'.[21] Furthermore, in Leavis's later and less famous study *Thought, Words and Creativity* (1976), he commends Lawrence's writing about international theatrical performance. Here Leavis recommends the chapter in Lawrence's *Twilight in Italy* (1916) entitled 'The Theatre', and argues that this piece revealed Lawrence to be:

> [A]s great a critic as there has ever been. It shows what penetration he had turned on Shakespeare. But what I want to stress at the moment is the ease with which he got on with all kinds of casually encountered people [. . .] This characteristic was the secret of his dramatic power.[22]

Later in *Thought, Words and Creativity*, Leavis went on to recommended two other essays that Lawrence had written about ritual drama ('The Dance of the Sprouting Corn' and 'The Hopi Snake Dance'), both of which had first appeared during 1924 in the journal *Theatre Arts Monthly*. Leavis declared, 'These, in their marvellousness, are truly important'.[23] Thus, although he may have been temperamentally disinclined to analyse plays, Leavis did recognize the power of the theatrical in Lawrence's work.

The publication of *D.H. Lawrence: Novelist* was followed by the Lady Chatterley trial in 1960, further raising Lawrence's public profile. The trial concluded with Penguin acquitted of obscenity, and the publisher then shifted two million copies of *Lady Chatterley's Lover* within the year.[24] At this point, Lawrence's dramatic work finally attracted popular attention. After all, his plays avoid sentimentality, cherish ambiguity, and describe the disorder of personal relationships in a way that looked strikingly modern during the decade that saw the introduction of Britain's Abortion Act and Divorce Reform Act. For example, the main male character of *The Daughter-in-Law* discovers that he has impregnated a woman who is not his wife, and then regrets having ever married at all; *A Collier's Friday Night* depicts a father who spends his time drinking at the pub before returning home to berate his wife as 'you begrudging bitch'; and when a corpse appears in *The Widowing of Mrs Holroyd*, it is not the body of a faithful husband whose grieving wife has always loved him, but the carcass of a lascivious drunk whose wife was on the cusp of fleeing to Spain with another man.[25] In the 1960s, such storylines found a new purchase, and *The Widowing of Mrs Holroyd* became the first of Lawrence's plays to appear on television, when Granada showed Ken Taylor's hour-long adaptation in 1961.[26]

This broadcast received positive reviews, and the reports reached a young theatre director, Peter Gill, who then mounted a version of *A Collier's Friday Night* for the English Stage Company at the Royal Court in 1965. This pared-down production had neither sets nor properly printed programmes, but nevertheless delighted the newspaper critics, with the *Daily Telegraph* noting that Lawrence's work manifests 'a true feeling for the stage and for dialogue that encourages acting'.[27] In the same year, Heinemann published *The Complete Plays*, making available all eight of Lawrence's full-length theatre scripts for the first time (as well as two incomplete plays). Next, in 1967, Peter Gill went on to produce *The Daughter-in-Law* at the Royal Court, with *The Times*'s critic Irving Wardle declaring:

> Peter Gill's beautiful production two years ago of Lawrence's first play, *A Collier's Friday Night*, exploded in one night the idea that Lawrence the dramatist could safely be ignored. Mr Gill has now followed it up with a later piece which, like much of Lawrence's dramatic output, had only appeared in academic journals before the collected edition of 1965. And again the production leaves you amazed that such a work could have been neglected.[28]

Gill now realized that this play, *The Daughter-in-Law*, together with *A Collier's Friday Night* and *The Widowing of Mrs Holroyd*, might form a trilogy of work all set in the domestic spaces of mining towns that resemble Eastwood, the location in the English Midlands where Lawrence was born and raised. Between February and April 1968 the Royal Court therefore performed these three plays together in repertory for a season, and the works of this 'Eastwood Trilogy' have tended to be grouped together since that time. A 1969 Penguin paperback edition published the three scripts alongside an introduction by Raymond Williams, who dismissed the notion that the plays 'were a sideline, or even a mistake' and argued that instead Lawrence presented 'a theatre of ordinary feeling raised to intensity and community by the writing of ordinary speech'.[29]

Of course, Lawrence had scarcely been thinking about creating a grouping of three dramas when he wrote those pieces. There are in fact five plays that would have an equally good claim for inclusion as part of an 'Eastwood Trilogy': *A Collier's Friday Night*, *The Widowing of Mrs Holroyd*, *The Merry-go-Round*, *The Daughter-in-Law* and *Touch and Go* are all set in or around recognizable versions of Lawrence's hometown. Even *The Fight for Barbara*, which has an Italian setting, nonetheless features a male protagonist who is the son of a coal miner and who uses the language of Lawrence's English Midlands ('Not a scroddy atom' (243)). Still, from 1969, three of Lawrence's best plays had become available in the sort of paperback edition that suited both the student budget and the amateur thespian in need of inexpensive scripts that could be easily marked up during rehearsal. Michael Marland also published a version of *The Widowing of Mrs Holroyd* and *The Daughter-in-Law* in 1968, which the *Times Literary Supplement* reviewed by saying that *The Daughter-in-Law* was 'a fine and moving piece of work' that 'ought to be as well known as *Sons and Lovers* and the best Nottinghamshire stories'.[30]

The 'Eastwood Trilogy' of plays at the Royal Court received widespread critical praise, with this depiction of working-class life having a particular appeal in the era following the 1944 Butler Education Act, which enabled many poor British children to transcend the material circumstances of their parents, and to feel a consequent pang of recognition at encountering Lawrence's theatrical vision. In *The Times*, Michael Billington described *The Widowing of Mrs Holroyd* as 'a powerful, controlled piece of writing, full of rich dialect, quiet humour and strong emotional collisions', and when he saw the Royal Court's subsequent performance of Lawrence's comedy, *The Merry-go-Round*, he wrote in the *Guardian*, 'The deeper the Royal Court ventures into D.H. Lawrence's plays, the more obvious it becomes that the British theatre has been sitting on a goldmine'.[31] Following such enthusiasm, in 1975 Sylvia Sklar published an academic study of Lawrence's plays in which she urged 'that all of Lawrence's plays should be looked at with attention by everyone who has the best interests of the English-speaking theatre at heart'.[32]

The rediscovery of Lawrence's work at the Royal Court came in the wake of John Osborne's 1956 play *Look Back In Anger*, a contemporary, realistic drama about the dissatisfactions of existence in the English Midlands.[33] Osborne's success – followed shortly afterwards by that of Arnold Wesker – heralded the arrival of the 'angry young men', who felt determined to depict the lives of ordinary people on the stage, and were willing to offer a penetrating critique of society, even if that analysis involved the upsetting or unpalatable. By these lights, Lawrence's drama looked prescient. After all, here was another writer of central England whose working-class drama was passionate, committed and grittily realistic, and whose plays had been set around the kitchen sink for more than forty years. Indeed, when Lawrence's *The Fight for Barbara* appeared in 1967 at London's Mermaid Theatre, the *Daily Mail* commented: 'We are getting used to the idea that Lawrence was no mean playwright and this first performance of a play he wrote in 1912 is further evidence [. . .] If this play had seen the light of day sooner, *Look Back in Anger* might not have seemed so original.'[34]

However, although Osborne's early work now garnered a great deal of attention, a set of competing revolutions in theatre taste had also been set in motion during this period. Samuel Beckett's *Waiting for Godot* premiered in English in 1955, and Bertolt Brecht's Berliner Ensemble first performed in London in August 1956, so there developed, as Toril Moi puts it, 'a modern scepticism that makes us feel that ordinary language and everyday actions fail to provide good enough expression of pain and joy.'[35] A living playwright could try to navigate through such changing theatrical currents. John Osborne, for example, acted in a production of Brecht's *The Good Woman of Setzuan* in late 1956, incorporated epic elements into his 1957 play *The Entertainer*, and produced a full-blown Brechtian work called *Luther* in 1961.[36] Needless to say, a dead dramatist could scarcely respond to varying theatrical tastes in the same way. After the successful staging of Lawrence's plays at the Royal Court in 1968, they had been firmly established, in the words of Michael Billington, as 'a superb example of stage naturalism at its microscopic best', and this perception may have been off-putting to some producers and directors who viewed such a style as passé.[37] To his credit, Peter Gill tried to draw attention to the broader range of Lawrence's drama by producing *The Merry-go-Round* at the Royal Court in 1973, but a number of the other plays from outside the established 'Eastwood Trilogy' – such as *The Fight for Barbara* and *The Married Man* – remained largely ignored and have hardly ever been seen in production.[38] As we shall see in Chapter 4, Lawrence can scarcely be thought an unexperimental dramatic writer: his early theatrical realism was far from formally conservative, and his later thinking about theatre repeatedly moved him into the orbit of Europe's avant garde. But perhaps what might have been needed in order to sustain interest in Lawrence's drama into the 1970s was for a professional company to stage his late plays *David* or *Touch and Go* in a Brechtian manner, or to perform his comedies from 1910 to 1912 by exaggerating their surreal and fantastical elements.

Influence on playwrights

Nonetheless, Lawrence did exert an influence over the following generation of playwrights, with such dramatists often proving themselves ahead of the academics in analysing Lawrence's writing. For instance, in 1973, the literary critic Frank Kermode pointed out that:

> Chapter XVI of *Lady Chatterley's Lover* contains what has become the most controversial passage in all of Lawrence's novels. The fact that it describes anal intercourse was long ignored; nobody mentioned it at the 1960 trial [...] As in *Women in Love*, the climactic sexual act is an act of buggery, conceived as a burning out of shame.[39]

David Lodge has declared that Kermode 'radically and convincingly reinterpreted Lawrence', yet, in truth, such sexual ideas had not been completely overlooked before Kermode.[40] Samuel Beckett, for one, had read Lawrence's prose and found 'lovely things as usual and plenty of rubbish', having probably first encountered *Lady Chatterley's Lover* in Paris between 1928 and 1930.[41] In 1955 Beckett published his own novel, *Molloy*, in English, mocking the kind of eroticism found in Lawrence's late work. In *Lady Chatterley's Lover*, as Kermode highlights, Lawrence had written in exultant terms:

> Though a little frightened, she let him have his way, and the reckless, shameless sensuality shook her to her foundations, stripped her to the very last, and made a different woman of her. It was not really love. It was not voluptuousness. It was sensuality sharp and searing as fire, burning the soul to tinder.[42]

In *Molloy*, the Beckettian version is rather more deflating:

> [I]n I went from behind. It was the only position she could bear, because of her lumbago. It seemed all right to me, for I had seen dogs,

and I was astonished when she confided that you could go about it differently. I wonder what she meant exactly. Perhaps after all she put me in her rectum. A matter of complete indifference to me, I needn't tell you. But is it true love, in the rectum?[43]

In this way, Kermode's discussion of Lawrence's 'controversial passage' had already been anticipated in the prose of one of the twentieth-century's greatest dramatists.

Beckett was not the only prominent playwright to parody the sort of desires that characterize Lawrence's work. Tennessee Williams deeply admired the Nottinghamshire writer, found many autobiographical similarities between himself and Lawrence, and included in his own plays a number of Lawrentian ideas, as Norman Fedder highlighted in a book-length study of 1966.[44] Indeed, the poet William Jay Smith described how the young Williams's 'great god was D.H. Lawrence', and describes the American playwright's 'lyrical Laurentian outpourings'.[45] Even Williams's most famous work – *A Streetcar Named Desire* (1947) – has at its heart the distinctly Lawrence-like theme of a woman with social pretentions finding herself forced into sex with a relatively base man. In fact, in 1939 Williams wrote to Lawrence's widow Frieda to tell her, 'I am a young writer who has a profound admiration for your late husband['s] work and has conceived the idea, perhaps fantastic, of writing a play about him, dramatizing not so much his life as his ideas or philosophy which strike me as being the richest expressed in modern writing'.[46] This epistler then visited Frieda in Taos and promised to create just such a dramatic script about Lawrence. Williams made several abortive attempts at drafting this, including an unfinished four-person drama about Lawrence's wartime experiences that was only rediscovered by Gerri Kimber in 2014.[47] However, the best-known, and only complete drama that Williams managed to produce about Lawrence was a one-act play published in 1951 under the title *I Rise in Flame, Cried the Phoenix*.[48] Williams admired the way that, as he put it in his preface to the play, 'Lawrence felt the mystery and power of sex, as the primal life urge, and was the lifelong adversary of those who wanted to keep the subject locked away in the cellars of prudery'.[49] But although Williams appreciated Lawrence, and felt inspired by the boldness of Lawrence's erotic vision, the younger man also proved willing to mock his hero and to draw a contrast between Lawrentian sexual rhetoric and the reality of life as lived. In *I Rise in Flame*, Lawrence might be the man whom some women think is 'the oracle of their messed-up libidos', but he is also revealed as an irritable woman-hater, whose personal sexual skills had little connection with the purple passages of his novels.[50] In Williams's play, Frieda responds to one of Lawrence's admirers in the following way:

> Bertha. He's more than a man.
>
> Frieda. I know you always thought so. But you're mistaken.
>
> Bertha. You'd never admit that Lorenzo was a god.
>
> Frieda. Having slept with him ... No, I wouldn't.[51]

Unsurprisingly, the real-life Frieda put some distance between herself and Tennessee Williams's script, commenting, 'When I read this short play, I forgot that it was supposed to be Lawrence and me'.[52]

Later in the twentieth century, Alan Bennett took a similar approach to Williams in debunking Lawrence. During 1968, the Royal Court's version of Lawrence's 'Eastwood Trilogy' had been praised in *The Times* for reawakening audiences 'to what naturalism should be: the art of riveting the attention by telling the truth about ordinary life'.[53] But Alan Bennett's play *Enjoy* (premiered 1980) mocks the idea that we might be getting the unmediated 'truth' in such performances. In *Enjoy*, the local council has sent a silent observer to watch a family of one of the last back-to-back houses in Leeds, in order to record a vanishing mode of existence. The father tells this observer:

> So it's me you're watching? Not her. What for? There's only me, sitting. (*Pause*) And that's not real, not accurate. Because you're here too. You spoil it. Go away and I might be natural [...] And don't think you're going to pick up any information about me and her either. Our so-called sexual relations.[54]

Here Bennett made the case that such apparent demonstrations of working-class authenticity are deliberately manufactured and fabricated for presentation before an audience. According to Bennett's way of thinking, Lawrentian notions of sex were particularly unreal and disconnected from the actual realm of lived experience, and Bennett showed this through a Rabelaisian reimagining of the corpse-washing from Lawrence's play *The Widowing of Mrs Holroyd*, a scene that audiences and critics had found particularly affecting at the Royal Court in 1968. In Bennett's *Enjoy*, when the women prepare the body, there is a phallic intrusion that is entirely absent from Lawrence's original scene:

Mrs Clegg. Good garden rhubarb! What's that? Oh, Connie.

(*They cling to one another, gazing at Mr Craven's body and at one part in particular.*)

Mam. And you said he was dead.

Mrs Clegg. He may still be dead.

Mam. That's not dead. That's alive. That's life, that is.

Mrs Clegg. It may not be. It may just be a side effect. The muscles contract. The body plays tricks. The dead often seem to grin. This doesn't mean they are happy.

Mam. One touch of the flannel. The sly bugger. And me thinking he was all dead and decent.[55]

The inappropriate tumescence (as well as the name Connie) moves the scene away from *The Widowing of Mrs Holroyd* and towards a comic reimagining of *Lady Chatterley's Lover*. Thus, if the Royal Court productions had often been understood as offering a straightforward realism in 1968, by 1980 Bennett had emphasized the potential for a far more surreal dynamic in Lawrentian drama.

Lawrence and women

These examples from Samuel Beckett, Tennessee Williams and Alan Bennett reveal the ways in which Lawrence's writing finds echoes in work by some of the most famous dramatists of the later stage. And it was fitting that these playwrights should set about critiquing Lawrentian ideas about sex and gender, because such ideas damaged Lawrence's reputation very soon after the Royal Court produced his 'Eastwood Trilogy' in 1968. At this juncture, F.R. Leavis's moral seriousness began to look embarrassingly dated, and a new generation of critics began to cast Lawrence's overall achievement in an extremely unflattering light. Perhaps most influentially, in 1970, Kate Millett identified in some of Lawrence's writings 'a combination of political fascism and male supremacy.'[56] She highlighted some of the misogynistic constructions that are found in Lawrence's work, arguing – with deliberately provocative rhetoric – that here was a writer whose literary descriptions might be accused of 'penetrating the female victim and cutting out her heart – the death fuck.'[57]

Millett provided a much-needed counterblast to parts of Lawrence's oeuvre and to aspects of the burgeoning Lawrence industry. It is certainly possible to find instances of misogyny in Lawrence's writing; indeed, it becomes an increasingly pronounced strain in his later work, and does colour his ideas about theatre. For example, the characters of his novels repeatedly dwell on the pejorative associations of the term 'actress', and in a non-fictional essay of 1928 he wrote:

Beware, oh modern woman, the age of fifty. It is then that the play is over, the theatre shuts, and you are turned out into the night. If you have been making a grand show of your life, all off your own bat, and being grand mistress of your destiny, all triumphant, the clock of years tolls fifty, and the play is over. You've had your turn on the stage. Now you must go, out into the common night, where you may or may not have a true place of shelter.[58]

Such an extract, with its combination of casual ageism and misogyny, indicates why Kate Millett's viewpoint needed articulating with some urgency after Lawrence assumed a preeminent cultural position in the 1960s.

Yet Lawrence's writing is more nuanced and varied than Millett's analysis allows. For example, at one point in his non-fictional writing about theatre, Lawrence describes his visit to an exclusively male theatre show in Italy, and says he was, 'thankful we hadn't a lot of smirking twitching girls and lasses in the audience. This male audience was so tense and pure in its attention'. Yet his professed satisfaction with the situation is undermined by the repeated challenges that he makes of those around him. At first he enquires 'why there are no women – no girls', and when he is told that the theatre is too small, Lawrence states again, 'But, I say, if there is room for all the boys and men, there is the same room for girls and women'.[59]

In more recent years, Anne Fernihough has emphasized the way that Lawrence's sympathetic reading of feminist writings profoundly shaped his novel *The Rainbow*, while Andrew Harrison has discovered an unpublished manuscript from 1924 in which Lawrence railed against the *Adelphi* magazine's 'automatic meat lust' and against the tendency of one male writer to view each member of the opposite sex 'as a piece of lurid meat'.[60] Similarly, one of the most striking features of Lawrence's dramatic work is that it insistently expresses a kind of proto-feminism. When he thought about the playhouse, Lawrence realized that the theatrical form allowed a male viewpoint to predominate, and that the women portrayed onstage often functioned as little more than male fantasies. He wrote:

> Why are the women so bad at playing this part in real life, this Ophelia-Gretchen rôle? Why are they so unwilling to go mad and die for our sakes? They do it regularly on the stage.
> But perhaps, after all, we write the plays. What a villain I am, what a black-browed, passionate, ruthless, masculine villain I am, to the leading lady on the stage; and, on the other hand, dear heart, what a hero, what a fount of chivalrous generosity and faith![61]

In his own plays, Lawrence therefore allowed a thoroughly different kind of woman to dominate. Not a figure who would go mad and die for the sake of a man, but a woman, usually from the upper tier of the working class, who was forthright and independent. For example, *The Widowing of Mrs Holroyd* shows how the title character has already planned her escape from marriage even before her husband suffers a fatal mining accident, and after he dies she comes to believe that she controlled his destiny all along, reflecting that, 'He'd have come up with the others, if he hadn't felt – felt me murdering him' (107). In the final scene of that play, the male character, now dead, is utterly passive and inert, by contrast with the two onstage female characters who remain active and in control of the family. Similarly, in *The Daughter-in-Law*, Minnie speaks to her mother-in-law and criticizes 'strong women like you, who were too much for their husbands' (350), yet by the end of the play Minnie's own husband begs his wife, 'I want thee to ma'e what tha can o' me' (359). Meanwhile, *The Fight for Barbara* concludes with Barbara's decision to reject patriarchal expectations, as she declares, in the style of Nora Helmer: 'Nor more will I have men like you interfering with my affairs behind my back, Papa!' (273). Thus, in Lawrence's theatrical work, male agency is often necessarily or voluntarily subordinated to the female. Indeed, the playwright Amy Rosenthal has observed that the female characters of Lawrence's dramas 'blaze with life. I struggle to believe that these characters sprang from a man who hated women'.[62]

Furthermore, the very titles of Lawrence's plays – *The Widowing of Mrs Holroyd*, *The Daughter-in-Law*, *The Fight for Barbara* – give an indication of which characters will hold the spectators' attention, and such naming feels particularly notable in an English stage tradition that remains dominated by Shakespearean scripts, none of which is named after a lone female character. The practical business of staging Lawrence's plays certainly reveals his positive bias towards the female. Even today, playmaking remains a male-dominated business where it is extremely difficult for women to develop an onstage career. But Table I.1 shows how Lawrence's main period of playwriting (1909–1913) was characterized by a consistent bias in favour of female performers.

Of the fifty named characters that Lawrence included in these plays, twenty-eight of them were female, a ratio of 56 per cent female to 44 per cent male. By comparison, an acting company putting on a version of Shakespeare's *Hamlet* will be dealing with cast of named characters that is 11 per cent female, and even when a play containing such an iconic female role as Shaw's *Saint Joan* opened in 1924 still only 8 per cent of the cast needed to be female.[63]

In his dramatic scripts, Lawrence reveals the humdrum details of female working-class life (featuring cycles of conflict, and preparing food, and washing clothes) with the sort of unflinching and unsentimental commitment that would make his scripts appear groundbreaking in the era of *Look Back in Anger*. For instance, at the start of *The Widowing of Mrs Holroyd*, we watch

Table I.1

a woman laying out a pile of washed clothes, one of the everyday actions that dominated the lives of such women for many years. As Mick Wallis and Simon Shepherd put it, it is this task that 'takes over the living space [...] the stage is giving over real time to the display of women's work, in all its difference, and seriousness, and effort'.[64] The leading theatre historian Christopher Innes argued in 2002 that:

> [I]t may be difficult to appreciate how unconventional such a depiction of human existence would have seemed to Lawrence's contemporaries. The sharp contrast with the sanitized image of the worker in more traditional plays – including those of Galsworthy – was intended to shock (and may have contributed to keeping Lawrence's work unperformed).[65]

Lawrence's plays are usually set in mining communities, but tend to focus on the female area of the home rather than the male zone of the colliery. In this way, Lawrence gives domestic drudgery a kind of dignity by paying close attention to it, with all of its rhythms and conflicts. Richard Hoggart's analysis of working-class women points to Lawrence's sensitivity in highlighting the overlooked lives of the poor, with Hoggart remarking that 'many old working-class women have an habitual gesture which illuminates the years of the life behind. D.H. Lawrence remarked it in his mother'.[66] By asking an audience to sit down and attend to the striving layer of the working class in provincial England, Lawrence ensured that the sort of lives which were considered by political and artistic elites to be marginal or uninteresting might take centre stage. And at certain moments in his dramatic oeuvre this process of recovery becomes more explicit: for example, in *A Collier's Friday Night*, Ernest says to Maggie, 'You never tell me *your* side', to which she responds, 'There's nothing to tell', and Ernest retorts, 'As many things happen for you as for me' (30).

Of course, Lawrence fails to offer a solution to the problems of the female working-class characters, a fatalism for which he has been justifiably reproached in some left-wing criticism.[67] But what he did do in his plays, to his credit, is articulate something of the everyday troubles and desires of those who had, until then, been largely ignored, or condescended to, by the realm of cultural production. In this respect, Lawrence asks bourgeois spectators the same question that Anabel enquires of her middle-class companions in his 1918 play *Touch and Go*, where she sees questions about redistribution as being beside the point, and asks rhetorically, 'Do you think they would *live* more, if they had more money? Do you think the poor live less than the rich – is their life emptier?' (392). When Philip French reviewed Lawrence's plays in 1968 he wrote that the Royal Court actors 'never betray Lawrence's truth by attempting to alleviate it with sentimentality, caricature or the suggestion of false hope. They do not, in short, patronise these people'.[68] By putting the – often difficult to understand – dialect of Eastwood under the spotlights, Lawrence also ensured that the theatre event became defamiliarized for middle-class patrons in the same way that it might often have been alienating for audience members from his own background. If a working-class Eastwood boy needed to strive hard to understand the classical references or social codes of much of the contemporary stage, his own drama ensured that those from well-heeled backgrounds would have to put in a comparable amount of effort and concentration, and would encounter similar moments of bewilderment.[69]

In 1927 Lawrence wrote an assessment of the Italian realist writer Giovanni Verga, and observed that the second half of the nineteenth century had witnessed a Europe-wide tendency 'to pour too much emotion, and especially too much pity, over the humble poor [...] the tragic fate of the humble poor was the stunt of that day. *Les Misérables* stands out as the great monument to this stunt'.[70] In Lawrence's plays the working-class characters refuse pity and certainly avoid humility, instead appearing with complex motives and desires, as the opposite of the tendency that he identified in Hugo. From today's perspective, Lawrence's work constitutes a reversal of the pejorative stereotyping that Owen Jones identifies in modern 'newspapers, TV comedy shows, internet forums, social networking sites and everyday conversations. At the heart of the "chavs" phenomenon is an attempt to obscure the reality of the working-class'.[71] If such modern stereotyping works by obscuring how such life is lived, then Lawrence sought to do precisely the opposite and to bring specific details of working-class existence, particularly working-class female existence, into sharp relief.

Current status

In recent years, Lawrence's 'Eastwood Trilogy' has enjoyed a regular, if sporadic, history of production and, perhaps because of the richness of its fictional women, has often attracted some of the country's best-known female actors. In 1985, the Hollywood-bound Alex Kingston – in the part of Minnie Gascoyne – toured a RADA version of *The Daughter-in-Law* to Nottingham.[72] Two years afterwards, the BAFTA-award-winning Annette Crosbie starred as Mrs Lambert in *A Collier's Friday Night* at the Greenwich Theatre, alongside a young Jane Horrocks who, after appearing in this dialect-play, went on to become famous for performing with a strong, working-class Lancashire accent.[73] Then, during 1995, Katie Mitchell directed the established film-and-television actor Zoë Wanamaker as the title character in a BBC2 version of *The Widowing of Mrs Holroyd*. Wanamaker had already, in 1975, acted as Clara in a staging of the play at Richard Eyre's Nottingham Playhouse, and now her television portrayal won praise from the *Guardian* for leading the audience 'through a series of well-judged character studies: from bitter, dignified housewife, uncertain lover, to widow overwhelmed by guilt and grief'.[74] Scenes from that script were then performed in Feburary 1999 as part of the National Theatre's '100 Plays of the Century' series.[75] Following that, in 2002, Anne-Marie Duff played Minnie in the Young Vic's version of *The Daughter-in-Law*, and commented:

> I first read *The Daughter-in-Law* when I was 18 – I found it in the Uxbridge Library one afternoon – and I loved it, though in hindsight, I don't think I really understood it. I had just discovered Lawrence and was devouring his work. When I found out the Young Vic were [*sic*] reviving it, I was ecstatic [. . .] I can't really understand why his work isn't fashionable because it's so brilliant. When I was at the Drama Centre, the other half of my year put on *A Collier's Friday Night* and I remember thinking what an amazing chamber piece it was [. . . *The Daughter-in-Law*] is full of brilliant lines. Lawrence has this incredible capacity for lancing the boil, striking home, hitting the bull's-eye. No one is ever let off the hook when a character is being evasive or cowardly. It's exhilarating to play because all the characters are so tied up in each other.[76]

More recently, the New Vic in Stoke-on-Trent recruited RSC director Fiona Buffini and film actor Joanna Croll for a 2012 production of *The Widowing of Mrs Holroyd*, while the following year the Sheffield Crucible staged *The Daughter-in-Law* with sitcom actor Lynda Baron playing the dominant matriarch. When Katie Galbraith reviewed the latter production in *The Stage* she praised the female roles, interpreting the play as essentially a battle between two women, the 'commanding' Lynda Baron in the part of the mother-in-law 'who controls everything', and Claire Price, the 'wonderfully seething' daughter-in-law.[77] In the *Guardian*, Alfred Hickling commented that this production revealed Lawrence's playwriting as being 'so ahead of its time'.[78]

That production at the Sheffield Crucible was directed by Paul Miller, who shortly afterwards took charge as artistic director of the Orange Tree Theatre, the first purpose-built theatre-in-the-round in London. When Miller arrived at the Orange Tree in 2014, he decided to present *The Widowing of Mrs Holroyd* as his inaugural work. And, as with his previous Lawrence production, Miller's 2014 staging received plaudits from both left- and right-leaning newspapers. In the *Observer*, Susannah Clapp praised the female acting in this 'bracing battle of the sexes' and in the *Daily Telegraph*, Dominic Cavendish commended 'a powerful, autobiographically influenced portrait of a miserable marriage'.[79]

Indeed, in the early years of the twenty-first century, other leading British newspaper critics similarly extolled the virtues of Lawrence's theatre. The *Daily Telegraph* reviewer, Charles Spencer, had, in 1994, condemned Lawrence as the 'appalling bearded loony' whose playwriting comprised 'a hilarious parody of all the clichés of Northern working-class drama'.[80] But Spencer underwent a Damascene conversion when watching *The Daughter-in-Law* at Watford's Palace Theatre in 2006, and afterwards described an 'arresting and beautiful play' by a 'fresh and original dramatist', whose playwriting 'rigorously avoided the usual sentimentality and melodrama of the age'.[81] In 2012 Spencer's revised judgement was endorsed by *The Times*'s theatre critic, Benedict Nightingale, who published a book portraying the Lawrence plays at the Royal Court as being one of the world's '*Great Moments in the Theatre*', and described how the 1968 production of *The Widowing of Mrs Holroyd* 'left the audience stunned with admiration and emotion'.[82] Discussion of Lawrence's plays also began to creep into the undergraduate seminar room, with Mick Wallis and Simon Shepherd's popular guide to theatre, *Studying Plays* (which went through three editions between 1998 and 2010) repeatedly using *The Widowing of Mrs Holroyd* and *The Daughter-in-Law* in order to illustrate ideas about the semiotics of the playhouse.[83]

Quite understandably, when critics acclaim Lawrence's drama they usually focus upon these three plays of the 'Eastwood Trilogy'. His other five plays are less accomplished, and have tended to be ignored, as have the broader theatrical concerns that Lawrence made manifest in his novel writing. Keith Sagar asserts that Lawrence had essentially finished working as a dramatist by 1913, and that the author then felt able to 'write FINIS under that stage of his life from which the colliery plays had drawn their life-blood'.[84] Yet, *The Theatre of D.H. Lawrence* will examine the way that the theatrical concerns of the 'Eastwood Trilogy' continued to pervade Lawrence's writing beyond this point, with such concerns revealing a writer who remained attuned to various advanced ideas about drama, and who felt determined to see his own writing performed on the playhouse stage even in the very final years of his life.

After 1913, Lawrence wrote only two full plays (*Touch and Go* and *David*) and two incomplete theatrical pieces (*Altitude* and *Noah's Flood*), yet those later dramas offer an important corrective to certain critical interpretations of Lawrence's work. For example, his unfinished 1924 comedy *Altitude* is relatively slight, and largely unfunny if you do not know the characters being parodied, but it does strive to highlight the hypocrisy of white attitudes towards indigenous people. In this skit (the title of which points to the idea that living at 7,000 feet above sea level might cause the residents of Taos in New Mexico to behave somewhat oddly), a white American character repeatedly bosses a Native American, telling him to 'Fetch a pail of water', 'chop some wood', 'Put some water in the kettle' (543–546); but at the same time the white character spends her time claiming that she is on the Native-American side and asserting the superiority of Native-American civilization. During the year that he wrote this sketch, Lawrence also composed a savagely satirical essay about the way that wealthy and white tourist audiences viewed, with condescension, the profound spirituality of traditional Puebloan performance. He wrote scathingly about the ignorance of affluent spectators (with their comments, 'Why, he sure is cute! He says he's dancing to make his corn grow. What price irrigation, Jimmy?'), and thus, in his late theatrical work, Lawrence explored a deep affinity with the subaltern.[85]

Of course, a number of Lawrence's comments about theatre and performance do contain racist assumptions and assertions. For example, in the first version of his essay 'The Spirit of Place', written in 1917–1918, Lawrence includes an anti-Semitic reference (deleted from his later revision of the piece), observing that the white American population in the USA had been left 'Uprooted' in an alien environment where its members had to be 'always calculated', and that such similar characteristics could 'be found in the Americans and the Jews. Hence the race talent for acting'.[86] Yet as the example of *Altitude* shows, this often self-contradictory and argumentative writer did question and critique hegemonic views, including the era's damaging attitudes to the racial Other (notably, his Jewish-American actor-friend, Ida Rauh, was one of the few people accompanying him at the time of his death). Arguments about Lawrence may often proceed through polemic statements that characterize him in binary terms, but his late dramatic writings reveal him as a figure capable of undermining his own assumptions and prejudices as he went along. Thus, although Lawrence wrote few plays after 1913, and although none of the later scripts is particularly well known today, the theatrical pieces that Lawrence did compose during this mature period are often deeply revealing about the author's developing ideas and attitudes, as we shall see later in this volume.

Nevertheless, Lawrence faced a number of problems in actually getting any of his plays to the stage, a disappointment that largely discouraged him from scripting new theatre pieces as his career progressed. Still, he continued to find inspiration in theatrical tropes and examples, and his later writings show a sustained cross-fertilization between his thinking about drama and his composition of novels and short stories. For Lawrence, going to the theatre, performing in skits and writing plays could scarcely be separated from his broader creative drive. Just as an actor's basic job is to use the single human body to portray a number of different characters, so Lawrence's fiction often works by presenting versions of Lawrence in which different aspects of his own life and personality are erased, embellished or invented; revealing a kind of thespian delight in role play and identity change. During his lifetime, as well as in the years since his death, Lawrence's plays may often have struggled to find life on the theatre stage but, as we shall see, theatrical concerns continue to inhabit and infuse some of his best known and most accomplished novels.

CHAPTER 1
WRITING LAWRENCE'S PLAYS:
BECOMING A DRAMATIST, 1885 TO 1910

Eastwood

D.H. Lawrence was born, the fourth of five siblings, in the small mining town of Eastwood, near Nottingham, in September 1885. His father, Arthur, was a collier, who had worked a twelve-hour day, five days a week from the age of seven: and for at least ten years before D.H. Lawrence's birth Arthur had worked as a 'butty', a reasonably well-paid position that involved supervising and paying three or four men to work on a particular section of the coal face.[1] Lawrence's mother had once aimed for a teaching career, but her family's slide into poverty, occasioned by an injury to her father, meant that before her marriage she found herself working in the lace industry instead.[2]

Socially and culturally, of course, there were many better places from where to cultivate a literary career. As John Worthen puts it:

[I]t was the healthy who survived best in Eastwood. There were regular epidemics: measles, diphtheria, diarrhoea, scarlet fever and whooping cough; in the late nineteenth century, respiratory diseases (tuberculosis and bronchitis) accounted for 17% of deaths in the area. The writer who died of pleurisy and tuberculosis in 1930, at the age of 44, remarked just before he died that 'I have had bronchitis since I was a fortnight old'.[3]

This environment may have appeared particularly unpromising for a would-be playwright. The main town in the region, Nottingham, was eight miles from Eastwood and had, as Joanna Robinson points out, long contained a high proportion of dissenters, which meant that local theatrical enterprises had often struggled to overcome the residents' autonomic hostility. From the 1860s, nonconformist preachers had been warning Nottingham's population that 'the Theatre must remain a power for mischief, and, therefore, must have the unqualified condemnation of the holy and good' and that drama constituted 'THE DESTROYER OF MORALITY, THE HOT-BED OF VICE, THE SINK OF SIN AND SHAME!'[4] Eastwood scarcely remained immune from such rhetoric: when Lawrence was 17 years old, even the curate of the town's Anglican church delivered a well-publicized sermon denouncing the playhouse 'as stained with the blackest vices and crimes'.[5] At home, Lawrence probably heard an echo of these views from his mother, who diligently attended the dissenting Congregational Chapel and set about instilling what Worthen calls a 'puritan stoicism' in her children.[6]

Such facts steer us towards the famous 1951 declaration about Lawrence made by F.R. Leavis in *Scrutiny*: 'when I think of the career that started in the ugly mining village in the spoilt Midlands, amidst all those apparent disadvantages, it seems to me that, even in these days, it should give us faith in the creative human spirit and its power to ensue fullness of life'.[7] However, although Eastwood remained physically unprepossessing, it was scarcely such a barren cultural wasteland as all that. One of Lawrence's local acquaintances, Enid Hopkin Hilton, recalled that the town afforded a number of opportunities for intellectual communion and cultural experience. 'Out of the shabby, often grimy houses', she wrote, 'emerged dedication, courage, ideas, fights for freedom, self-education, music and drama'.[8] She remembered how groups of travelling players often visited Eastwood during Lawrence's youth, with such actors producing work that was:

[A]mazing – dramatic, often tragic, and concerned with the triumph of virtue over sin. Generally the 'good' man won and secured the girl if she had not already been killed in the tragic parts. These plays were performed in any shed available, curtains occasionally rising at the wrong moment to reveal a partially dressed heroine.[9]

These travelling players included Teddy Rayner's 'Star Theatre', a family company that toured across the Midlands, and set up at the Eastwood statutes ground next to the Sun Inn, during Lawrence's early years.[10] Rayner's company probably charged admission of between two and six pence, advertised evening performances on a blackboard, and acted inside a worn tent before coal-oil flares.[11] Tuppence customers sat on planks, whereas those paying sixpence had seats furnished with a buttock-easing strip of carpet.[12] For Hilton, the memory of such performances proved long lasting, and she was not alone in this. In 1913, D.H. Lawrence wrote about sitting in a box at the Italian theatre and commented wryly, 'it's not like Teddy Rayners' (*Letters* I, 508).

Teddy Rayner's company played sensational dramas such as *Sweeney Todd* in locations across the Midlands. Nearby, in Belper, Rayner's actors performed *The Chilwell Ghost* – a notorious East Midland ghost story.[13] At Ilkley, they wrote and performed a play about the murderous Nottinghamshire resident, Charles Peace, only a fortnight after his execution in 1879, and on that occasion Teddy Rayner accidentally fired his stage gun directly into a member of the company's face, causing blindness for two days.[14] Elsewhere, when one of the Rayner actors performed in the company's popular *Maria Marten* (another drama about a notorious murder) one of the actors planned to perform a hanging scene by jumping from a makeshift stage of tables, but misjudged the leap and very nearly garrotted himself for real.[15] Little wonder that, in 1957, one of Lawrence's acquaintances remembered how the Rayner company 'got so carried away with their blood-and-thunder performance that they staged a real blood-letting performance on each other, much to our delight. Then we were getting 2 pennyworth'.[16]

When Lawrence set about forging a career as a novelist he would remember such bloodthirsty theatrical displays.[17] For example, his early novel *The White Peacock* (1911) describes a travelling theatre, 'gloriously named the "Blood-Tub"' where audiences spend their time 'watching heroes die with much writhing, and heaving, and struggling up to say a word, and collapsing without having said it'.[18] His 1920 novel *The Lost Girl* largely revolves around such a travelling theatre, and his later novel *Kangaroo* (1923) describes how 'there was murder in the air in the Midlands, among the colliers. In the theatre particularly, a shut-in, awful feeling of souls fit for murder'.[19]

That last description is scarcely flattering, yet Teddy Rayner's company evidently entertained large numbers of working-class men and women; consistently innovated with an array of different plays in order to keep the customers returning; and often sought drama in the tragedies, rumours and hauntings of life in the region. Indeed, in later years, Lawrence himself would script plays that likewise sought to represent the details of local experience. To take only the three dramas that Richard Eyre calls Lawrence's 'best plays': *The Widowing of Mrs Holroyd* dramatizes the death of the author's uncle in the Brinsley colliery; *A Collier's Friday Night* reimagines Lawrence's relationship with his own mother as he educated himself through Nottingham University College; and *The Daughter-in-Law* situates a domestic drama against the backdrop of the kind of local miners' unrest that the area witnessed in 1893 and 1908–12. Thus, just as the Rayner company had done, Lawrence sought to dramatize the deaths, the personal relationships and the newsworthy events that had affected Nottinghamshire. And, like the performers of the Teddy Rayner company, Lawrence sought to present such happenings in a local voice. Hence, in a play like *The Daughter-in-Law* he puts onstage the working-class dialect words of 'clat-farted', 'buggers' and 'stool-arsed' (305, 346), which would have attracted the censor's blue pencil if the script had ever been produced in public during the first half of the twentieth century.

Such language may have been associated with the uneducated and unscholarly, as evinced even by the knowing jokes of the local newspaper (where one 'Eestwud' correspondent declared 'Mester Nuespapur Mann – Aw shud lyke ta av a wurd a tu wi yo').[20] But in his plays, Lawrence treated this dialect form seriously, and used it ambitiously, showing how it might be used to describe the comedy and tragedy of the human condition just as well as the more 'refined' forms that dominated the established playhouses. In *The Uses of Literacy*, Richard Hoggart praises such dialect forms for revealing the 'remnants of a more muscular tradition of speech', and for showing how the working class might 'draw, in speech and in the assumptions to which speech is a guide, on oral and local tradition'.[21] For Hoggart at least, such working-class distinctiveness could function as an antidote to modern forms of mass entertainment that tend to present a 'uniformity' of experience, 'in which progress is conceived as a seeking of material possessions, equality as a moral levelling, and freedom as the ground for irresponsible pleasure'.[22] The distinctive voice of Lawrence's plays, then, which he developed from the earlier dramas of the Eastwood area, potentially offered a form of resistance to the approaching norms of the film-and-television era, in which mass entertainment has often consisted of the uniform and predictable, offered under the guise of anti-elitism but in reality, in Hoggart's terms, assisting 'a gradual drying up of the more positive, the fuller, the more cooperative kinds of enjoyment'.[23]

Shakespeare

In addition to performing stories about the local area, the Teddy Rayner company also staged Shakespeare. In a short essay of 1913 ('The Theatre') Lawrence described one of his very first childhood memories:

> [W]hen I was about seven years old, I went to Teddy Rainer's theatre in the Statutes ground at home: we used to long for the twopence it cost to go in! They played Hamlet once a fortnight. My mother would

let me go to see Hamlet, but not 'Maria Martin, or the Murder in the Red Barn'. I hung onto the form when the Ghost said, very deep:

''Amblet, 'Amblet, I am thy father's ghost'.

Then a voice from the audience came, cruelly disillusioned:

'Why tha h'arena – I can tell thy voice'.

Then I wanted to go dismally home – it was all untrue, and the Ghost wasn't a ghost.[24]

The seven-year-old Lawrence may have felt disappointed to discover that the theatre involved pretence, but he was soon making up his own 'little plays' for his school friends (giving them the instructions 'you are a bird, you are a rabbit, you are a flower', something that finds a later echo in the children's acting that opens act three of *The Widowing of Mrs Holroyd*).[25] And the early experience of watching *Hamlet* remained with him for a long time. That production of *Hamlet* was given a clear local inflection ('''Amblet'), with the dialect and audience interaction suited to the East Midlands, and Lawrence's own theatrical work would later strive for something similar: taking a quotation or plot-line from Shakespeare but making sure that it sounded like a distinctive product of Eastwood. Hence – to take only three examples – the colliers of Lawrence's play *Touch and Go* are described as 'the old Shylock of the proletariat' (367); the miner Lambert paraphrases King Lear in *A Collier's Friday Night* (51); and the butty's son Wesson in *The Fight For Barbara* casts his mistress as Desdemona (277).

Of course, the young Lawrence spent time reading as well as watching Shakespeare. One of the most important books in his home was the twenty-volume *International Library of Famous Literature*, a wide-ranging, if somewhat idiosyncratic, anthology edited by Richard Garnett. Lawrence's brother Ernest purchased this set at some point in 1900 to 1901, at the great expense of nearly nine pounds, when the young writer would have been about 16 years old.[26] One of Lawrence's close acquaintances remembered that this was 'One of the most treasured possessions of the Lawrence household' and that 'Lawrence must have made many literary acquaintances through the medium of these volumes'.[27] Indeed, the *International Library* contains a number of canonical dramatic moments – including Portia's trial scene, Hamlet's grief over Ophelia, and Faustus's damnation – to which Lawrence would allude in his own plays.[28]

Additionally, although Lawrence knew Shakespeare through the acting of the Teddy Rayner company, and from the books that sat on the shelves at home, when he reached 16 or 17 years old he also began to perform these scripts himself. In 1902, Lawrence made the acquaintance of a 15-year-old local school-monitress called Jessie Chambers, who became his girlfriend, and, in the congenial atmosphere of her family home, the two shared many magazines and books: 'a kind of orgy of reading' according to Chambers.[29] Part of this cerebral orgy involved Lawrence honing his sense of theatre by discussing Shakespeare and rehearsing Shakespearean scenes at the Chambers farm, where according to Jessie he proved an 'excited' and 'domineering' director.[30] Enid Hopkin Hilton remembered that acting out dramatic scenes was relatively common amongst Lawrence's Eastwood acquaintances, with locals such as Lawrence's friend and sometime lover, the suffragist Alice Dax, taking part in theatrical events:

> Alice formed a drama group with my parents' assistance; our thespian abilities were never outstanding, but the attempts were fun. We learned to conquer stage fright, as pretending to be someone else was a great relief. Soon I started writing my own plays and dragging playmates in as performers, family and other adults as the audience.[31]

Lawrence himself participated in similar performances at the Chambers household. Here, by acting out the parts, he developed a close personal identification with particular Shakespeare characters. When, for example, Jessie Chambers and Lawrence went to watch a production of *Macbeth* (likely that given by the well-known Frank Benson company at the Nottingham Theatre Royal in February 1903), Lawrence afterwards spent time rehearsing the protagonist's lines in the Chambers family home, memorably asking 'Is this a dagger I see before me?', and grasping an imaginary weapon.[32] Jessie Chambers described how 'Lawrence identified himself with the play, and for the time being lived in its atmosphere'.[33] Indeed, phrases from the play pepper his personal correspondence, with his early letters featuring recurring phrases such as 'Tomorrow, and tomorrow, and tomorrow' and 'Bubble, bubble/Toil and trouble' [sic] (*Letters* I, 60, 54).

On another occasion, Jessie Chambers recalled how the teenage Lawrence insisted several times 'We must read *Coriolanus* together', and that when they did so, Chambers 'wondered at his look of puzzled concentration, and felt that the play had a significance for him that I had not grasped'. Lawrence then told her: 'You see, it's the mother who counts', continuing, 'the wife hardly at all. The mother is everything to him'.[34] In August 1905 Lawrence then went, with Jessie Chambers and her brother, to watch a production of

Hamlet at the Nottingham Theatre Royal, with Cyril Este playing the main part.[35] After the show, Chambers reported that 'Lawrence was intensely excited. He went through *Hamlet's* soliloquy afterwards in our kitchen – "To be, or not to be . . .".[36] Of course, Lawrence's concern for *Hamlet* and for the mother–son dynamic in *Coriolanus* would soon be manifested in his own playwriting. In Lawrence's first play, the 1909 script *A Collier's Friday Night*, the son of the household, Ernest, enjoys a quasi-incestuous bond with his mother, making the father jealous. And in the 1913 play *The Daughter-in-Law*, the character of Luther experiences a similar maternal relationship, frustrating his wife, who believes that he has been ruined by his mother's demand to be loved above all other women. When Lawrence wrote the most famous articulation of these themes in his novel *Sons and Lovers* (begun in 1910 and published in 1913), it is notable that, just as in *Hamlet*, the mother figure is named 'Gertrude'.

However, by Easter 1906 Lawrence told Jessie Chambers that he had little intention of marrying her, and thereafter the two spent less time together, particularly between October of that year and June 1908, when Lawrence studied for his teacher's certificate at University College Nottingham. Here he continued to show a fascination for the dangerous mothers of the dramatic canon: in April 1908 he wrote (on behalf of his new girlfriend, Louie Burrows) to describe feeling eager to see a forthcoming undergraduate production of Euripides' *Medea*.[37] But more formally, at the university, Lawrence spent time engaged in the academic study of Shakespearean theatre, and his student notes provide intriguing clues about his developing dramatic thinking. For example, Lawrence, a writer whose plays would give the working class and women a central place on the stage, made unimpressed notes about the renaissance wit, John Lyly, writing, 'Lyly's first plays dealt largely with woman, + treated her none too respectfully. Later he turned to political drama. Lyly wrote rubbish for the aristocrats, but for the populace different men were writing'.[38] By contrast, Lawrence's notes admire Marlowe for having 'introduced real feeling' to drama, and for pursuing a career on the stage because this was: 'The only course open to a literary man of no fortune not willing to be a big man's dependent'.[39] Shakespeare, meanwhile, receives praise for depicting 'the rough pictures of the peasant as well as the refined creations of art', and for creating Puck, a character whose 'dress is the dress of the peasant, his work the farm-hand's talk – or the good wife's – and his pranks the awkward jests of crude-minded country people'.[40]

Nonetheless, Lawrence's student writing about theatre reveals him largely bored by the pedestrian essay topics that his tutors set. The Nottingham university approach was dominated by applying nineteenth-century morality and psychology to Shakespeare's characters, with such literary tactics having recently been approved by A.C. Bradley's *Shakespearean Tragedy* (1904). As a result, Lawrence ended up writing half-hearted disquisitions on, for example, a 'Character Sketch of Lady Macbeth' or 'The Fairies of "Midsummer Night's Dream"'. We might remember how, in his first play, *A Collier's Friday Night*, the autobiographical figure of Ernest complains that, at college, 'You have to fool about so much, and listen when you're not interested, and see old Professors like old dogs walking round as large as life with ancient bones they've buried and scratched up again a hundred times, and they're just as proud as ever. It's such a farce!' (27–28). Ernest complains that, 'if school pulls all your playthings and pretty things away from you, College does worse: it makes them all silly and idiotic, and you hate them' (27).

After all, in Eastwood, Lawrence had engaged in reading and acting Shakespeare's plays, personally embodying the heroes and villains in a way that would greatly affect his later writing. But by contrast, in the university classroom – perhaps like many an undergraduate – Lawrence felt divorced from the action and excitement of the drama; and he preferred instead the Saturday-night discussions, concerts and plays given by the Students' Association.[41] Indeed, during his academic life he wrote a poem 'From a College Window', and in the original version Lawrence explains how the student may feel separated from the real experience of life's theatre, with the narrator watching incidents in the street outside from behind a sheet of glass:

> These are fragments of an incoherent play, and we scoff
> As we look at the actors, and say in our souls we will never join
> Their ill-played drama, we, like gods in the window seat
> Uplifted in wisdom, half amused by the play in the street.[42]

This academic sense of distance had certainly not been known to Lawrence in Eastwood, where he had wholeheartedly flung himself into rehearsing, discussing and inhabiting the plays of Shakespeare. The 7-year-old Lawrence had first been initiated into the theatre by a boisterously received *Hamlet*, and his hometown had since hosted a number of other comic performers who mocked Shakespearean pretentions. For example, in 1896 the humourist Harry Liston spent time in Eastwood making jokes about *Richard III*; while in 1902, a performance by the Eastwood Amateur Dramatic Society included a satire on *Hamlet* by the local wit Cecil Berle.[43] Little wonder that Lawrence himself would write the irreverent poem 'When I Read Shakespeare', which declares:

And Hamlet, how boring, how boring to live with,
so mean and self-conscious, blowing and snoring
his wonderful speeches, full of other folks' whoring![44]

Likewise, the plays that he wrote after leaving university would continually return to Shakespeare, challenging and contradicting, but also seeking inspiration from that earlier literary master who emerged from a similarly unlikely background in the English Midlands.

Arthur and Ernest

In addition to the theatrical stimulation that the young Lawrence found at the family farm of Jessie Chambers and amongst the touring thespians of Eastwood, his own home may also have encouraged his ideas about performance. Lawrence's pious mother, admittedly, grew increasingly hostile to storytelling and entertainments during the writer's youth.[45] But other members of the household held an entirely different attitude. For example, Lawrence's father Arthur is sometimes characterized simply as a miner who was 'barely literate'.[46] But such a dismissive portrait ignores his broader interests, which included helping to organize local shows in Eastwood and at one time running a dancing class.[47] The author's youngest sister Ada remembered the improbable fact that her mother had first been drawn to this husband 'by his graceful dancing, his musical voice, his gallant manner and his overflowing humour'.[48] And something of this skill is recalled in Lawrence's play *The Widowing of Mrs Holroyd*, where the collier-father of the household drunkenly carouses at the pub. Although the collier's wife deplores this behaviour, his son nonetheless indicates admiration, reporting that there are 'lots of folks outside watchin', lookin' at my dad! He can dance, can't he Mam?' (65).

In 1899, Lawrence's father worked as part of a committee that organized a 'grand concert' at the Mechanics Hall in Eastwood. This event was held in aid of a local resident, Robert Clifton, who had probably been incapacitated in the mines. It featured an eleven-piece band, beginning with a rousing march called 'honest toil', and then included a variety of musical numbers, structured so as to appeal to Eastwood. For example, one humourist received loud applause for three comic songs, the last of which he promised to sing backwards, before whirling around so that the audience viewed the reverse of his head. The evening then concluded with the famous hymn 'Lead, Kindly Light' (1833) by John Henry Newman (1801–1890) that had a particular resonance for those who spent their days toiling in the mines with the ever-present danger of pit collapse:

> Lead, Kindly Light, amidst th'encircling gloom,
> Lead Thou me on!
> The night is dark, and I am far from home,
> Lead Thou me on!

Something of the way that Lawrence's mother viewed such theatricals is perhaps indicated in *Sons and Lovers*, where her fictional counterpart, Mrs Morel, waits up late at night for her husband to return from the pub and hears 'On a doorstep somewhere, a man [. . .] singing loudly, in a drawl, "Lead Kindly Light". Mrs Morel was always indignant with the drunken men, that they must sing that hymn when they got maudlin'.[49] Nonetheless, Arthur's concert was generally well received: it raised £17 for the injured man, and the Mechanic's Hall 'was crowded to its utmost limits', with the local newspaper praising Arthur and his committee 'for their untiring efforts to make what is one of the most charitable objects in the parish a grand success'.[50]

Indeed, the concert received sufficient acclaim for Arthur to arrange a similar event less than a year afterwards. On this second occasion, the show was held in a nearby pub, the General Havelock Inn, and the organizers again sought to raise money for another local man by presenting a programme that combined the comic and the sentimental.[51] This included the humorous ditty 'Some One to Mind the Children' and a more lachrymose item, the 1897 song 'Break the News to Mother', about a dying soldier who declares:

> Just break the news to mother,
> She knows how dear I love her
> And tell her not to wait for me
> For I'm not coming home.[52]

D.H. Lawrence's fictions include notoriously unflattering recreations of his father, and the younger man's dramatic efforts differed from Arthur's theatrical work in eschewing easy sentiment and avoiding any practical suggestions about how the circumstances of the local poor might be improved. Yet a similarity of concern does emerge in the fact that both father and son set about creating theatrical events that would revolve around the struggles of those families in the surrounding mining area. Indeed, the narrative of 'Break the News to Mother' is essentially that of Lawrence's drama *The Widowing of Mrs Holroyd*, which focuses on the death of an Eastwood miner, and the arrival of that news with wife and mother.

Arthur Lawrence was not the only member of the immediate family to have participated in this local world of performance. D.H. Lawrence's older brother, Ernest, was familiar with the Mechanics Institute, the venue where Arthur Lawrence's 1899 concert had been held. The institute was funded by the local colliery and contained a library with a large variety of works of fiction and bound magazines, and hosted the local literary group. As the *Eastwood and Kimberley Advertiser* noted, 'More than one young fellow owes his start in public life to the Literary Society, and to many a one it has been the means of providing an intellectual feast, and a key wherewith to open the door leading to a long vista of mental delights'.[53] The newspaper also observed of Ernest that at the Mechanics Institute library 'there was no more familiar figure than his, he was a great reader from a boy, and in his early teens he had become acquainted with most of the present day writers and many of the past'.[54]

When Ernest haunted the Mechanics Institute, it is unlikely that he could have avoided hearing about the local non-professional thespians who performed there in the 1890s, and an Eastwood Amateur Dramatic Society also organized and acted at the venue in 1900.[55] In large part, the audience's enjoyment of these shows came from seeing friends and neighbours dressed up in various outlandish costumes. It was amusing to see the familiar people from this small town dressed up as a 'Breton shepherd' or a 'man of the world'. The local newspaper drew particular attention to such costuming, pointing to 'Miss Ida Haynes making a capital peasant girl' and noting that 'Mr. Burns, although seldom called upon, made a really splendid old man, his "get up" being excellent'.[56] Eastwood's audiences evidently enjoyed the comic potential here in knowing what such local people were like in real life, and contrasting that knowledge with the costumed performers onstage.[57] Although we have no record of Ernest performing in a play, he did attend the Mechanics Institute for the annual Fancy Dress Ball, which was furnished with music by the same violinist who usually accompanied local dramatic performances.[58] In 1896, the 17-year-old Ernest was described by the

Eastwood and Kimberley Advertiser as having attended this ball dressed as 'a Scotchman', and so was clearly engaging with the same kind of make-believe fancy-dress world that motivated those who performed in amateur shows at the same venue.[59]

That Caledonian costuming made sufficient impression upon the young D.H. Lawrence for him, a decade and a half later, to fictionalize in *Sons and Lovers* (1913). In the novel, Mrs Morel worries about the 'brazen baggages' that her son William (the novel's version of Ernest) is meeting at dancing classes, and the situation deteriorates when William plans to go 'to a fancy dress ball. He was to be a Highlander. There was a dress he could hire, which one of his friends had had, and which fitted him perfectly. The Highland suit came home. Mrs Morel received it coldly, and would not unpack it'.[60] Then William put on his outfit in front of his brother Paul (the fictional D.H. Lawrence):

'See me in my black shorts!' he said, twisting round. Then he added: 'You see,'Postle, a real Highlander doesn't wear drawers – he covers his nakedness with a kilt. But if I happened to kick rather high, and all those ladies there – why – it wouldn't do! [...] You see, 'Postle, I can wear a kilt, because I'm a tidy size round where it sits. You'd be no good – as flat as [a] box lid. You must pray to the Lord for development in that quarter, or you'll never be able to wear a kilt'.[61]

For many years that last passage remained unknown, as Lawrence's editor Edward Garnett decided to cut it, presumably for the sake of decency, before publication, and it was only restored in the Cambridge edition of 1992. Yet the deleted passage shows how, for Lawrence, this realm of theatrical costuming was connected with some decidedly subversive sexual sub-currents. Lawrence reimagines his dead brother's dressing up, but specifically considers the tight shorts worn underneath the kilt, how they fit snugly around his brother's backside and how they might prevent the exposure of his brother's genitals. The kilt, in resembling a skirt, has an element of cross-dressing, whilst the hostility that Mrs Morel feels towards William's admirers carries strong overtones of jealous sexual desire. The realm of performance might therefore enable a reversal or questioning of Eastwood's workaday norms, and might involve the incestuous, the cross-dressed or the homosexual.

Alongside Ernest's Scottish costume, the Mechanics Institute ball of 1896 included local people dressed as international theatrical characters. One local woman attended in the guise of Marguerite, the main character in the

French novel *La Dame aux Camélias* by Alexandre Dumas, *fils*, which had been adapted into a famous stage play, while another woman attended dressed as the Colleen Bawn, the title character of a smash-hit melodrama by the Irishman Dion Boucicault. The fact that such costumes might be worn and identified indicates that, although shows in Eastwood drew on local performers and the ability of audiences to recognize local characters in humorous situations, the people of the town also looked outwards to a range of broader theatrical trends. Like them, the young Lawrence also engaged with the dramatists of France and Ireland, and such international elements can be discerned in his earliest attempts at playwriting.

Sarah Bernhardt

Sadly, Ernest Lawrence would die in October 1901, only five years after his appearance in Scottish dress at the Eastwood Mechanics Institute. But following Ernest's death, much of his interest in reading and performance was inherited by his younger brother. If Ernest had once been the dancer and the 'life and soul' of family games and songs, as his sister Ada remembered, D.H. Lawrence now became the figure whom 'the girls loved to dance with', the performer of stories, and the person who arranged house decorations ready for such revelries.[62] Where formerly Ernest had lingered at the Mechanics Institute, the venue now became a key site for the intellectual development of his younger brother, with D.H. Lawrence regularly accompanying Jessie Chambers to the library, something that she described as 'the outstanding event of the week'.[63]

Part of this bibliophilic journey of discovery involved Lawrence acquainting himself with broader European trends in drama and performance. One of the volumes that Ernest bequeathed to the household contained an extract of the dramatized version of *La Dame aux Camélias* by Alexandre Dumas, *fils* (the 1848 novel that had famously been adapted for the Parisian stage in 1852). The protagonist of that play was the prostitute, Marguérite Gautier, a character who became the most popular role played by the celebrated actor Sarah Bernhardt. Indeed, Bernhardt had been performing that character in England since 1881, to such acclaim that – as we have seen – one of the attendees at the 1896 Eastwood fancy-dress ball, attended by Lawrence's brother Ernest, had worn a replica costume.[64] Moreover, the Lawrence family possessed a printed photograph of Bernhardt playing her celebrated role, with the image lying amongst the pages of Ernest's books.[65]

Then, in June 1908, at the age of 63, Bernhardt arrived in Nottingham to play Marguérite inside the packed Theatre Royal. Here, spectators adored Bernhardt's performance, with its portrayal of the saintly but misunderstood courtesan, the tortured cries of passion and grief, and the memorable death scene. The *Nottingham Evening Post* praised 'the fire of her genius, causing an audience to forget everything except the fact that the greatest actress of her time is before them', and one of the most excitable of these audience members was the young D.H. Lawrence.[66] Before the show he boasted, 'Tonight I am going to see Sarah Bernhardt in *La Dame aux Camélias*. As Camille I think she will be thrilling' (*Letters* I, 55), and, indeed, his own feelings overwhelmed him during the performance. The day afterwards he contacted Jessie Chambers, who recalled:

[T]he play had so upset him that at the end he rushed from his place and found himself battering at the doors until an attendant came and let him out. He ran to the station to find the last train gone, and had to walk home. He added, 'I feel frightened. I realise that I, too, might become enslaved to a woman'. On the Saturday afternoon he came up and told us all about the play, and showed us how Sarah Bernhardt died in the last scene. He looked quite worn out with emotion.[67]

Ten days after the show, Lawrence himself described his feelings in a letter to his friend, the socialist and suffragist Blanche Jennings. He described being overcome by the sight of Bernhardt, who managed to become the 'incarnation of wild emotion'. Lawrence reflected:

I could love such a woman myself, love her to madness; all for the pure, wild passion of it. Intellect is shed as flowers shed their petals. Take care about going to see Bernhardt. Unless you are very sound, do not go. When I think of her now I can still feel the winsome, sweet, playful ways; her sad, plaintive little murmurs; her terrible panther cries; and then the awful, inarticulate sounds, the little sobs that fairly sear one, and the despair and death; it is too much in one evening (*Letters* I, 59).

In fact, Lawrence felt sufficiently moved by the experience to refer to it directly in his fiction. In *The White Peacock* (1911) the character of Lettie watches Bernhardt's performance and then starts impersonating the same 'mad clatter of French', while in *Sons and Lovers* (1913) Lawrence's fictional surrogate, Paul Morel, sees Bernhardt's Nottingham show and is so overcome by desire that – in another passage that was excised until 1992 – he accompanies his female companion straight home, cross-dresses in a pair of her stockings, and then has sex with her in the kitchen.[68] Perhaps, just as the sight of his brother dressed as a Scotchman enabled Lawrence to write about a kind of subversion of the everyday, so the idea of Bernhardt's acting opened up similarly transgressive possibilities.

A Collier's Friday Night

When he watched Bernhardt's performance, Lawrence realized the emotional power of the stage, and shortly afterwards he decided to become a playwright himself. His earliest dramatic script, *A Collier's Friday Night*, was completed in the year after he had watched *La Dame aux Camélias* (most probably in November 1909), and in this first play Lawrence drew extensively on his own family home in Eastwood. The most cursory biographical enquiry reveals that the main character of Ernest Lambert, the college-educated son of a mining family, is a version of Lawrence himself; that the fraught parental relationship described in the script between the butty-collier father and the aspirational mother offers a reimagining of the relationship between Lawrence's own parents; and that the intellectually curious Maggie Pearson is a fictional Jessie Chambers. Chambers herself commented that this play 'was about his home on a Friday night. Sitting there in the tiny suburban room, it troubled me deeply to see his home put before me in his vivid phrases.'[69]

Yet, although the play is rooted in the reality of Eastwood, there are repeated indications in *A Collier's Friday Night* that Lawrence also drew upon his knowledge of international theatre. The opening stage direction makes clear that a copy of Richard Garnett's *International Library of Famous Literature* should be positioned onstage, the edition in which Lawrence had probably first discovered both *La Dame aux Camélias* and the portrait of Sarah Bernhardt. Ernest goes on to read French poetry aloud, corrects the diary that he has asked his girlfriend to write in French, and drops French expressions into his speech. For example, when Ernest argues with Beatrice Wylde, he declares 'It's a case of *ennui. Vous m'agacez les nerfs. Il faut aller au diable*' ('It's a case of boredom. You make me nervous. Go to the devil'). The uncomprehending Beatrice asks Ernest's girlfriend, 'Translate for us, Maggie' (37), and such unintelligibility echoed one of the notable features of Sarah Bernhardt's acting in Nottingham. Lawrence knew that Bernhardt had the power to move the Theatre Royal's audience to tears, even though she spoke in French (one Nottingham newspaper reported a real-life spectator declaring between sobs, 'I wish – I knew – what – she was saying').[70] In Lawrence's first play, he therefore establishes a contrast between the distinctive Nottinghamshire dialect spoken by most of those onstage ('Hello, my duck' (8)) and Ernest's use of foreign language, which often marks the character as somewhat pompous and affected. At one point in A Collier's Friday Night Ernest reflects on the sensuous sound of performed French literature, 'It's so heavy and full and voluptuous: like oranges falling and rolling a little way along a dark blue carpet' (33). He is discovering beauty through his education in a way that can scarcely be imagined by his collier father: but we might also sympathize with that father who, after sweating in a pit all day, then has to listen to such ornate discussions of a world that he himself will never enter.

However, there is another connection between the Sarah Bernhardt performance and A Collier's Friday Night, in addition to the straightforward fact that both rely upon the theatricalized use of spoken French. When Lawrence watched Bernhardt, he had felt overwhelmed by feelings of entrapment, needing to beat the theatre doors in order to escape. His skill in constructing his own first play was to summon up a similar sense of claustrophobia. In A Collier's Friday Night, Mrs Lambert is trapped and stifled by the limited horizons of the mining village in which she lives, and ensures that her children are educated in order to escape. Her husband tries to find his own release through alcohol, having to spend his days enclosed in the pit before emerging and handing over his earnings in order to support the (to him, astronomical) cost of books for his son Ernest, who is notably failing to bring home a wage for the family. Ernest, meanwhile, is broadening his intellectual horizons at the same time that he remains physically rooted in a household where he faces both paternal aggression and stifling maternal love. Elsewhere, the minor characters feel equally confined: Maggie's relationship with Ernest is maladroit and largely unaffectionate, yet she is drawn to him by a need for intellectual companionship. Ernest's sister Nellie longs to escape with her boyfriend, but she is frustrated by his having to work in a shop until past ten o'clock at night. And even Nellie's friend Gertie has a boyfriend whom she finds tedious. In the cramped domestic setting depicted onstage, such tensions inevitably result in conflict, argument and threats of violence. Lawrence revealed how, in such a restricted space, working-class characters might continually be irking one another, with ostensibly minor incidents – most notably when one character eats some grapes intended for another – might provoke major eruptions of emotion, and become representative of a wider set of frustrations and anxieties. After all, in the real-life local mining community, Lawrence's paternal uncle Walter had killed Lawrence's cousin,

Walter junior, in 1900, after a similar miner's-kitchen row about whether the father or son of the household deserved to eat some eggs.[71]

Lawrence's first attempt at playwriting had therefore been affected by both real-life experience and Theatre-Royal drama, and this combination of influences meant that he managed to transcend a script like *La Dame aux Camélias* by rejecting straightforward heroes or villains. When he watched Bernhardt playing Marguerite, he and the rest of the audience had seen a tragic heroine, who, by the end of the play, has strived for nobility but been grievously wronged. Lawrence, however, declined to draw his characters in such binary terms. Ernest, for example, might be the figure who most closely resembles the author, but we are scarcely encouraged to view the character as laudable. Ernest treats Maggie, for example, with a mixture of brusqueness and condescension, particularly when commenting on the mistakes he finds in her diary. He may inspire great love from his mother, but this is the portrait of the artist as a young prig.

Similarly, Ernest's father, although a bully and a drunk, is not an unredeemable villain, but is portrayed with nuance and shading. At the start of the play, whilst the other characters spend their time sitting, reading and talking, he emerges limping and covered in black dust from the pit. It is Friday, so he has been busily labouring all week. But upon returning home, he is immediately greeted by his daughter scolding him for disturbing the furniture, his wife berating him for leaving dirty marks on the table, and his daughter's friend laughing at him because of the crude way he drinks his tea. It is little wonder that he eventually explodes, 'A man comes home after a hard day's work to folks as 'as never a word to say to 'im, as shuts up the minute 'e enters the house, as 'ates the sight of 'im as soon as 'e comes in th' room – – !' (13). He never becomes altogether likeable, but at least Mr Lambert is allowed to state his case and make the audience see why, from his perspective, his son – who blithely devours the house's food, money and wifely attention – might deserve treating with aggression. As Sylvia Sklar points out, 'We see, in Lambert's warm response to Gertie Coomber's polite conversation how readily he responds to being treated as a human being, and we sense his sufferings at the hands of a wife who feels herself a cut above him'.[72]

For readers of Lawrence's novels, some of these ideas will feel familiar. Indeed, Lawrence later recycled parts of *A Collier's Friday Night* when drafting *Sons and Lovers* (1913). In each case, the mother of the main character expresses jealousy at the intellectual companionship that has developed between her son and his girlfriend; both texts depict the main character's father as a dipsomaniac miner who rages home from the pub; and in both works the father very nearly punches his son in the face.[73] Indeed, when *Sons and Lovers* comes particularly close to the script of *A Collier's Friday Night*, the novel deploys the language of the playhouse: at one point in the book where Lawrence most obviously recycled the material from his earlier drama, he concluded the scene by picturing the mother, in thespian style, rehearsing what has just happened: 'mechanically she went over the last scene, then over it again, certain phrases, certain moments coming each time like a brand red-hot down on her soul; and each time she enacted again the past hour'.[74]

Nonetheless, in *A Collier's Friday Night*, Lawrence had done more than warm up for his later novel: he had created a drama that stands as an accomplished piece of theatre in its own right. In 1891, G.B. Shaw had published *The Quintessence of Ibsenism*, arguing that the best modern drama might avoid stereotypes and instead describe the ambiguous rights and wrongs of any particular situation.[75] Shaw felt that such plays might guide spectators away from easily settled opinions, towards a realm of complexity and difficult discussion. In his very first script, D.H. Lawrence had managed to achieve what Shaw was advocating, with the economy of the dramatic form bringing a sharp focus to Lawrence's writing. As John Worthen correctly points out, 'Writing a play, he is unable to introduce the kind of moralizing commentaries which interfere with the 1909–1911 versions of "Odour of Chrysanthemums"; nor does he have the problems of his uncertain fictional narrators'.[76] Instead, the job of reaching judgements is left open to us, as spectators, to debate and to question; and any moralizing is likely to reveal much about our own attitudes towards family, class and gender.

Croydon and Synge

In October 1908, the 23-year-old Lawrence left Nottinghamshire for Croydon, where he gained work as an assistant teacher at Davidson Road School. Here he developed further his taste for live performance, and took the opportunity to watch shows in London as frequently as possible. Jessie Chambers recalled going with Lawrence to watch plays by John Galsworthy (with whom Lawrence would dine in 1917) and Alfred Sutro (who would send £10 to a struggling Lawrence in 1914), as well as opera by Gilbert and Sullivan.[77] Lawrence's other visitors from Nottingham also got dragged to the capital's theatre, to watch shows including Strauss's *Elektra* and Puccini's *La fanciulla del West*.[78] Catherine Carswell remembered how she had accompanied Lawrence to Tolstoy's *Living Corpse*, but that her companion had been so 'appalled by what he considered to be the falsity and ineptitude of its stage appeal' that the duo had to leave mid-way through the performance, making Carswell 'question indeed if he ever found enjoyment in witnessing a play unless it might be one of the older classics'.[79] Lawrence was indeed reading a great number of classical playtexts at this time, with Jessie Chambers pointing out that, in addition to Sophocles, 'Gilbert Murray's translations from Euripides were a great delight. He gave me *The Trojan Women*, which I think was his favourite, and he passed on to me *Medea*, *Elektra*, *The Bacchae*, and Aristophanes' *Frogs*'.[80] But Lawrence also watched and read contemporary drama and had been impressed by a performance of the now forgotten society play *Don* by Rudolf Besier in 1909, as well as admiring Chekhov's *The Seagull* and *The Cherry Orchard* by 1912.[81]

Indeed, after Lawrence had moved to Croydon, his theatrical commitments grew so extensive that he began to describe them in quite exasperated terms. In 1911 he wrote to Louie Burrows:

> I am frightfully busy this week. On Monday I was up at Covent Garden to hear *Siegfried* – Wagner – one of the *Ring* cycle that I had not heard. It was good, but it did not make any terrific impression on me. And now George [D.H. Lawrence's brother] has asked me to take a friend of his – a Nottingham chap – to the theatre tomorrow evening – in London. The man is quite a stranger in London (*Letters* I, 327).

In *The White Peacock,* his novel of 1911, Lawrence's autobiographical character Cyril moves from Nottinghamshire to London, where playhouse attendance is presented as the norm. When Cyril is visited by the Nottinghamshire horse-dealer George, the former notes, 'At night, after the theatre, we saw the outcasts sleep in a rank under the Waterloo Bridge'.[82] Any further details – such as the specific show that was seen – remain unmentioned, but the sentence is nonetheless revealing. At the time, there may have been few Nottingham horse dealers in attendance at the average London theatre, but for Lawrence the detail is entirely unremarkable and workaday: *naturally* a visitor to the capital would be taken to the theatre.

In Croydon, Lawrence even began to consider his own life according to dramatic schema: during 1910 he thought of his relationship with a woman to whom he proposed sex, Helen Corke, in terms of lines from Hauptmann's play about infidelity, *Elga* (*Letters* I, 164). And when Lawrence had to return to Eastwood to visit his dying mother later that year, he compared his disappearances from Croydon to the evasions of Algernon Moncrieff, telling one friend that 'you will think I have a sort of "Mr. Bunbury"' (*Letters* I, 185). Indeed, Lawrence may also have been using the theatre for some real-life Bunburying at around this time: he actually watched John Galsworthy's play *Strife* with his on-off partner Jessie Chambers in Nottingham in September 1909 but, at the same time, told his other girlfriend Louie Burrows that he was unable to see that show because he remained stuck in Croydon, writing to say 'I wish I were in Nottingham at this moment – it is two o'clock – to be going with you to the theatre. I should very much like to see *Strife*' (*Letters* I, 138).[83]

As Jessie Chambers noted, during this period when he lived in Croydon, the voraciously bibliophile Lawrence also 'seemed to read everything.'[84] One of the playwrights who now had the biggest effect on Lawrence's thinking was the Irish dramatist John Millington Synge. Synge's work had caused riots in Dublin in 1907, but he died in March 1909, with his premature death then being widely discussed in the English newspapers. The *Manchester Guardian*, for example, mourned his passing by declaring that 'no one with a sense for the higher values in letters could touch his word and not feel that it had authentic greatness.'[85] Synge remained in the headlines throughout 1909: in that year, London's Afternoon Theatre premiered Synge's anticlerical play *The Tinker's Wedding*; various English organizations hosted public lectures on Synge; and the Abbey Theatre performed his dramas in Manchester.[86] Lawrence's interest was piqued, and he wrote to Blanche Jennings in November 1909 to ask, 'Have you got any of Synge's plays – the *Playboy of the Western World* – I should like to read them: but I know the little volume beginning or ending with *Riders to the Sea*' (*Letters* I, 142). That volume (published in the Vigo Cabinet Series in 1907) allowed Lawrence to read the tragic *Riders to the Sea* (1905) along with Synge's comedy *In the Shadow of the Glen* (1904). But he also sought out Synge's most famous script, as Jessie Chambers reported, 'He was a diligent searcher of the second-hand bookstalls and barrows in Surrey Street, Croyden [. . .] He came across *The Playboy of the Western World* in a tattered condition, had it bound, and sent it to me.'[87] He went on to recommended 'Synge's fine dramas' to Jessie's brother Alan, and later wrote to Sally Hopkins to declare that Synge's play 'Riders to the Sea is about the genuinest bit of dramatic tragedy, English, since Shakspere, I should say: and you can read it in half an hour' (*Letters* I, 260–261).[88]

The Widowing of Mrs Holroyd

Lawrence felt most affected by Synge's short tragedy *Riders to the Sea*, and transplanted the action of this play to Eastwood when he came to write his next play, *The Widowing of Mrs Holroyd*. In fact, Lawrence originally planned to tell his tale as the short story, 'Odour of Chrysanthemums', but in September 1910 the planned publication of that work in the *English Review* had stalled, so Lawrence redrafted the piece as his second stage script, and as a result both his short story and drama have broadly the same plot: they both revolve around a wife in a mining community who worries about why her husband has failed to return from work; both texts then feature the arrival of that miner's mother; and both include the subsequent news that he has suffocated in the mine. The two pieces conclude with the two women washing the corpse, with the mother commenting on the beauty of her dead son's white skin.[89]

Lawrence's drama may thus have been conceived as a short story, but *Riders to the Sea* always lurked in the background, and may have convinced Lawrence to develop the narrative for the stage. Synge's original play had first been produced in Dublin in 1904 by the Irish National Theatre Society (which became known as the Abbey Theatre later that year), and the drama is set amongst fishing folk on the remote Aran Islands, off Ireland's west coast. The action revolves around Maurya, a mother who experiences the death of her sixth and last son, with all of her other male offspring already having died at sea. Synge's tragedy thus shows how the islanders' closeness to the Atlantic provides them with a livelihood, but also keeps them in close proximity to death. When Lawrence read Synge's script he realized that he could create an Eastwood version. As with Synge's play, he would position a group of men and women in a location where daily life might involve an elemental and potentially fatal battle with nature. Thus, whereas the men of *Riders to the Sea* repeatedly return to the ocean, even after disaster, the men of Lawrence's *The Widowing of Mrs Holroyd* return to the mines, and in each case the dramatic action revolves around the womenfolk of these communities who are left to survive and to mourn. Both dramas are set by the fireplace of an early twentieth-century cottage kitchen, and so focus insistently upon female space and female concerns.

As with his first play, Lawrence could draw upon real-life events about which he knew. In February 1880 his Aunt Polly had lost her husband – Lawrence's paternal uncle James – in an accident at Brinsley Colliery near Eastwood. James had been 'holing' when the roof collapsed on him. At the time, Polly and James lived in Vine Cottage, a house standing only feet away from the colliery entrance, and Polly was eight months' pregnant with Lawrence's cousin Alvina. Polly herself then died in 1895, leaving her three teenage children as orphans.[90] Unsurprisingly, the family continued to re-live the trauma of James's death in the ensuing years, and Lawrence particularly remembered his grandmother's thoughts of her dead son, 'Like a blessed smiling babe he looked – he did that' (*Letters* I, 199). Indeed, the fictional mother in his play *The Widowing of Mrs Holroyd* speaks almost identical words when she sees the corpse (109).

Part of the play's power, then, is derived from its strong sense of local affect, rooted in one of the regular colliery tragedies of the Nottinghamshire pit communities. Yet, at the same time, the construction of the piece is influenced by Lawrence's reading of Synge, with the closest parallels occurring as *The Widowing of Mrs Holroyd* reaches its conclusion. In Synge's *Riders to the Sea*, Maurya complains:

> I've had a husband, and a husband's father, and six sons in this house – six fine men, though it was a hard birth I had with every one of them and they coming to the world – and some of them were found and some of them were not found, but they're gone now the lot of them.[91]

Lawrence re-worked that line so that the mother of the dead man in his play announces:

> I'm sure I've had my share of bad luck, I have. I'm sure I've brought up five lads in the pit, through accidents and troubles, and now there's this. The Lord has treated me very hard, very hard (100–101).

In *The Widowing of Mrs Holroyd*, the body of the dead miner Holroyd is then carried onto the stage, just as the dead fisherman's corpse arrives in Synge's work. Lawrence's stage direction specifies that, as the body appears, the covering slips to reveal the dead miner covered in pit dirt, recalling Holroyd's battle with the mine just as the corpse in Synge's play is clad in a sail to illustrate the dead man's struggle against the ocean.

Synge's drama had provoked grumbling when first seen, because, as the *Irish Times* put it, the 'long exposure of the dead body' was 'repulsive' and 'quite unfit for presentation on the stage'.[92] A decade later, Lawrence's work provoked similar approbrium. The Stage Society refused to produce *The Widowing of Mrs Holroyd* in 1914 because 'you could not satisfactorily conclude an evening's entertainment with the laying out of a dead body and twenty minutes of weeping, wailing and washing'.[93] Eventually an amateur group in Altrincham premiered the play in 1920, after which Lawrence's friend, the novelist Catherine Carswell, complained that:

To do justice to the Altrincham plays and the Altrincham audience, no sniggering was elicited by the scene where the dead miner's body is washed by his women. All the same, I felt that in a play so realistically written and produced, a body-washing scene was theatrically unacceptable. Either it must be done 'off' with only the voices and the footsteps of the women to give it reality, or the stage must be darkened to a firelight glow.[94]

When *The Widowing of Mrs Holroyd* received its first professional British production in 1926, reviewers for publications such as the *New Statesman* and *Outlook* expressed similar disapproval.[95] Indeed, the difficulty that the company found in staging the play's conclusion is revealed by the prompt book from that 1926 staging, which ends with the note, 'Unfasten belt, stand up. Very slow. Very Slow. Picture'.[96] Presumably, the sight of Mrs Holroyd unfastening her husband's belt, as the play's final line suggests she is about to do, had given inappropriate connotations to this part of the play (anticipating Alan Bennett's bawdy rewrite of the scene in *Enjoy*), and a frozen tableau had eventually proved more effective. Nonetheless, later in the century, other critics would discuss the conclusion of Lawrence's script very favourably, particularly in relation to the work of Synge. For example, in 1968 *The Times*'s reviewer, Irving Wardle, watched the Royal Court production of the play and felt that those final lines of Lawrence's play 'bring you closer to tears than Synge's keening islanders'.[97] In 1973, the *New York Times*'s critic, Julius Novick, made a virtually identical observation.[98] Yet, as we shall see, other work from the Irish dramatic canon also influenced Lawrence when he set about writing his first plays, and he developed a particular affinity for Yeats's writing, an appreciation that came about largely because of Lawrence's innovative methods of teaching drama in the schoolroom.

Davidson Road School

When Lawrence began teaching at Davidson Road School in Croydon he quickly realized that this institution had a close connection with the world of professional theatre-making. From 1908, the Actors' Orphanage Fund rented the nearby premises of 32–34 Moorland Road, as a home for the orphans and illegitimate children of actors. Thus, almost as soon as he arrived, Lawrence noted that of his fifty pupils, 'Six are the orphans of actors and acresses [*sic*], who live in the Actors home near us. They are delightful boys, refined, manly, and amiable. The other week we had Beerbohm Tree and Cyril Maude [two well-known actor-managers] and other big actresses and actors round to see them in school' (*Letters* I, 97). In this environment, Lawrence thought it appropriate to introduce the practical study of drama to the curriculum, in a way that had the potential to surprise some educationalists. The headteacher Philip Smith remembered how a visiting school inspector arrived in Lawrence's classroom:

> [The] intrusion was unexpected and resented. A curious wailing of distressed voices issued from a far corner. The sounds were muffled by a large covering black-board. The words of a familiar song arose from the depths:
>
> > Full fathom five thy father lies;
> > Of his bones are coral made.
>
> The class was reading *The Tempest*. The presentation expressed the usual thoroughness of Lawrence's attitude to the exercise in progress. It must not be spoiled by even official comment. Lawrence rushed with outstretched hands to the astounded visitor: 'Hush! Hush! Don't you hear? The sea chorus from *The Tempest*.'[99]

Lawrence had long been engaging in this kind of activity at Jessie Chambers's house, and so continued with a practical approach as a teacher, by contrast with the more conventional approach of a text-based classroom reading, which he found stultifying (as expressed in his 1915 novel *The Rainbow*, where Ursula complains that 'Most tedious was the close study of English Literature').[100] Elsewhere, he described how characters might appear quite different in performance from in a printed text, declaring 'Hamlet in the book seems to me a very messy person, but the Hamlets I have seen on the stage have been positively nasty'.[101] When in Croydon, he probably also discovered a new interest in sharing such pedagogical ideas with his younger sister Ada, who had gained employment in the tin-roofed New Eastwood Council School at the same time as he was engaged in his first teaching job, and who took a similar classroom approach to him.[102] Indeed, at one point in 1911, when Lawrence contracted double pneumonia, Ada and her Eastwood pupils had been due to perform a play called *Slightly Mixed*, and the *Eastwood and Kimberley Advertiser* reported that: 'Great consternation and regret was felt by the performers when it was found that Miss Lawrence, who had worked so hard in training the children, and was the [musical] accompanist, had been called away to nurse her brother, who is lying seriously ill at Croydon.[103] Still, when D.H. Lawrence was not poleaxed, his own drama teaching was clearly filled with energy and enthusiasm. Indeed, a theatrical sensibility infused his broader classroom technique: for example, he taught poetry by focusing on the sound of performance, the 'rhythm and the ring of words', and taught history by arranging 'the boys in two sides and they *fought* the battle of Agincourt'. Little wonder that his headteacher described Lawrence's English teaching as 'for the time, unorthodox'.[104] At one point, Lawrence asked his Croydon students to act out *As You Like It*, 'as if the front of the class were a stage', in order to make 'the boys enjoy it' (*Letters* I, 245). There may have been limited space in the schoolroom, but an expansive sense of fun infuses Lawrence's own reimagining of the Shakespearean play in the script he wrote at around the same time, his third play, *The Merry-go-Round*.

The Merry-go-Round

There can be little doubt about the influence that teaching *As You Like It* had upon Lawrence's latest play, a comedy set in Northrop (a phonetic variant of Newthorpe, the village located a mile-and-a-half from Eastwood). *The Merry-go-Round* begins by presenting the dying Mrs Hemstock, whose two children, Harry Hemstock and Susy Smalley, each suspect the other of attempting to inherit their mother's shop earnings of £500. The drama is therefore set up as a working-class version of Shakespeare's *As You Like It*, which begins after the recent death of Sir Rowland de Boys, and presents two of the nobleman's sons as being at loggerheads, with the eldest having inherited most of the estate and now refusing to pass any money to the younger son, Orlando. The Shakespearean parallels are inexact, but Harry Hemstock goes on to win the approval of a religious baron (who has previously disliked Harry) by saving him from a night-time assault by two women, just as Orlando repairs the relationship with his noble brother by saving him from being devoured by a forest lioness.

Lawrence's play goes on to follow *As You Like It* by depicting a set of confused lovers; female characters who are mistaken for men; and a central heroine in Nurse Broadbanks who, like Shakespeare's Rosalind, functions as the intelligent and witty heart of the drama. As Susan Carlson points out, although Lawrence shifts the focus away from the nurse in act five of *The Merry-go-Round*, 'All Lawrence's attention to Nurse Broadbanks – the complex plot set up largely around her controlling and tempering of others and his placement of wit, depth, and power in her – suggests that he intends her to be the main carrier of the play's intellectual weight'.[105] The nurse is herself involved in the various romantic confusions that ensue, before, at the end of *The Merry-go-Round*, there is a contrived Shakespearean ending when three groups of couples agree to marry. At this final moment, one of the characters suggests, 'It's "As You Like It"', only be corrected by another: 'It's "As You *Lump* It"' (190), and that qualification confirms that, although Lawrence's text relies on Shakespearean comedy, *The Merry-go-Round* avoids a straightforward retelling. The marriage conclusion, for example, has been undermined from the start by Mrs Hemstock's assertion that 'a husband only changes a lonely corner into a lonely house' (121), while, at another point, Lawrence almost veers off into a different Shakespearean piece altogether. At the end of act four, *The Merry-go-Round* looks closer to the tragedy of *Hamlet* than anything comic: Harry Hemstock is so grief-stricken by the death of his mother that he needs to 'go rummagin' down i' the loose ground like a moudiwarp, to look at the coffin' (185), and when he then decides upon a hasty marriage, another character comments, 'It'll look nice, that will – his mother buried yesterday' (186).

This varying tone, and somewhat meandering plot, mean that *The Merry-go-Round* is less admired than Lawrence's two earlier attempts at playwriting. Yet the piece contains a number of innovative features, and when Peter Gill staged a version at the Royal Court in 1973, the *Guardian* critic Michael Billington declared, 'No other native dramatist dealt so intelligently with personal relationships [...] Lawrence's delight in vagaries of human character and refusal to make moral judgments gives the play its supreme vitality'.[106] Like its predecessors, *The Merry-go-Round* features sharp regional language that has led even a harsh critic of the play, Arthur Waterman, to praise the 'wonderful dialect of homey images'.[107] The script also shows Lawrence's formal ambition in ranging beyond domestic drama and into offbeat comedy. One of the things that has damaged Lawrence's reputation as a writer is the notion that he was angry and mirthless. As Hilary Spurling put it in her review of his plays in 1968, 'It is Lawrence's humourlessness which defeats him in the end, banishing any trace of objectivity, dramatic tact, intelligence even'.[108] Similarly, in 1994, Charles Spencer declared, 'He takes himself so seriously, but you can't prevent yourself from sniggering'.[109] Yet, in *The Merry-go-Round*, Lawrence anticipates some of the best-known British comic performances of the later twentieth century. For example, the uptight baron who *'speaks with a very foreign – German – accent'* (123) is a forerunner of the comic staple of television sitcoms such as *Fawlty Towers* and *'Allo 'Allo*. The last-minute, multiple-marriage shenanigans at the church (as well as the death that occurs in the play) anticipate British romantic movies in the mould of Richard Curtis's *Four Weddings and a Funeral*. And the doctor–nurse relationship is full of the kind of innuendo that would characterize the *Carry On* films (something strongly suggested by the poster that advertised the 1973 Royal Court version of the play).[110] For instance, the nurse compares the doctor to the Pears Soap baby, 'He won't be happy till he gets it' (164); an old miner who wants to marry the nurse sends for her because 'he feels hot inside, an' believes he's got an inflammation' (173); and when the medical duo first meet they say:

> Nurse. Fancy you keeping your old shyness.
>
> Dr Foules. (*flushing*) I don't know that I do –.
>
> Nurse. I should have thought it would have worn off – all the experience you have had (128).

Ooh matron! Thus, even though his mother was dying at the same time as he wrote *The Merry-go-Round*, Lawrence managed to infuse the piece with a forward-looking sense of humour, much of which had been derived from the lively teaching sessions that he led at Croydon.

W.B. Yeats

Outside those formal lessons, Lawrence even helped to stage full-scale productions at Davidson Road School, one of which was a short 1902 comedy that had been co-authored by W.B. Yeats and Lady Gregory, *The Pot of Broth*. Lawrence painted the set, and adapted the script for performance, which took place on 30 November 1910. Indeed, he may have felt particularly enthusiastic about becoming involved in a Yeats production at this time, having recently met the Sligo poet in person. He had spoken with Yeats and Ezra Pound in December 1909, and subsequently gushed, 'Aren't the folks kind to me: it is really wonderful' (*Letters* I, 145).[111] The encounter with these *littérateurs* clearly triggered some kind of longer-term theatrical response in Lawrence, as he took to impersonating both men as his party-piece for many subsequent years.[112]

Unfortunately, on the evening that his schoolboys actually performed *The Pot of Broth*, Lawrence missed the play because he had to travel back to

Eastwood, to care for his mother in her dying days. Nevertheless, his colleague Arthur McLeod reported that the show had been well received, and the headmaster praised Lawrence's work in adapting it. Lawrence responded:

> I'm glad the concert went well – and proud that my awning should so approximate the work of Almighty God as to deceive people into a belief in its reality – unless you're telling me an amiable fib, for which I forgive you. Philip [Smith, the headteacher] had better read some of my prose before engaging me as school play-wright: it'll cure him of desiring me (*Letters* I, 193).

Later in the year, Lawrence set his students a composition exercise to write 'a newspaper account of any event', and one particularly sycophantic (or canny?) pupil responded by writing 'I found this jewel, "A Pot of Broth" an Irish play, was perfectly performed under the direction of Mr MacLeod [*sic*], before gorgeous scenery, exquisitely painted by Mr Lawrence' (*Letters* I, 246).

As noted, Lawrence started writing his play *The Merry-go-Round* at the same time as staging *The Pot of Broth* in Croydon, and his drama reveals at least one notable element taken from the earlier work. *The Pot of Broth* begins with the threat that the onstage action will be upstaged entirely by a chicken, as the audience hears shouts and footsteps and a frightened bird's cackling, and one character shouting 'Stop that old schemer of a hen flying up on the thatch like as if she was an eagle!'[113] In *The Merry-go-Round*, a live goose called Patty appears on the stage in the opening scene as a crucial part of the action, to be caressed and heaved into the air. Lawrence's humorous effect is heightened by the avian references adorning the rest of the play: for example, one of the characters is given the name of 'Dr Foules', another character is told 'Shut up, you old chuck! Shoo!' (145), and a third character starts '*flapping her arms suddenly*' (179). Lawrence had learned, from Yeats and Gregory, about the comic purpose of using a marauding bird in the opening sequence of a play, and here reveals the delight of a man who has obviously had great fun in the classroom with reading and preparing the opening sequence of *The Pot of Broth*.

In addition, *The Merry-go-Round* features an extensive use of dialect, with the Hemstock characters speaking some of the broadest Eastwood that is found anywhere in Lawrence's writing. This too was probably influenced by the strong Kiltartan dialect included in *The Pot of Broth*, which Lawrence and his schoolboys had delved into at the same time as he began writing *The Merry-go-Round*. But Lawrence failed to realize that this aspect of *The Pot of Broth* was shaped mainly by Lady Gregory, who co-wrote the piece (according to Yeats, she 'helped me as she has helped in every play of mine where there is dialect [...] This play may be more Lady Gregory's than mine').[114] Not knowing about this shared authorship, Lawrence – like many commentators and critics in the twentieth century – held a relatively dismissive view of Gregory, writing in later years, 'do you know I *can't* read dear Lady Gregory: too much of an insipid old stew' (*Letters* IV, 105). Lawrence had of course met face-to-face with Yeats; Yeats was the smiling public man; and when Lawrence met Frieda he began a relationship with a woman who had already acted as German translator of Yeats's early play *The Land of Heart's Desire*.[115] So the bias towards Yeats is understandable, even if the ageist and misogynistic language with which Lawrence dismissed Gregory remains less comprehensible.

Nevertheless, Lawrence was clearly excited by Yeats. And by April 1912, when Lawrence felt determined to get some of his playwriting seen by an audience, he understood from his friend Edward Garnett that Yeats's old manager at the Abbey Theatre, Ben Iden Payne, might produce one of the early Eastwood plays on the stage.[116] Unsurprisingly, Lawrence reacted by writing: 'It is huge to think of Iden Payne acting me on the stage [...] Of course I will alter and improve whatever I can, and Mr. Payne has fullest liberty to do entirely as he pleases with the play' (*Letters* I, 384).

Finally, for Lawrence, after that invigorating period of play-reading and theatrical discovery, his own experiments in scriptwriting appeared on the threshold of success. In his first three playtexts – *A Collier's Friday Night*, *The Widowing of Mrs Holroyd* and *The Merry-go-Round* – he had found a distinctive dramatic voice by blending the French theatre of Sarah Bernhardt and the Irish theatre of the Abbey playhouse together with his own observations of life in Eastwood, including his Nottinghamshire-inflected readings of Shakespeare. Now Lawrence simply had to get his work onto the stage, and Yeats's former manager would be the ideal person to help facilitate this. However, as we shall now see, during this next phase of Lawrence's theatrical life, very little went according to plan.

CHAPTER 2
THE FRUSTRATION OF STAGING:
DRAMATIC STRUGGLES, 1911 TO 1930

Granville Barker

By 1911, Lawrence had completed three plays, *A Collier's Friday Night*, *The Widowing of Mrs Holroyd* and *The Merry-go-Round*. But he had very little knowledge about the world of the theatre professional. He had spent much time reading through the dramatic canon, performing amateur dramas and visiting the playhouse. Yet he knew next to nothing about the mysterious process by which theatres selected their scripts, cast the main parts and rehearsed pieces for performance. Nonetheless, Lawrence was scarcely writing his plays in order that they should remain on paper: he wanted to see them on the stage.

Lawrence now sent copies of his three plays to the writer and critic, Ford Madox Hueffer, informing Hueffer that these scripts were designed for actors. *The Widowing of Mrs Holroyd*, Lawrence emphasized, was 'an act-able play' and *The Merry-go-Round* 'shall be playable', although he also confessed that he had little idea about how to proceed – asking plaintively 'what am I to do with these plays?' (*Letters* I, 199).[1] Hueffer wanted to help, but offered somewhat cackhanded assistance, mislaying two of the three scripts that Lawrence sent him. Worryingly, these were the only copies in existence, but Hueffer nonetheless forwarded the one play he had not lost, *The Widowing of Mrs Holroyd*, to the actor, director and playwright, Harley Granville Barker.

At first glance, Barker looked like the ideal producer for Lawrence's work. Barker had, after all, managed a celebrated three seasons of what he called 'the uncommercial drama' between 1904 and 1907 at the Court Theatre.[2] Under Barker, the Court had showcased the work of young British dramatists whose plays took, in the words of Desmond MacCarthy, 'a critical and dissenting attitude towards contemporary codes of morality.'[3] During 1909 Barker then produced John Galsworthy's play, *Strife*, which was praised by the *Nottingham Guardian* for conveying meaning through 'a twitch of the mouth, a change of expression, or even a movement of the hands', and the play influenced the subtleties of Lawrence's stagecraft after he watched the production in Nottingham that year.[4]

However, unknown to Lawrence, mid-1911 was a bad time to approach Barker with new playwriting. Between June 1908 and February 1910 Barker had directed only one play, and his 1910 effort to run a repertory theatre based on new work 'all grounded in a naturalistic style' proved a box-office disaster, receiving criticism in *The Stage* because 'the morbid and the sour-visaged predominated'.[5] In this atmosphere, Lawrence's realistic descriptions of poverty and corpse-washing were the last thing Barker needed. In any case, by the summer of 1911, Barker had become producer at the 278-seat Little Theatre in Adelphi, and had found great commercial and critical success with Shaw's class-based comedy, *Fanny's First Play*, which meant the playhouse gave a long run of that play throughout 1911 and did not require an extensive array of new submissions.[6] Barker therefore returned his copy of *The Widowing of Mrs Holroyd* with a note saying 'read it with much interest but afraid I don't want it' (*Letters* I, 298).

Edward Garnett

Into the breach stepped Edward Garnett, the literary editor who would have a major influence on Lawrence's writing career. In August 1911, Garnett worked as English agent for the US magazine, the *Century*, and approached Lawrence for submissions.[7] By October, Lawrence had sent Garnett the one complete play that Hueffer had not lost, *The Widowing of Mrs Holroyd*, and despite the piece having been rejected by Granville Barker, Lawrence emphasized to Garnett that this was really intended 'for the stage – I tried to make it end up stagily', adding, 'The first scenes are good' (*Letters* I, 309).

Garnett mooted the idea of publishing a volume of plays, but this stalled because two-thirds of them had been lost by Hueffer (who started asserting that he had 'never had them' and 'didn't know anything about them', although he eventually located them in the Authors' Club during March 1912 (*Letters* I, 309, 376)). Nonetheless, even whilst the prospect of publication receded, Garnett looked likely to provide Lawrence with a route into professional production. After all, Garnett had written a play called *The Breaking Point* that had become one of the best-known works of the contemporary British stage, creating a scandal when originally accepted for production in 1907 because the plot revolves around the suicide of a woman who becomes pregnant after an affair with a married man. Unsurprisingly, the censor refused a licence on the grounds of indecency.[8] But Garnett, with his top-notch literary connections, challenged this judgement, and the play became the centrepiece of an anti-censorship campaign.[9] Indeed, *The Breaking Point* grew so notorious that Lawrence worried for his own reputation when he forwarded copies of Garnett's plays to Louie Burrows, and warned her, '*Don't show them to your people: it will be enough for them that *The Breaking Point* is censored, to make them look at me very askance*' (*Letters* I, 325).

However, although *The Breaking Point* had achieved notoriety, it remained poorly written, something that was apparent to G.B. Shaw, who worried that it might provoke unintended 'roars of laughter' if performed.[10] When the play finally reached the stage for a members-only production in 1908 the critical verdict indeed proved damning: even Garnett's own son declared, 'The agony was prolonged and the effect was nightmarish.'[11] D.H. Lawrence praised the script to Garnett himself, declaring, 'It is a fine, clean moulded tragedy, *The Breaking Point*. I have always got such a lot of non-essential stuff in my work' (*Letters* I, 317). However, Lawrence's private opinion remained less flattering. After he had finished reading *The Breaking Point* he forwarded it to Louie Burrows and told her, 'I don't care for Garnett's plays – they are not alive' (*Letters* I, 325).

Still, Lawrence obviously wanted to impress Garnett, and drew upon *The Breaking Point* during a renewed bout of playwriting. In a fertile period during 1912–13, Lawrence scripted *The Married Man*, *The Fight for Barbara* and *The Daughter-in-Law*, and each of these works evokes Garnett's *The Breaking Point* in the complicated marital and extramarital relationships that Lawrence describes. After all, although Garnett's work had been a theatrical disaster, Lawrence admired the script's challenge to conventional morality and authority.

The Married Man

The play that Lawrence wrote after reading *The Breaking Point* was *The Married Man*, which includes some exposition that recalls Garnett's work. Garnett's *The Breaking Point* begins with a stilted scene that allows a man-of-the-world attitude to dominate the stage. At this opening moment, two male characters discuss the fact that one of them has separated from (although not divorced) his wife, and has since impregnated his new girlfriend. Likewise, in Lawrence's *The Married Man*, two men discuss the fact that one of them has separated from (although not divorced) his wife, and is now living the life of a 'gay bachelor', including dalliances with some 'fine girls' (195).[12]

In part, *The Married Man* took inspiration from Lawrence's own personal life at the time. Shortly before writing the play, Lawrence felt keen to tell Garnett that:

> My sister and I were at a bit of a dance last night at Jacksdale – mining village four miles out. It was most howling good fun. My sister found me kissing one of her friends goodbye – such a ripping little girl – and we were kissing like nuts – enter my sister – great shocks all round, and much indignation. But – life is awfully fast down here (*Letters* I, 369).

This 'fast' life of casual female acquaintances being kissed 'like nuts', without any great emotional attachment, is precisely the one that is described in the play. Furthermore, one of the main characters of *The Married Man* is a thinly disguised version of Lawrence himself: the character of William Brentnall is (like Lawrence at the time) convalescing from an illness and (like the young Lawrence) is often called 'Billy'. At the start of the play, Brentnall visits his friend George Grainger (the 'Married Man' of the title) just as, in the final week of March 1912, Lawrence had visited his old schoolfriend George Neville.[13] During this real-life reunion of 1912, Lawrence found his acquaintance to be 'Don Juanish': Neville was living alone while his wife and newborn child stayed in Stourbridge (*Letters* I, 373). Within a month of this trip, Lawrence had completed *The Married Man*, depicting a character called George who is in a similar situation, living apart from his wife Ethel and baby son James, with all three fictional characters bearing the same first names as the real-life Neville family.

In *The Married Man*, George has impregnated Ethel and then married her during the third trimester of her pregnancy, but after openly admitting paternity he was 'kicked out' (223) of prudish Wolverhampton, and now feels fondness for neither wife nor child. Indeed, he has only visited his wife once in six months since the wedding. Instead, George works as a doctor in a small village, where he pursues other women who remain ignorant of his marital status, although the truth is revealed during the course of the play, and at the end he embraces and agrees to live with both bride and baby. That final vision of domestic happiness is, however, entirely undercut by the very last words of the play: George's comment to an approving Brentnall, 'Shut up, fool' (235).

George's confident closing assertion to his wife that 'You're the only girl I could have married' (235) has also been thoroughly demolished by the earlier action of the play itself. The plot proceeds by showing the men swapping their partners at random, and this is shown most vividly in the central third act of the play, which involves the characters dancing in changing combinations. Exactly how this choreography works is quite difficult to discern in the printed script, but the dynamic would be clear in performance, where the three main changes in dancing partnerships outlined in Table 2.1 would be observed.

These bodies in motion form shifting and recombining partnerships, making this part of Lawrence's play feel something like a forerunner to Samuel Beckett's drama of movement *Quad* (1981), in which the dancers circle around something unseen at the centre of the stage. As with Beckett's play, Lawrence offers more questions than answers: the couples of this part of *The Married Man* meet and interact largely at random, and indeed Lawrence brings the last couple, Tom and Gladys, onto the stage without any explanation, they fail to appear in the rest of the play and are perhaps simply there to illustrate a point about the arbitrary nature of romantic entanglement.

Furthermore, a biographical reading of the shifting pairings of this scene throws up something rather disconcerting: in using the names Ada and

Table 2.1

1				
Sally + George	Ada + William	Emily + Jack		
2				
Sally + William	Ada + George	Emily + Jack		

At this point there is the surprise arrival of William's fiancée Elsa, with another married couple Tom and Gladys

3				
Sally + George	Ada + Tom	Emily + Magneer	Elsa + Jack	William + Gladys
		(Magneer = previously the non-dancing musician)		

Emily, Lawrence was using the names of his own sisters, and yet the autobiographical figure of William Brentnall begins this dance by partnering Ada, and repeatedly kissing her, at the same time that the fictional Ada calls Brentnall by Lawrence's real-life family nickname (she calls Brentnall 'his knobs' (213) just as the young Lawrence had been known as 'Billy White-nob').[14] This fictional incestuousness, then, allowed Lawrence to consider the idea that romantic partnerships might be random enough to incorporate even the most unconventional and taboo of unions.

In *The Married Man*, Lawrence also extended some of the dramatic enquiries that he had conducted in his earlier plays: for example, the Magneer characters of this play continue to speak in the Eastwood dialect, and the sexual theme allowed Lawrence to test the skill at comic innuendo that he had explored in earlier scriptwriting. The Calladine sisters also enabled Lawrence to continue his investigations into female independence. These twenty- and thirty-something sisters, who are the main subject of the attention from George and Brentnall, are living together without husbands or father, and so are free to explore their emotions and desires without the constraints of patriarchal control, and with the ability to perceive that, as one of them puts it, 'You men are all alike' (206).

Regional repertory theatre

In *The Married Man*, Lawrence had therefore echoed the risqué topics of Edward Garnett's playwriting, and there may have been a canny calculation in this emulation. After all, Lawrence had written dialect-drama that no one wanted to stage, but Garnett had successfully managed to find actors who would put similar plays into production. For example, Garnett's *The Breaking Point* had been produced in 1908 by the Stage Society, which specialized in mounting censor-baiting shows and whose actors could cope with the moments of Exeter dialect in that text ('Good evening, Zur! [...] They've sent I on to tell 'ee').[15] Garnett's next produced play, *The Feud*, needed delivering in a quasi-northern English dialect – with characters saying things such as 'I don't see that aught is wrong' – and was first performed in April 1909 by Annie Horniman's company at the Manchester Gaiety, which had been founded a year and half before and which set about producing work that engaged with the particular language and concerns of the local area.[16] Another Garnett play, *Lords and Masters*, then received a Manchester production in May 1911, with both this and *The Feud* appearing there under the direction of Yeats's former manager, Ben Iden Payne. In May 1912 Payne agreed to produce another Garnett effort, *The Spanish Lovers*, at the Little Theatre in London. Of course, Garnett's work continued to be savaged by the critics, who made comments such as 'A play of this kind is a test for any company'.[17] But Lawrence saw that, regardless, Garnett at least had found professional theatre companies that would stage such drama, with Lawrence always feeling 'keen to hear' about these events (*Letters* II, 98–99). During rehearsals for the 1912 production, Garnett offered to introduce Iden Payne to Lawrence, who responded with great enthusiasm. Lawrence had, after all, seen Iden Payne's company at Nottingham's Theatre Royal two months earlier, and felt so excited by the prospect of working with Iden Payne that he wrote to Garnett, 'of course I don't expect to get money by it. But it's ripping to think of my being acted' (*Letters* I, 384).

Lawrence and Iden Payne then chatted together, but the meeting hardly proved a success. Payne failed to offer a proposal of a production, but merely suggested changes to one of Lawrence's existing scripts. Shortly afterwards, Lawrence wrote to Garnett, declaring that Payne 'rather amuses me – He was going to show me what he wanted altering, but now says I know what wants doing without his troubling' (*Letters* I, 389). Thus Lawrence had failed to make his way into the world of the professional theatre through Ben Iden Payne, just as he had failed to make it through Granville Barker. A second opportunity had gone begging, and it had looked a good one. After all, the Manchester Gaeity theatre was part of a regional repertory movement that had sprung up from 1907, and involved a number of new British companies staging plays by writers such as John Joy Bell, James Sexton and Harold Brighouse, whose stage characters spoke in dialect and addressed the particular histories and concerns of people in urban areas outside London.[18] Lawrence's work, with its detailed engagement with Nottinghamshire life and Nottinghamshire dialect, obviously had the potential to dovetail with such a movement.

However, the repertory theatres that might have proved most sympathetic to Lawrence's work enjoyed a relatively brief flourishing. Most of those companies suffered from financial problems, with the most boldly experimental productions – such as Hauptmann's sacrilegious *Hannele* (1893) at the Liverpool Repertory Theatre in spring 1913 – proving toxic at the box office. In the wake of that production, in December, Lawrence met with Lascelles Abercrombie, the poet who worked as play-reader for the Liverpool Repertory Theatre and whose verse-drama *The Adder* had recently been staged there during the same season as *Hannele*. Abercrombie's play *The Adder* is concerned with the issue of illegitimate fatherhood, troubled family bonds, and is written in dialect, and Lawrence may have recognized an affinity with his own writing, judging Abercrombie 'one of the sharpest men I have ever met' (*Letters* II, 118). However, at the time of their meeting, the Liverpool Repertory Theatre had just experienced a financially woeful year, and now faced possible closure, with its director and chairman having resigned.[19] If Abercrombie and Lawrence chinwagged about drama, it would have been in this miserable context, and Liverpool was not alone. By 1914 the Glasgow Repertory had closed, while the Manchester Gaiety had appointed Douglas Gordon as manager, a traditionalist who brought back the old stars of the touring companies.[20] The work of the regional repertory theatres between 1907 and 1914 aligned with Lawrence's own theatrical aesthetic but, particularly through his contact with Abercrombie, the Eastwood man is likely to have realized the fleeting nature of that opportunity.

In addition, Edward Garnett had never mastered scriptwriting sufficiently well in order to function as a reliable theatrical guide, and – aware that his own reputation had suffered because of his persistence with drama – he increasingly shepherded Lawrence towards novel-writing. After all, Lawrence published his first novel *The White Peacock* in 1911, produced the follow-up *The Trespasser* by 1912, and – as his mentor Garnett evidently felt – now required encouragement to complete *Sons and Lovers* in 1913. Lawrence needed to avoid developing a self-destrutive relationship with the theatre like that of Garnett, who was himself counselled by playmaking friends such as William Archer and John Galsworthy to write novels rather than dramas.[21] Lawrence did make supportive noises, pointing out that Garnett's productions had been treated 'rather meanly' (*Letters* I, 469) and denouncing hostile reviewers as 'Fools – they're all fools' (*Letters* I, 414). But, like Garnett's other friends, Lawrence realized that Garnett was writing in the wrong medium, declaring of Garnett's 1912 play *Jeanne D'Arc* that, 'It seems to me a human record rather than a play' (*Letters* I, 469–470). With such criticism ringing in his ears, Garnett felt determined to steer Lawrence in a different direction; and indeed, under this influence, Lawrence now described his own recent dramatic scrips rather dismissively as 'candidly impromptus. I *know* they want doing again' (*Letters* I, 477).

Frieda

Perhaps Lawrence ought to have persisted with Ben Iden Payne. After all, Iden Payne knew the regional repertory movement extremely well, had produced the work of Edward Garnett, and showed a clear interest in Lawrence's drama. But during the following year, Iden Payne travelled to work in the USA, where he remained until after Lawrence's death. Besides, at the time that Lawrence arrived for their *tête à tête*, the writer himself was feeling distracted by other life events, and had the feeling that his own future lay elsewhere.

In early March 1912, Lawrence met Frieda Weekley, wife of one of his professors at Nottingham University College. Although Frieda had a husband and three children, she and Lawrence began a love affair, and Lawrence brought Frieda to London in April when he met Iden Payne. Lawrence then opted out of attending *The Spanish Lovers*, the script that Garnett had written and Iden Payne was then producing. Instead, by 3 May 1912, Lawrence and Frieda had travelled to Germany together, with Lawrence telling Garnett, 'I wanted to see it, but as things are, I want to go to Germany more' (*Letters* I, 386).

Lawrence, then, hardly concentrated on making the best possible impression with Iden Payne, whose show it would have been tactful to attend. However, despite Lawrence's lovestruck escape with Frieda, he remained intensely interested in theatre and performance. During the short period between first meeting Frieda and travelling to Germany, Lawrence completed his play *The Married Man*, a work that (with its overlapping personal relationships) owed something to the situation in which Lawrence and Frieda now found themselves. When the duo arrived in Germany, they then saw a Passion play in Beuerberg, a version of Ibsen's *Ghosts* in Munich and may also have attended the theatre in Bad Tölz.[22] Then, after three months in Germany, the duo continued through Austria to a new base on the edge of Lake Garda in Northern Italy, where Lawrence continued pursuing his theatrical interests, despite the fact that neither he nor Frieda spoke Italian, and despite being chronically short of money. Towards the end of 1912, the pair watched Verdi's *Rigoletto* in Saló, as well as a touring version of Ibsen's *Ghosts* at nearby Gargnano.[23] By the start of 1913, Lawrence had also watched Gabriele d'Annunzio's play *The Light under the Bushel*, Silvio Zambaldi's comedy *The Wife of the Doctor* and a version of Shakespeare's *Hamlet* that conjured up childhood memories of performances in Eastwood.[24] Lawrence also wrote a review of those Italian theatrical experiences in a piece called 'The Theatre' that would appear in the *English Review* by September 1913, and that would be revised and expanded for his 1916 volume of essays, *Twilight in Italy*.[25]

The Fight for Barbara

In Italy, during October 1912, Lawrence also wrote a new play based on his current situation, *The Fight for Barbara*. The plot of this drama revolves around the married Barbara Tressida, who has abandoned her husband for Jimmy Wesson, the working-class son of a butty collier. Barbara and Wesson have (according to her husband) had sex in her house on their first meeting, and, three weeks later, have fled to Italy together, where the play is set and from where Barbara's husband and parents try to persuade Barbara to return. This plot came close enough to the real-life situation of Lawrence and Frieda Weekley for Lawrence to assert that 'much of it is word for word true', and for Frieda to claim 'it's all of it really lived' (*Letters* I, 466–467). Indeed, she responded by penning her own – now lost – biographical skit, which she entitled 'Paul Morel, or His Mother's Darling'.[26]

As a result, critics have mainly tended to explore *The Fight for Barbara* in biographical terms. Yet, as Ian Clarke has argued, the play also deserves to be seen in the 'appropriate late Victorian and Edwardian theatrical context'.[27] After all, certain parts of the play come closer to what Lawrence had seen on the stage than anything he had known in real life. Frieda herself wrote, after Lawrence's death, that 'the setting is the setting of the villa, the kitchen with its copperhaus is the kitchen of the Villa Igéa, the postman at the door, the pretty girl with the milk & the butcher, very real. But of course ~~many~~ some of the characters are not real people'.[28] For example, Lawrence had only met Frieda's father once, at a time when the two men communicated only in broken French, and when Lawrence and Frieda were keeping their love affair a secret and pretending simply to be friends.[29] But in *The Fight for Barbara*, Lawrence depicted Barbara's father arriving in consternation at his daughter's adultery, and demanding that the lower-class Wesson now 'leave her' (272). Such a scene followed the best-known part of the play that had deeply affected Lawrence in 1908, *La Dame aux Camélias*, where the character of Marguerite is confronted by Armand's father, who tries to persuade her to give up Armand. This part of *The Fight for Barbara* also recalls a parallel scene in a different play that Lawrence had recently grown to know well, Edward Garnett's *The Breaking Point*, where there is another confrontation between a woman's father and her lover. Indeed, the language used in *The Fight for Barbara* suggests that Lawrence had drawn specifically upon his friend's work: in Garnett's play the lover admits that he is 'criminally to blame', whereas in Lawrence's script the lover is told that he has committed 'a criminal act' (272).[30]

Furthermore, *The Fight for Barbara* allowed Lawrence to extend some of the ideas in the drama he had written earlier that year. A few months before, Lawrence had written his play *The Married Man*, which begins with two characters discussing sex and contraception. Now, *The Fight for Barbara* starts with a variant on the same idea, by showing Wesson 'in dressing-gown and pyjamas' and Barbara 'holding her blue silk dressing-gown about her' (239–240). A version of Frieda had also fleetingly appeared in *The Married Man* as the character of Elsa Smith, a beautiful German-speaking woman who expresses relaxed views about those who might break their marriage vows. Now, in *The Fight for Barbara*, such a figure becomes the title character, not just commenting on the potential infidelity of others, but willing to conduct her own adulterous relationship. Even some of the language of the earlier play is recycled. For example, in *The Married Man*, one female character declares that 'men are all alike' (206), whereas in *The Fight for Barbara*, Barbara repeats and extends that thought: 'All men are alike. They don't care what a woman wants. They try to get hold of what they want themselves, as if it were a pipe. As for the woman, she's not considered – and so – that's where you make your mistake, gentlemen' (293).

One of the most notable things about *The Fight for Barbara* is that Lawrence makes more explicit some of the pro-woman views of his earlier drama. Barbara is a figure of independence who refuses to submit to existing male structures of power and makes the argument for gender equality, telling her lover, '*I* want there to be no upper hand. I only want both of us to be free to be ourselves' (248). Barbara is thus established as the main force of agency in the play, although those around her often – comically – fail to realize this. When Barbara's mother arrives she continually appeals to Wesson to return her daughter, while Barbara repeatedly interrupts to point out, 'But Mama, what I do I do of myself' (259); 'But if I chose to do it, Mama, it is my affair'; 'But Mama, I'm not a horse that is to be kept' (260). Barbara's father then arrives in the play and makes exactly the same mistake of appealing to Wesson, causing Barbara to explode: 'What right has he to come bullying Wesson behind my back. *I* came away with him – it was *I* who suggested he should come to Italy with me when I was coming to see Laura. So when you have anything to say, Papa, say it to me, – if you dare' (273).

By contrast with Barbara's power, the men that she must decide between – her lover and her husband – are diminished figures, who both make threats of physical violence against her but ultimately exert little authority. Barbara mocks her lover, and although he eventually feels provoked enough to seize her, that reaction makes small difference as she continues to criticize him (with notably phallic jibes) for having been a 'shrivelling creature whom Mama scolded' (270) and for acting like a 'poor worm' (274). Her husband's threats of violence and grabbing of Barbara have still less effect upon her behaviour. Indeed, with both her lover and her husband having threatened to kill her, Barbara simply responds with wry resignation: 'Not twice in one *night*' (296).

At the start of the play, Barbara tells her lover Wesson, 'you want to humble me [...] and make me nothing – and then swallow me. And it's *wrong*. It's *wrong* for you to want to swallow me. I am myself – and you ought to leave me free' (247). She does eventually decide to remain living with him, but only after he has acknowledged that she should not be treated in this way: Wesson comes to the conclusion that 'You were too big a mouthful for him to swallow, and he was choking himself' (298). The play then ends with Barbara asking Wesson to 'Love me a fearful lot!' (299), a statement that sounds docile but is laced with irony, coming as it does from a character who has been anything but submissive until that point, and thus providing a resolution that is as undermined as the one which concluded *The Married Man*.

Those dramatic scripts of 1911–1912, then, help to show Lawrence's developing thinking about theatre, as well as his ideas about sex and gender, and about his own personal situation. Yet *The Merry-go-Round*, *The Married Man* and *The Fight for Barbara* have never enjoyed sustained attention from theatre producers. In part, the convoluted plot of *The Merry-go-Round*, the textually opaque choreography in *The Married Man* and the dominant biographical reading of *The Fight for Barbara* may have worked against these scripts being recognized as potentially effective stage pieces. In subsequent years, there is no sign that Lawrence ever did the editorial 're-casting' (*Letters* I, 477) he told Garnett they needed. Frieda suggested of *The Fight for Barbara* that 'no doubt he would have rewritten it, if he had seen it again, as he did most of his things'.[31] But, in the event, those three scripts were found only after Lawrence's death, in the Heidelberg attic of his German sister-in-law, having apparently been forgotten by the author during his lifetime.

The Daughter-in-Law

However, in a flurry of twelve days' writing at the start of 1913, Lawrence wrote another play that would be far better remembered. Having recently experimented with the quasi-Shakespearean piece, *The Merry-go-Round*, a comedy of movement in *The Married Man* and a society drama in *The Fight for Barbara*, he now returned to draft a realistic play written in a heavy Eastwood dialect, *The Daughter-in-Law*. He described the new work to Edward Garnett: 'I am going to send you a new play I have written. It is neither a comedy nor a tragedy – just ordinary. It is quite objective, as far as that term goes, and though no doubt, like most of my stuff, it wants weeding out a bit, yet I think the whole thing is there' (*Letters* I, 500–501).

Indeed, *The Daughter-in-Law* has been hailed by Lawrence's biographer Mark Kinkead-Weekes as 'not only well made but (arguably) Lawrence's best, and his most original play'.[32]

The real skill of Lawrence's writing here is in depicting the working-class characters of the Nottinghamshire mining district in difficult and sometimes desperate circumstances, but removing the audience's ability either to locate moral responsibility for those circumstances or to find easy solutions to the characters' problems. Indeed, the very start of the play presents a conundrum: the young miner Joe Gascoyne has been injured at work but is being refused compensation. Do we think he actually deserves money? He was *at* work when he was injured: but, as it turns out, he was fooling around and not actually *working* at the time when the accident occurred.

A more complex dilemma then appears in the shape of Joe's brother Luther, who has recently married but suddenly learns that he has impregnated a woman who is not his wife (here Lawrence recycled an idea from the dialect poem he had first written in 1911, 'Whether or Not').[33] Should we blame Luther for the predicament? At the time that he had sex with this woman he had no knowledge that he was going to get married and is profoundly upset when told about the pregnancy. Perhaps it is the pregnant woman's fault? Yet she is described as 'poor' and 'simple' (314), and will now have to bear the social and financial burden of raising the infant.

Rather than resolving this argument, the blame is then deflected towards another character entirely. Luther's mother argues that his wife Minnie could have married him years ago and thus prevented this whole situation, but instead Minnie kept him waiting, uncertain and discouraged, leading him to seek out another girlfriend. However, when Minnie appears, she in turn argues that such a delay was scarcely her fault: Luther is a mother's boy who remained long unprepared for marriage, and even now Minnie strongly hints that she remains sexually unsatisfied by him. In any case, Minnie's own grim family background is alluded to: she is an orphan and her mother was 'treated scandylos by Jim Hetherington' (310), so perhaps the current situation is therefore Jim Hetherington's fault for doing whatever he did to Minnie's mother and thus making Minnie so wary of marriage.

Responsibility is thus endlessly deferred, with Joe going on to suggest that they blame Liz Varley, a local acquaintance who encouraged the now-pregnant woman to go out to the alehouse where meetings with Luther occurred; or maybe Jim Horrocks, Liz's boyfriend, who corralled the future parents into a double-date at the pub. Minnie herself consistently blames her misfortunes on her mother-in-law, the indomitable Mrs Gascoyne, for being overly possessive towards Luther and Joe: 'You kept him, like a child [. . .] You didn't care what women your sons went with, so long as they didn't *love* them' (348). But as Mrs Gascoyne explains, she actually does not wish to hold on to Luther indefinitely, repeating the maxim 'My son's my son till he takes him a wife' (315, 343). Mrs Gascoyne has, after all, already married off her four older sons and has been protecting the younger two only because 'they'd run theirselves into danger and lick their lips for joy' (358). Her sense of Luther's and Joe's self-destructiveness is proven correct throughout the play: the piece opens by describing the unfortunate results of Luther's amorous and Joe's accident-prone activities, and closes with them almost dying amidst pit strikes. In any case, although Minnie blames her mother-in-law, she has to repeatedly qualify her criticisms (349, 358), and the play ultimately makes clear that Minnie herself is simply a younger version of the strong matriarch.

In *The Daughter-in-Law* all of these complex personal interactions take place against a broader background of miners' strikes, whose morality and efficacy are also opened to debate. At one stage (321–322), the argument proceeds as in Table 2.2.

In this way, Lawrence's finely balanced play presents the many ambiguities of everyday working-class life, with its dilemmas and arguments as vexed as anything faced by any other section of society. Lawrence does not offer solutions to the problems of the poor because, as *The Daughter-in-Law* makes clear, such problems are multi-factoral, shifting and perhaps ultimately intractable.

Innovative though this drama may have been, it was not entirely *sui generis*, and, like Lawrence's other plays of 1912–1913, *The Daughter-in-Law* borrows from *The Breaking Point*, the censored play by Edward Garnett. As with Garnett's script, *The Daughter-in-Law* begins with the discussion of an unplanned pregnancy, and both plays then portray the ensuing pressures that might be faced by female characters. Indeed, the two dramas share some specific stage business: for example in Garnett's *The Breaking Point* when one woman is surprised by her father, she jumps and drops the plate that she is holding, almost starts to cry and '*flushes*'.[34] In Lawrence's

Table 2.2

Minnie's View	*Luther's View*
The miners are going on strike simply because they want a holiday.	The miners are striking because they deserve a proper minimum wage for a day's work in the mines, as demanded by the Miners' Federation in the early years of the twentieth century.
The local coal seams are growing thin: in this situation, the company cannot afford to pay higher wages to the colliers.	The company has no excuse for scrimping on workers' wages: it has built a new electric plant and is providing high wages and new houses for the managers.
High wages are required for the managers if the company is going to be able to attract good managers in the first place. Good managers are required so that the pits make money.	Those managers make the pits profitable by cutting wages for everyone else.
Her husband lacks ambition: he is 'not much of a workman' and taking part in a strike will damage his prospects of promotion.	'Thee shut thy mouth'.

The Daughter-in-Law, Minnie's brother-in-law arrives, deliberately smashes a plate, and Minnie weeps and '*flushes*' (323).

When Lawrence finished writing *The Daughter-in-Law* in 1913, he sent it to Garnett, as he had done with his five other plays, emphasizing that the text needed to 'have a chance on the stage' and that 'I don't think it lacks the stuff for the theatre' (*Letters* I, 501). Shortly afterwards, Lawrence told Garnett, 'I believe that, just as an audience was found in Russia for *Tchekhov*, so an audience might be found in England for some of my stuff, if there were a man to whip 'em in. It's the producer that is lacking, not the audience' (*Letters* I, 509). But Garnett had been discouraging about Lawrence's recent dramatic efforts, only really praising *The Widowing of Mrs Holroyd*. In response, Lawrence made his best-known statement about the contemporary stage, writing to Garnett that: 'I am sure we are sick of the rather bony, bloodless drama we get nowadays – it is time for a reaction against Shaw and Galsworthy and Barker and Irishy (except Synge) people – the rule and measure mathematical folk. But you are of them and your sympathies are with your own generation' (*Letters* I, 509).

Still, *The Daughter-in-Law* remained disappointingly unpublished and unperformed throughout Lawrence's lifetime. So Lawrence, continually pursued by money worries, decided to recycle the script in order to create the short story 'The Last Straw' ['Fanny and Annie'] (written in 1919 and published in 1921).[35] The short story echoes the plot of the earlier play, presenting a socially pretentious woman with an inheritance who has returned to her industrial hometown in order to marry a man who, during the long wait for marriage, has had sex with another women who is now pregnant. In the rewrite, Lawrence of course made a number of changes, including the fact that 'The Last Straw' is notably less sentimental than *The Daughter-in-Law*. But the overall narrative shape of the short story, as well as particular lines of dialogue, reveals how heavily Lawrence relied on his earlier dramatic script.

The Stage Society

The Daughter-in-Law thus led Lawrence to express hostility towards theatrical contemporaries such as Shaw and Granville Barker, and to realize that he might have to redraft his dramas as short stories in order to find an audience. Yet the playhouses that promoted Shaw and Granville Barker still provided Lawrence with his most likely route into theatrical production, and in 1913 Lawrence received a promising invitation from the Stage Society in London, an organization that aimed to present scripts which were artistically impressive but that might prove commercially toxic. Furthermore, the Stage Society was a private club, so could produce dramas that remained censored from the general public, staging notable productions of banned plays including Shaw's discussion of prostitution in *Mrs Warren's Profession* (1902) and Granville Barker's abortion play, *Waste* (1907).

In June 1912, the Stage Society had scored a notable hit by producing *Hindle Wakes*, a recent play by one of the writers associated with the Manchester Gaiety, Stanley Houghton.[36] Houghton's drama revolves around the working-class mill-girl, Fanny Hawthorn, whose family discovers that she has just spent a dirty weekend with a wealthy, and already betrothed, son of an industrialist. The drama begins in the kitchen of a working-class Lancashire home, ends with an assertion of female independence, and includes the working-class dialect of north-west England: 'Stop thy crying. Thou'd better get upstairs to bed. Happen thou's fagged out'.[37] With newspaper critics widely praising the 'agreeable novelty' of Houghton's play, the Stage Society now sought to replicate the success.[38] The following year, after the publication of Lawrence's *Sons and Lovers*, the novelist and playwright Arnold Bennett recommended the Eastwood man's work to the Stage Society, whose management then contacted Lawrence in December 1913, enquiring if he could provide any suitable theatrical pieces.[39]

However, at this point Lawrence was worrying about redrafting. He found it relatively easy to set down his dramatic ideas, but he had been spending a great deal of time in 1913 revising *The Widowing of Mrs Holroyd*, feeling bruised by those earlier rejections by Iden Payne and Granville Barker.[40] He declared in April 1913 that although he thought it a 'jolly fine play' he had 'been very busy reading the play to Frieda. It wants *a lot* of altering. I have made it heaps better' (*Letters* II, 58).

Such revisions to the text meant that, when contacted by the Stage Society he worried that it was 'in such a state they could not read it' (*Letters* II, 127): the society would have to wait until the following year when a printed copy was due to appear. In the end, he did send some proofs in advance of publication, but the state of that submission remains unclear. Today, the only surviving copy of *The Widowing of Mrs Holroyd* is the one printed in 1914 – the original manuscript, typescript and proofs are lost – and as John Worthen and Hans-Wilhelm Schwarze have shown, Lawrence continued revising the piece until the eleventh hour, adding changes onto the proof copy that mean today it is impossible to tell whether all of those intended revisions are incorporated into the final printed text.[41] Thus, Lawrence may well have sent an unimpressive version to the Stage Society that indicated that the work remained unpolished or incomplete.

In the event, the Stage Society rejected the play 'after long consideration'.[42] After all, the organization had looked to Lawrence following the working-class triumph of *Hindle Wakes*, but Houghton's drama started with the tragic news of a drowning and ended with comedy. According to that model, Lawrence's narrative was all wrong, making precisely the reverse journey: Mrs Holroyd begins the piece in humorous vein by imitating '*a man brushing his hair and moustache and admiring himself*' (64) but ends with her keening over the dead body of her husband, and the Stage Society found this an unacceptable conclusion to the show.

Esmé Percy

Still, Lawrence continued to wish for a theatrical production for *The Widowing of Mrs Holroyd*, and in March 1914, made contact with Edward

Marsh, the well-connected editor of *Georgian Poetry*, who promoted the verse of some of the best-known figures in the regional repertory movement, Lascelles Abercrombie and John Drinkwater. Lawrence declared his desire for one of Marsh's acquaintances to put *The Widowing of Mrs Holroyd* 'on the stage', although he added pessimistically, 'But probably you won't care for the play anyway' (*Letters* II, 152).

This eeyorish attitude proved justified, as Marsh's fleeting interest came to nothing, but prospects for a production improved again after the publication of the US edition of *The Widowing of Mrs Holroyd*, to which *The Times* gave a fulsome review, saying: 'this play has the qualities of finished craftsmanship [...] it is finely built and perfectly shaped'.[43] Following that praise, three separate actors contacted Lawrence about mounting the play, of whom Esmé Percy emerged as the most convincing.[44] Percy had been an actor at the Gaiety Theatre in Manchester since 1911, and so knew the appeal of regionally inflected writing. In August 1915 he suggested staging Lawrence's work in repertory theatres outside London (*Letters* II, 382), and Lawrence knew that this actor had the capability to do the work well: Percy had headed Iden Payne's company in a performance of Shaw's *Man and Superman* at Nottingham's Theatre Royal that Lawrence had watched in March 1912, when Percy acted with what the Nottingham press called 'an incisiveness and a naturalness'.[45] Thus, on 23 August 1915, Percy met with Lawrence to discuss staging *The Widowing of Mrs Holroyd*, contemplating a production that would be seen in Edinburgh, Glasgow and Manchester.

However, once again the plans came to nothing, largely because of the World War, which in December 1916 saw Percy enlisting in the army, where he remained until 1923 (*Letters* II, 384). By 1916, then, the theatre makers Lawrence had attempted to cultivate in order to get his work onto the stage had scattered: not only had Esmé Percy joined the troops, but Iden Payne had decamped to New York and Granville Barker had effectively finished working as a director and was now at the Western Front.[46] Lawrence's attempt to court these people had been largely a wasted effort.

Still, Esmé Percy did remain loyal to *The Widowing of Mrs Holroyd* and, on eventually emerging from the army, did direct the play's first professional production in England, for the Stage Society in December 1926. By this time, of course, Lawrence had cemented his reputation as a novelist rather than a playwright, although he still indicated to Percy a continuing willingness to revise the drama to make it successful for performance (*Letters* V, 604).

What Lawrence may not have known is that, in the intervening years, his play did enjoy some success in the USA. When the published version of *The*

Widowing of Mrs Holroyd appeared there in 1914, the *New York Times* hailed 'D.G. Lawrence' as 'the author of a most terrific bit of realism'.[47] There followed the first performance – anywhere – of a Lawrence play, in the 450-seat Little Theater, Los Angeles, on 26–31 December 1916. The feminist and patron of the arts, Aline Barnsdall, had opened this venue two months earlier, and her patrons included Charlie Chaplin, Douglas Fairbanks and Cecil B. DeMille. Her company now staged *The Widowing of Mrs Holroyd*, which played to capacity houses under the direction of Irving Pichel, who would later find fame as a film actor and director (playing Fagin, for example, in the 1933 *Oliver Twist*).[48] The *Los Angeles Times* declared the Lawrence piece 'poignant, gripping, and vivid in its startling realism', describing it as the 'most grewsome [*sic*] and the best acted play in Los Angeles today'.[49] But sadly, there is no clue to be found about this triumph in any of Lawrence's surviving letters. After all of his worries about getting his plays onto the stage, it appears that, when that was finally accomplished, and accomplished successfully, he remained entirely ignorant of the fact. The encouragement that he might have needed in order to develop his writing for the stage remained denied to him.

Ireland

By 1916, then, a number of those who could potentially have been Lawrence's theatrical allies – most notably Esmé Percy, Iden Payne and Granville Barker – had been lost to the British stage. Lawrence had also received scant encouragement about his playwriting from his well-connected editor and mentor, Edward Garnett, and the World War hastened the demise of a repertory-movement style that might have suited his theatrical aesthetic.

To make matters worse, Lawrence began to view his own dramatic influences as increasingly suspect. As we have seen, his early writing had been deeply affected by the plays of Synge and Yeats, as produced by the Irish National Theatre Society at the Abbey Theatre in Dublin. In July 1914, when contemplating the production of *The Widowing of Mrs Holroyd*, Lawrence had even considered travelling to the source of that work's inspiration, declaring, 'We are going to Ireland at the end of this month' (*Letters* II, 198). However, those plans came to nothing, and in 1916 Lawrence felt shaken by the outbreak of the Easter Rising in Dublin, a bloody insurrection that proclaimed Irish independence and left some 450 people dead.[50] After all, Lawrence had recently befriended Francis Birrell (see *Letters* II, 319), the son of Augustine

Birrell, the British chief secretary for Ireland who now faced resignation and a barrage of criticism for his handling of the situation. In the post-Rising period, Lawrence then contacted friends including Lady Ottoline Morrell, E.M. Forster and Lady Cynthia Asquith to say how much the event disturbed him, describing feeling 'shocked' (*Letters* II, 611–612) and filled with 'misery and shame' (*Letters* II, 603). He also took to mocking the leaders of the 1916 rebellion in his letters (calling them 'windbags and nothings' (*Letters* II, 611)) as well as in his 1924 novel *The Plumed Serpent* (which revolves around an Irish rebel's widow). In the novel that Lawrence was writing during Easter 1916, *Women in Love*, Gudrun reflects, 'who can take the nationalisation of Ireland seriously? Who can take political Ireland really seriously, whatever it does?', and he also mocked Irish separatist in his later novellas, 'The Captain's Doll' and 'The Ladybird'.[51] Perhaps Lawrence's feelings were inflamed by the fact that most of the British soldiers who died in the 1916 rebellion came from the ranks of the Sherwood Foresters, a regiment from the Nottinghamshire and Derbyshire communities that Lawrence knew so well.

Lawrence must have realized that the Irish drama he had so admired had in fact prepared the ground for this revolutionary event. After all, the Abbey Theatre had set about illustrating the distinctiveness of Irish life on the stage in order to demonstrate Ireland's independence from Britain, and a number of the playhouse's personnel had fought in the rebellion. But Lawrence may not, in his earlier career, have seen where these artistic ideas were leading. Indeed, his friend, Beatrice Elvery had shared his enthusiasm for Yeats's playwriting, and felt so 'impressed' by Yeats and Gregory's insurrectionary drama *Cathleen ni Houlihan* that she had made a large picture based on the title character. But Elvery said she subsequently felt disarmed to find her painting hanging at the boys school that Patrick Pearse, the Irish rebel leader, had founded: she declared, 'I met one of the boys from the school and he told me that this picture had inspired him "to die for Ireland"! I was shocked at the thought that my rather banal and sentimental picture might, like Helen's face, launch ships and burn towers!'[52]

After the Easter Rising, Lawrence felt keen to meet Beatrice Elvery and her husband Gordon Campbell, to 'see what one might make out of the confusion. You must tell me about things' (*Letters* III, 49). Elvery and Campbell had been in Dublin in the immediate aftermath of the rebellion, and, as Elvery put it, 'drove round looking at the ruins and hearing all the stories'.[53] The structure of Beatrice Elvery's account of the Rising implies that she went straight from febrile Dublin to a meeting with Lawrence, where he spent his time 'thumping the back of the chair and denouncing everyone'.[54]

Farjeon and Goldring

Yet, although Lawrence felt appalled by developments in Irish politics, he soon made the personal acquaintance of two theatre-makers who had an intimate knowledge of Ireland's leading playhouse. In Berkshire during 1918, he developed a friendship with the Englishman Herbert Farjeon, who had recently become an Abbey Theatre playwright. Farjeon's first drama, *Friends* (a slight one-act comedy written in quasi-Irish dialect and set in the fictional Irish town of Glengannon) had premiered in Dublin during November 1917.[55] The play proved successful enough for the Abbey to revive it in October 1918, at the time that Lawrence was enjoying close conversations with its author; and Farjeon's theatrical success in Ireland now inspired Lawrence to begin scripting his own first new play since 1913. However, Lawrence's drama contrasted starkly with the guiding philosophy of the Abbey: if Yeats's theatre had set about articulating Irishness difference in order to press for political independence, Lawrence now set about writing a script that portrayed regional distinctiveness but which criticized the very idea of revolutionary upheaval.

Lawrence then met another Englishman with Dublin connections, the quixotic left-wing publisher Douglas Goldring. After the Easter Rising of spring 1916, Goldring had travelled to live in Dublin, excited by the international socialist revolution that he believed was heralded by the rebellion. He felt that the fighting had been stamped 'with a democratic character, making it indeed the first heroic skirmish in that universal revolt against capitalist government which has already transformed Russia and will sooner or later work shattering changes in England and Germany.'[56] In Dublin, Goldring became friends with W.B. Yeats (who ended up being Goldring's landlord and a lifelong friend of Goldring's mother-in-law) and through Yeats, Goldring became aware of how theatrical propaganda had influenced the organization of the Easter Rising.[57] As a result, Goldring felt excited by the revolutionary potential of the theatre, observing: 'Playwriting was very much in the air of Dublin – all literary Irishmen seemed to have written as least one play – and in the enthusiasm of the moment I wrote a four-act play called "The Fight for Freedom", to herald the breaking of the "Red Dawn". It was an ingenuous piece of Communist propaganda.'[58]

Goldring considered Lawrence to be in the vanguard of the same movement, and vowed to stage *The Fight for Freedom* alongside the drama of Lawrence. Goldring discerned that 'there is growing up now in England, as steadily as the new Irish nation is growing up in Ireland, a new English nation of which the skilled artisan class forms the backbone', and that this new nation 'politically has a marked tendency towards "Bolshevism", to use the latest journalese adjective. Mr. D.H. Lawrence seems to me to be the great national poet of the new nation'.[59]

Of course, such views scarcely cohered with what Lawrence himself thought about his own work: he hardly wanted to be the guiding light of a Marxist revolution. Yet he felt intrigued by Goldring, who wrote to Lawrence in 1919, and the two men met that autumn. Goldring had now returned to England and was attempting to establish the 'People's Theatre Society', which would produce dramas that were broadly sympathetic to radical socialism. One of the plays that was central to Goldring's thinking was Lawrence's *The Widowing of Mrs Holroyd*, and Lawrence felt so keen to get this script into professional production that he endorsed Goldring's plan and even insisted that Goldring's Irish wife 'should play the part of "Mrs. Holroyd"'.[60] That play was in fact premiered by the non-professional Altrincham Garrick Society near Manchester in 1920, but when Goldring saw that performance he felt even more convinced that 'if a company of amateurs could put on the play successfully, in the provinces, surely, with all the talent at our command, we could do the same in London'.[61] Lawrence felt impressed by Goldring's enthusiasm, and agreed that the communist 'People's Theatre Society' would give the first professional production of *The Widowing of Mrs Holroyd*, and would then premiere a brand new play by Lawrence, the first one written for five years, a piece called *Touch and Go*.

Touch and Go

Aside from Lawrence's friendship with the Abbey-Theatre playwright Herbert Farjeon, one of the other reasons why Lawrence had turned back to playwriting in 1918 was that he had struggled to get his novel *Women in Love* published, with the exigencies of wartime leading several publishers to reject the manuscript.[62] In October 1918 Lawrence therefore redrafted part of his unpublished novel as the theatre work *Touch and Go*, and the dramatic piece revolves around the character of Gerald Crich from the novel (named Gerald Barlow in the play). In both cases, Gerald has taken over the management of a local colliery from his father, who, in the face of violent strikes, has vainly attempted to run the mining operation according to a benevolent kind of Christian egalitarianism. That approach having failed, Gerald has subsequently made the mines profitable by introducing new methods of industrial production, and has done so with scant regard for the job losses and dehumanizing effect of such reforms. He is consequently hated by the workers, and his industrial reforms themselves are described in virtually identical terms in both the novel and the drama.[63] This subject matter, with its central clash between Labour and Capital, made Douglas Goldring believe that the piece would fit well with the revolutionary left-wing agenda of the 'People's Theatre Society'.

However, Lawrence's new play *Touch and Go* was actually written in reaction to all the revolutionary action, militaristic violence and rapid social change of the age, and scarcely endorses Goldring's politics. Goldring himself later reflected that 'I was completely unaware of it until I read his letters to Lady Cynthia Asquith, he loathed pacifists, idealists, and all the people at whose feet I was at this time sitting'.[64] If Goldring had been influenced by the dramas of revolutionary Dublin that urged military rebellion, Lawrence's new play ultimately shows that such actions are incoherent and faintly risible.

Lawrence wrote *Touch and Go* at the end of October 1918, at the same time as the armistice negotiations that would end the World War, and the play is a response to the preceding bloodshed and slaughter. At the start of the play, a '*stumpy memorial obelisk*' (371), honouring the victims of the conflict, is the only property specified by Lawrence as being on the stage (based on the real-life memorial that stood outside Eastwood's Sun Inn). The traumas of the recent fighting are never addressed directly, but the European conflagration constantly threatens to intrude upon the action. For example, like many of her male counterparts, Anabel has just returned from France at the start of the play, and she wonders about the status of Armenia, site of one of the war's most notorious massacres.

An atmosphere of death and loss therefore pervades the play's opening scenes, with Anabel also remembering that her Norwegian lover died during the war years (having been killed – with a nod to *Hamlet* – on the ice). She now returns to the Nottinghamshire mine-owning Barlow family, whose son Gerald had once been her lover before she abandoned him for the Norwegian. But Gerald's family has itself experienced 'our share of sorrow and of conflict' (392), having lost two children 'through sudden and violent death' (392).

Despite all this grief, the play shows how the forces of Labour and Capital are spoiling to continue a war. On the side of Capital, the mine-owner's wife, Mrs Barlow, explicitly urges renewed bloodshed. 'We need a few veins opening', she declares: 'Between me and the shameful humble there is war to the end, though they are millions and I am one. I hate the people. Between my race and them there is war, between them and me, between them and my children, for ever war, for ever and ever' (387).

Her son Gerald is also enthusiastic about renewed conflict, whilst on the opposing side the forces of Labour are equally prone to murderous violence. In the final scene of the play, the mineworkers take Gerald and Anabel as prisoners, and almost stamp Gerald to death. However, his murder is prevented by the realization of a common humanity, as Anabel screams out the repeated refrain, 'He's a man as you are' (428). Thus, in this final scene set before the memorial obelisk, and with voices singing the wartime song 'There's a long, long trail a-winding' (426), Lawrence ultimately signals a retreat from the excessive violence committed in recent years by those who, like Gerald, believe that they are part of a 'righteous cause' (418).

Galsworthy

In scripting the play in this way, Lawrence began and ended his play in an outdoor space that looks very different from the kinds of intimate domestic interiors that had been the hallmark of his earlier dramas. In *Touch and Go*, the first and final scenes occur at open-air meetings, where Labour leaders address the colliery workers, and this setting had, in fact, been borrowed from Galsworthy's play *Strife*, which Lawrence had watched in Nottingham during 1909, and which featured a much-praised central section with a group of striking tin-plate workers positioned around their fiery, revolutionary leader. On that occasion, the *Nottingham Daily Express* noted how Galsworthy's dramaturgy had drawn the real-life audience into sympathy with the onstage crowd, pointing out that Galsworthy's Labour leader had 'fired not only his mimic audience but the larger audience of the theatre with his fervid speech and manner.'[65]

Lawrence may have been thinking about Galsworthy as he wrote *Touch and Go* because in 1917 he had met the writer for the first and only time. The two men had an unsuccessful lunch date, after which Lawrence declared Galsworthy a 'Sawdust bore' (*Letters* III, 183) and Galsworthy pronounced that Lawrence was 'Obsessed with self. Dead eyes, and a red beard, long narrow pale face. A strange bird.'[66] Nonetheless, Lawrence presumably remembered feeling impressed by *Strife*, and attempted to emulate Galsworthy's play in 1918 when setting down *Touch and Go*, which draws heavily upon the father–son relationship of Galsworthy's drama. In both plays, the elderly father has built up the capitalist enterprise and long acted as company chairman, but differs with his son about the way to progress in the future.

Lawrence also emulated Galsworthy by including in *Touch and Go* a scene equivalent to that of the revolutionary leader before his audience, a moment that had been so well praised in *Strife*. But Lawrence ensured that the crowd scene of his play would avoid inspiring his real-life audience with enthusiasm for left-wing upheaval. Thus, Lawrence's socialist characters repeatedly undermine their own pro-revolutionary arguments. For example, the character of Job Arthur, the Labour leader who finally urges brutal overthrow of the mine owners, is first seen declaring that such a course of action would be to take the milk cow, then 'kill the cow, and share up the meat' (374). Another socialist orator, who starts the play by asking the colliers, 'Couldn't you contrive that the pits belonged to you, instead of you belonging to the pits[?]' (373), ends up – in the final scene – acknowledging that overthrowing the masters would simply mean 'you'll set up another lot of masters, such a jolly sight worse than what we've got now' (424).

The closing moments of *Touch and Go* are therefore dominated by the thoughts of Gerald and Anabel's friend, Oliver Turton, who urges the workers, 'if you wanted to arrange things so that money flowed more naturally, so that it flowed naturally to every man according to his needs, I think we could all soon agree. But you don't. What you want is to take it away from one set and give it to another' (430). Although these words of Oliver evidently draw upon those of Karl Marx, the sentiment is muddled and naive.[67] Oliver broadly dismisses a redistributive agenda, as simply being the haggling or bullying politics of those who would rekindle the violence and sorrow of the First World War; and leaves the audience wondering about exactly how to establish a 'better way' without the need to 'take away from one set and give it to another' (430–431). In fact, Lawrence altered the very final words of his play in order to make the ending even more ambigious. Lawrence's closing lines had originally read:

Gerald.   […] Has somebody got my coat?

Job Arthur.   What about the clerk's wages, Mr Barlow [?]

Gerald.   You hold your tongue, do you see – I'll put up notices tomorrow about what we'll do. I'm the Justice of the Peace for this district, you know – so we'll keep the peace for as long as we can – I've said we're quits –[68]

But Lawrence felt dissatisfied with that conclusion and altered his manuscript, so that the play's final words instead read:

> Gerald.   [...] I think we ought to be able to alter the whole system – but not by bullying, not because one lot wants what the other has got.
>
> Voice.   No, because you've got everything.
>
> Gerald.   Where's my coat? Now then, step out of the way – (431).

In the first version, Gerald was at least planning to take some kind of action as a result of his violent confrontation with the workers: he declares that tomorrow he will put up some notices about 'what we'll do'. Yet in the revised version, Gerald makes no such vow, and instead, when he is reminded that the workers remain dissatisfied about existing levels of inequality, he simply demands that they move away from him. Thus, a play that, at the start, looks like it might endorse revolution, ends up by showing that such upheaval is wrongheaded, and refuses to provide any clarity about what, if any, societal change should now proceed. John Galsworthy may have scripted a scene of revolutionary oratory that, in Nottingham, had 'grip and intensity' that 'quite carry the audience away', but Lawrence's drama highlights the inconsistencies of such oration, and never really allows the audience to feel enthusiastic about the potential of left-wing revolution.[69]

Another failure

Nonetheless, it was a mark of how desperately Lawrence wanted to see his work on the stage that, despite having written his play around such a message, he declared himself 'in sympathy' with Douglas Goldring's efforts to launch the revolutionary left-wing 'People's Theatre Society' (*Letters* III, 374). When the possibility arose that Goldring might stage a series of 'People's Theatre Society' dramas at the Royal Court, Lawrence declared 'I should love to be in it' (*Letters* III, 372) and, despite the fact that none of his previous six plays had yet been performed by any professional group in Britain, Lawrence took practical steps to prepare a production-ready version of *Touch and Go*, telling his acquaintances that it '*might* be acted' (*Letters* III, 293) and then that it 'will be acted' (*Letters* III, 299–300).[70] Goldring mooted the idea of staging Lawrence's script as the inaugural work of the 'People's Theatre

Society', and Lawrence confirmed 'I want it to be the first production, and I want it to be a success' (*Letters* III, 374–375).

However, the contrast between Lawrence and Goldring was shown in the introductions that the two men then wrote to their plays, which were due to appear in print alongside one another in a series called 'Plays for a People's Theatre'. Goldring's introduction to his own drama *The Fight for Freedom* declared a desire to see 'the miners, the transport workers, the postmen and the police – all interesting themselves in the establishment of a Labour theatre'; and looked to Dublin as a model, 'I should like to see the Clyde starting a theatre of its own on the lines of the Dublin Abbey Theatre. It would soon produce a school of playwrights, just as the Abbey Theatre has produced a school of playwrights.'[71] By contrast, Lawrence had grown suspicious of Irish politics, refused to endorse Marxist radicalism, and so wrote in his preface that 'A People's Theatre' was simply a theatre in which the seats are inexpensive, and which produced plays 'about people' (364). As for revolutionary change, he wrote, 'We shall crawl from under one cartwheel straight under another' (368).

Unsurprisingly, Goldring's own theatre company eventually outvoted him and refused to stage any of Lawrence's work. Instead the 'People's Theatre Society' mounted an expensive production of a Serbian play, Srgjan Tucic's *The Liberators*, which provided a predictable box-office failure that caused the group to fold.[72] At this time, Lawrence waited in Italy and hankered after news about a production of his drama that would never happen, feeling increasingly frustrated with Goldring. When *Touch and Go* was then published as the second, rather than the promised first, volume in Goldring's play series of 'Plays for a People's Theatre', Lawrence felt tricked. His politics could not have been further from the utopian revolutionary socialism of Goldring's *The Fight for Freedom*, which actually appeared as the first volume in the series, and Lawrence's quarrel with Goldring ended bitterly. When Lawrence thought about how things had turned out with *Touch and Go*, he declared Goldring a 'sly journalist' whose enterprise was 'damned and doubly damned'. 'Curse the sly mongrel world' wrote Lawrence, whose work had once again failed to reach the stage (*Letters* III, 469).

Nottingham

Nonetheless, later in 1920 Lawrence found another chance to see his plays acted, when Compton Mackenzie's mother attempted to establish a repertory theatre in Nottingham, and aimed to showcase Lawrence's dramas in the town. Virginia Mackenzie had run a girls' theatre club in London since 1915, and after the death of her husband in 1918 wanted to give her two daughters the opportunity of regularly acting on the professional stage.[73] She therefore converted a playhouse that stood about a mile outside Nottingham town centre, the Grand Theatre on Radford Road, into a repertory theatre. She refurbished this 34-year-old venue and reopened it in September 1920 with a first-night performance of *The School for Scandal*, which ended with Virginia Mackenzie herself on the stage, holding and kissing her two daughters, and delivering a speech in which she vowed 'to give Nottingham all that was true and brilliant and clever'.[74]

As with the repertory theatres that emerged before the First World War in cities such as Manchester, Liverpool and Glasgow, Virginia Mackenzie sought to promote the work of local people, including amateur singers and actors from the area. Her Nottingham Repertory Theatre also staged a poetic play called *Tale of Young Lovers* by nearby resident Cecil Roberts; the religious play *Raymond Lull* by a local clergyman; and a play about Nottingham hero *Robin Hood* with music by Bernard Page, a member of a well-known musical family in the county.[75]

Naturally, then, this theatre manager turned towards Lawrence's plays, and when approached by Compton Mackenzie about this, Lawrence responded from his base in Taormina, Sicily:

> About the theatre thrilling but terrifying! You know my horror of the public! Well, it's a phobia of phobias in Nottingham. Nottingham! Cursed, cursed Nottingham, gutless, spineless, brainless Nottingham how I hate thee! But if my two plays could be thrown so hard into thy teeth as to knock thy teeth out, why then, good enough [...] I should like to see the things done and done properly. Oh, if there were actors! I'd like to be there to beat the actors into acting. What terrifying thrills ahead! (*Letters* III, 509–510).

Despite Lawrence's professed hatred for the town, these theatrical developments in Nottingham – and the prospect of seeing his own work staged there – clearly excited him, and proved sufficiently intriguing for him to use his family connections in order to find out more about the repertory enterprise. In October 1920 he wrote to Compton Mackenzie: 'I wonder how you find Nottingham. I dread it for you because I loathe the town. But I hope all goes merrily. Tell me about it. I'll write to my sister. You might have tea with her in some café' (*Letters* III, 609). Little over a fortnight later he wrote again, to say that he had learned about the production of Compton Mackenzie's play *Columbine*, one of the best productions at the Nottingham repertory theatre: 'Heard from my elder sister, that Nottingham thought it a great success' (*Letters* III, 616). Lawrence then made sure to see Compton Mackenzie in person on two or three occasions in London later that year.

Sadly, Virginia Mackenzie never really understood how to make her venture financially viable, and the theatre soon needed bailing out by Nottingham's wealthy magnates.[76] Before she took charge, the Grand Theatre had been a low-price but popular venue, focusing on melodramas and pantomimes, with special tramcars bringing spectators from Nottingham market.[77] But that audience vanished when Virginia Mackenzie increased ticket prices and altered the repertoire, even though, during the death throes of the venture, she invited stock companies to the theatre, and the very last production was a rather sad, twice-nightly melodrama called *The Savage and the Woman* ('Reminiscent of the old "Grand" days' and featuring a villain with 'black moustache and "Ha! Ha!"').[78] Finally, on a last Sunday performance in 1923, less than three years after the start of the project, the final item on the programme was simply a question mark. At that point in the evening the stage remained empty, and the audience looked towards a box on the right, where Virginia Mackenzie stood wearing a long widow's veil. In tears, and with her head bowed, she explained that the experiment was ending and that the theatre would close.[79] The *Nottingham Journal* observed sympathetically that: 'Among the many reasons assignable for the lack of success with which they have been faced, there is none which lays blame upon Mrs Compton, her versatile daughters, and the company which they gathered round them. They have done much'.[80] The building did struggle on for a short time as a theatre, but by 1925 the venue had been reconfigured as a cinema, where talkies appeared from 1930. Lawrence's plays came tantalizingly close to being performed here, but had never appeared in the venue by the time that it was bulldozed in 1964.[81]

David

Throughout all of these disappointments, Lawrence had continued his own acting performances. Since 1913, Lawrence's own output of plays had substantially decreased, but he continued participating in various skits and sketches with his friends. Brigit Patmore knew Lawrence after he arrived in London from Nottingham, and remembered that 'our lunches used to be great fun, for he was a remarkable mimic and he was fond of acting'.[82] In the following years, such fondness for acting could be seen in various ways:

1914: Lawrence participates in an awkward Christmas play about the doomed marriage of John Middleton Murry and Katherine Mansfield.[83]

1915: Lawrence and his friends perform a twenty-minute comic play by the Austrian playwright Arthur Schnitzler (*Letters* II, 256).

1916: Lawrence co-writes a (now lost and thoroughly cruel sounding) comedy with the composer Philip Arnold Heseltine about a woman who had been impregnated by Heseltine (*Letters* II, 508).

1917: Lawrence directed his friends Richard and Hilda Aldington (the poet 'H.D.') in a satyr play about Adam and Eve, in which Frieda played the serpent with commendable enthusiasm by wrigging and growling on the floor (and had to be reminded that serpents do not growl).[84]

There are also, of course, a number of third-party accounts of Lawrence having violent public arguments with Frieda throughout his marriage, and these accounts have adversely affected the author's reputation.[85] But perhaps if we look at Lawrence's broader theatrical tendencies, and his consistent urge to act and perform in front of friends and acquaintances, then we might wonder about whether these accounts really indicate any kind of truth about the private reality of the Lawrence marriage, or whether the public rows were simply another form of role play.

Lawrence certainly continued playing acting games with his acquaintances into the 1920s. One of his visitors remembered him having 'acted out the Midland dialect' when in the USA, and Mabel Dodge Luhan recalled that when Lawrence was staying with her in New Mexico, 'The only time he appeared to relax' was at tea-time dramatic performances. 'He could imitate anything or anybody. His ability to identify himself intuitively with things outside himself was wonderful'.[86] Dodge Luhan remembered:

He loved to act and was perfectly unselfconscious about it [...] We used to laugh until we were tired. One night we acted a scene that represented me taking Tony to Buffalo to introduce him to my mother! Lawrence was my mother [...] That was so funny we couldn't finish the act![87]

Indeed, Lawrence – when he was not being a female impersonator – described his whole time in New Mexico during the mid-1920s as being like an actor in a bewildering stage show. He wrote, 'here am I, a lone lorn Englishman, tumbled out of the known world of the British Empire on to this stage: for it persists in seeming like a stage to me'.[88]

One of those who joined such theatrical games in New Mexico was the actor Ida Rauh, who founded a theatre company in Provincetown, directed the premiere of at least one of Eugene O'Neill's plays and also – according to Lawrence's friend, the artist Dorothy Brett – bore 'an amazing resemblance to Sarah Bernhardt'.[89] Lawrence and Ida Rauh were, according to Brett, the 'stars' of these theatrical games, and Lawrence's last attempts at playwriting were inspired by this process of acting opposite Bernhardt's doppelganger.[90] He wrote the theatrical sketch *Altitude* in 1924, which includes a character named Ida, and then Lawrence asked Ida Rauh 'what kind of a play do you like best?', to which she responded, 'I like stories from the Bible best'.[91] He then set about writing his drama *David* as well as an unfinished play, *Noah's Flood*. Unfortunately, Lawrence fell severely ill during the writing process, but did manage to complete *David* by May 1925, with Frieda declaring that, 'The poignancy of "David" is partly a result of Lawrence's own escape from the valley of death'.[92]

Despite all of the rejections of the past decade and half, Lawrence had again written *David* as a stageable drama. Indeed, when he told his agent about the play in May 1925 Lawrence wrote 'I don't care about having it published' (*Letters* V, 257), declaring 'It is a good play, and for the theatre. Someone ought to do it' (*Letters* V, 270). After the agent expressed doubts, Lawrence declared, 'I don't want it published unless it is produced' (*Letters* V, 274). Lawrence had, after all, begun the script after enjoying his own acting with Ida Rauh in Taos, and when he penned *David* he explained: 'I am a bit tired of plays that are only literature. If a man is writing "literature", why choose the form of a play? And if he's writing a play, he surely intends it for the theatre. Anyhow I wrote this play for the theatre, and I want the theatre people to see it first' (*Letters* V, 274). 'Playgoing', he declared, 'isn't the same as reading. Reading in itself is highbrow. But give the "populace" in the theatre something with a bit of sincere good-feeling in it, and they'll respond' (*Letters* V, 274). Here is part of the tragedy of Lawrence: in drama, he persisted with an art form where his skill remained largely unrecognized throughout his lifetime, yet he longed to make a breakthrough into that world. Other contemporary modernists, such as Yeats and Pound, had written plays for a coterie audience, believing that – as Pound put it – 'My whole habit of thinking of the stage is: that it is a gross, coarse form of art. That a play speaks to a thousand fools huddled together whereas a novel or poem can lie about in a book and find the stray persons worth finding.'[93] But Lawrence had never forgotten the power of the theatre to affect the 'populace' rather than the 'highbrow'. He remembered those Eastwood audiences of his childhood, and knew that such spectators would scarcely read his novels, but could be profoundly moved by theatrical performance. When, in early 1921, he visited a puppet show in Palermo, he found himself packed onto a back bench of a theatre, squashed amongst about fifty boys, soldiers and elderly men, but rather than feeling claustrophic or alienated by the fact that 'I can hardly understand anything at all', Lawrence relished the shared physical experience of sitting cheek-by-jowl with others in this noisy situation, and reflected that, 'Truly I loved them all in the theatre: the generous, hot southern blood, so subtle and spontaneous, that asks for blood contact, not for mental communion or spirit sympathy. I was sorry to leave them.'[94]

David had been written for Ida Rauh to bring to life onstage and, when Lawrence had finished it, both he and Frieda wrote to say they hoped she liked it (*Letters* V, 250). But when Rauh finally read it aloud with Lawrence she showed 'no enthusiasm', and simply declared in a tired voice, 'I am too old, Lorenzo; too old to play the part of Michal'.[95] Rauh had expressed excitement about the piece during its composition, but now, when she read the finished script, she distanced herself from it immediately.

Her reluctance probably related to the fact that, strangely, for a piece Lawrence had clearly designed with Ida Rauh in mind, this play is no star vehicle. Lawrence reflected, 'you'd have much preferred a more personal play, about a woman. Probably you would – and naturally. But I myself am a bit tired of personal plays, "about a woman". Time we all sank our personalities a bit, in something bigger' (*Letters* V, 276). Lawrence had actually created an ensemble piece, and his most ambitious piece of playwriting, stretched across sixteen scenes of uneven length, in a way that parallels the epic theatre of Bertolt Brecht. In writing *David*, Lawrence ignored conventional plotting, and instead created a non-realistic montage of isolated scenes, broadly showing how David displaces Saul, the king who falls from God's favour and – like Macbeth – can only envisage a rival's 'seed [. . .] rising up' (488). One of the most remarkable features of the original manuscript is the way that the spoken text repeatedly stops in order for Lawrence to write down chants and sometimes musical notation, indicating the drama's proto-Brechtian integration of singing and speech.[96] Indeed, Lawrence eventually wrote ten musical pieces for incorporation in the play.

In the ensuing years, Bertolt Brecht would emphasize the role of the individual actor as part of a collective: he used the word 'partner' to describe his performers, and condemned the 'bad habit of letting the dominant actor, the star, also "steal the show" by having all the other actors at their beck and call [...] the actors should sometimes swap roles with their partners during rehearsal, so that the characters can get from one another what they need'.[97] In *David*, D.H. Lawrence attempted something similar, although he expressed his reasoning more crudely, writing: 'my God, there's many a *nigger* who would play Saul better than Forbes-Robertson could do it' (*Letters* V, 274). Today, that language sounds repellently racist, although Judith Ruderman has recently emphasized that Lawrence was writing in an era of race theory when such extreme language would not have necessarily been idiosyncratic.[98] Furthermore, Lawrence was also arguing that a star performer like the actor-manager Sir Johnston Forbes-Robertson could unbalance the play, whereas Lawrence wanted a 'whole company of better men', who might be 'niggers' or 'Jews or Italians or Spaniards or Celts to do the thing properly' (*Letters* V, 274). Despite the colonial attitudes Lawrence expressed, he had encountered a great deal of condescension in his own life, and wanted to avoid a form of theatre in which white men who had been educated at Charterhouse would declaim beneath the spotlights.

Lawrence had in fact begun writing *David* out of his responsiveness to Ida Rauh's Jewish heritage, and hoped that putting his 'company of better men' onto the stage in an ensemble piece might extend the theatrical project that he had begun years ago. After all, Lawrence had long been writing plays about a group dynamic rather than one central character, and he had focused attention on members of the Eastwood working class who were denied a voice in the realm of cultural production. That final play *David* might appear like a departure from his earlier work in its biblical subject matter and its proto-epic form, yet, like those Eastwood plays, *David* also strives for a kind of inclusivity. The text relies on the story and language of the King James Bible, but destabilizes that central text of English Protestantism by giving it a wider resonance. One of the things Lawrence worked hardest to revise was the conventional Judeo-Christian terminology for God: as he redrafted his drama, he repeatedly swapped the term 'Lord' for words such as 'Deep' (438), 'Might' (441) and 'Fire' (454).[99] Hence, the original manuscript has Samuel saying to David, 'The Lord pours himself out on thee. The Lord sealeth thee. Thou are no more thine own, for the Lord hath claimed thee the length of thy days. When thou goeth in, it shall be because of the Lord'. But Lawrence then scribbled out that wording, and replaced it with: 'The Glory pours itself out on thee. The Chooser chooseth thee. When thou goeth in, it shall be at the whisper of the Mover.'[100] In this way, the kind of animist religious beliefs that Lawrence associated with the Native Americans became increasingly important to the play.[101] A multicultural casting of this drama, incorporating the vocal delivery of the Eastwood working class as well as that of the Pueblo Indians, would perhaps best have reflected his aims and preoccupations. But of course no theatre company existed that could easily provide such a staging.

As it was, Ida Rauh suggested that the play might suit the New York Theatre Guild, which had been founded in 1918 in order to produce uncommercial work, and had already shown an ability to cope with the experimental biblical material of playwrights from the British Isles. In 1922 the company had premiered G.B. Shaw's five-play cycle *Back to Methuselah*, which begins with Genesis, and ends with a woman being born from a giant egg in the year 31,290 AD.[102] During July 1925 Lawrence asked Rauh to contact the Theatre Guild's managers and tell them to expect his new play. But in truth, although Lawrence's drama is fascinatingly experimental, it badly wants pruning. Lawrence himself seemed to admit this when he described how 'if the speeches are too long – well, they can be made shorter if necessary' (*Letters* V, 274). The copy arrived at the Theatre Guild towards the end of the summer (*Letters* V, 281), but the company soon declined it. 'Damn them' declared Lawrence (*Letters* V, 303).

Disappointingly, then, in spite of all Lawrence's intentions, *David* appeared first in print rather than in the playhouse. The reviews of the publication were laudatory, and prompted the Stage Society to perform the piece in May 1927. Here was, perhaps, a chance to make amends for the company's original rejection of *The Widowing of Mrs Holroyd* in 1913–1914, but Lawrence knew that *David* was 'a much more difficult play to put on, I must go and help' (*Letters* V, 613). However, although Lawrence had lunch with the prospective director and planned to be in England to see the production (*Letters* V, 543, 545), the production was repeatedly postponed from its original date of autumn 1926. As compensation for Lawrence, Phyllis Whitworth at the Stage Society did engage Esmé Percy to produce *The Widowing of Mrs Holroyd* in December 1926, although by this time Lawrence had left England (for the final time) and was in Florence. Nonetheless, the thought of seeing *David* on the stage was sufficiently seductive for Lawrence to plan his return trip, but during the month of the eventual production in May 1927 he suffered from a tubercular attack, and had to apologize, 'I am more sorry than I can say about my not coming to *David*' (*Letters* VIII, 102).[103] He continued to give advice about costumes and about how to deliver the lines, as well as about how to edit the work for performance, advising that the actors get rid of 'anything that makes the movement drag [...] cut the longish mouthfuls and spit it out quick and sharp. Anything rather than let it be long-drawn-out and a nuisance' (*Letters* VIII, 102).

Undoubtedly, if he had not been so ill, Lawrence would have travelled to see his work professionally performed in 1927. But the dying man's fears about how *David* would be produced in his absence proved prescient. The *Sunday Times* described the audience's 'ennui', while an *Observer* reviewer commented, 'We were bored, bored, bored', although he did acknowledge that, with some extensive editing, this 'would be quite a play'.[104] The *Manchester Guardian* similarly pointed out that the script might be restructured, in the style of G.B. Shaw, to make the prophet Samuel emerge more clearly at the centre of the work.[105] Lawrence, in response, wrote, 'They say it was just dull. I say they are eunuchs, and have no balls. It is a fight. The same old one' (*Letters* VI, 72). However, five months later, upon reflection, Lawrence told the German playwright and novelist Max Mohr, 'of course the whole play is too literary, too many words. The actual technique of the stage is foreign to me' (*Letters* VI, 204). Lawrence did continue translating *David* into German in the hope of a Berlin performance, but he realized, as any subsequent director who considers a production of *David* must realize, that the writer who is hunched over the typewriter, and who has limited contact with the methods of professional production is likely to create a wordy script that needs extensive adjustment before stage presentation. When Cambridge Festival Theatre revived the piece in 1933, the programme announced that, although the actors valued and enjoyed the script, one of the scenes had been 'found in rehearsal to be impossible dramatically'.[106] In 1968, Philip French deemed *David* 'the only one of the eight completed plays that I shouldn't care to see staged'; and in 1984 Peter Hall declined to produce the script at the National Theatre because 'despite the original form and argument of the play, there are many problems of style and characterisation which stand in the way of the successful production'.[107] Lawrence himself never had the opportunity to make the necessary alterations through the experience of professional theatre himself, and less than three years after realizing that he had included 'too many words' in his latest drama, he was dead. During his lifetime, he had spectacularly failed in his ambition of becoming a successfully performed playwright.

CHAPTER 3
THE DRAMA OF LAWRENCE'S FICTION: PLAYWRIGHT AS NOVELIST

From stage to page

Lawrence finished six dramatic works between 1909 and 1913. But after 1913 he wrote only two complete plays in the seventeen years before his death. As we have seen, Lawrence experienced a repeated failure in getting his scripts to the stage, and – as this chapter will show – he diverted his theatrical energies towards novel and short-story writing instead. A contemporaneous working-class figure like Seán O'Casey made his way as a dramatist because he was taken under the wing of the Abbey Theatre, whose directors edited and reshaped his early scripts to make them suitable for the playhouse.[1] But Lawrence remained less fortunate, and although he tried to ingratiate himself with the kind of theatre producers who might have developed his craft as a playwright, he never received the same encouragement as O'Casey. Consequently, as John Worthen suggests, 'Lawrence's finest work as a dramatist may well indeed turn out to be not in his plays at all, but in the narrative of his fiction.'[2] This chapter therefore turns to Lawrence's novels and short stories – in a broadly chronological order – to see how these writings, although never intended for performance, are pervaded by notions of drama. I will also develop the idea that there is also a certain thematic consistency in Lawrence's novelistic use of the theatre. Today, Lawrence is best known as a writer who dealt with explicitly sexual themes, and such an emphasis has allowed academics to bracket him with the experimentalists of high modernism: as Pericles Lewis points out, 'particularly in their portrayals of sexuality, his novels challenged the traditions of English fiction.'[3] At a popular level too, as Steven Bailey and Chris Nottingham emphasize, Lawrence has secured a solid reputation as a 'mucky man' and 'a writer of "filth"'.[4]

Yet the depictions of sex that appear in Lawrence's novels and short stories very often intersect with, and depend upon, his ideas about the theatre. As we shall see, both his first published work of 1907 and his final completed story of 1928 revolve around a combination of sexual desire and festive drama being staged in the English midlands. These two texts mark the boundaries of a career during which Lawrence's fiction repeatedly explores, probes and problematizes the relationship between the erotic and the dramatic. By tracing such ideas through Lawrence's fiction, we can see how sex in his writing is connected with highbrow theatre such as operatic and Shavian performance, as well as with popular dramatic forms including circus, music hall and portable theatre. Furthermore, during his late career, Lawrence's writings often prove prescient about forthcoming developments in drama and performance, as the author uses that connection between theatre and the erotic in order to warn about the displacement of live drama by cinema shows, to consider the looming age of fascist theatricals, and to describe something akin to the theatre of cruelty that would shortly be articulated by Antonin Artaud.

Christmas

Despite experiencing a prolonged failure in getting his written scripts to the stage, Lawrence nonetheless participated in acting games with his friends and acquaintances throughout his life.[5] Jessie Chambers remembered that, during the writer's early years, Christmas proved a particularly 'wonderful time' for such performances, when there would be 'always thrilling charades at our house, with Lawrence directing things'.[6] Jessie's elder sister remembered one such evening at Christmas time in Eastwood, when Lawrence cross-dressed as an 'old crow to fetch down her lazy son' and then played the part of an over-excited preacher, yelling 'Repent!' and 'Hell-fire for everyone!' Indeed, he played both parts so convincingly that he made his audience 'shiver' and was told, 'You acted a bit too well'.[7]

However, after 1901, such festive performances became tinged with sorrow after the death of Ernest. Lawrence's sister Ada remembered that until that point, at Christmas:

> Mother always took part in our games and joined in our songs. He [Ernest] had been the life and soul of them. After he died she would stay in the kitchen in her rocking chair, pretending to read. We knew where her thoughts were, and it always cast a shadow over our fun.[8]

Ada recalled that, one Christmas Eve after 1901, Lawrence had decided to organize festivities in the house. He used candles to wax the floor, after which he danced with the local women, and then:

Someone suggested ghost stories, and we trooped downstairs into the parlour, put out the light and gathered round the fire. Bert [D.H. Lawrence], of course, told the tale, plunging into a ghastly adventure until our hair nearly stood on end. When he reached the most thrilling point he hesitated. Suddenly there was a most horrible banging and clattering just outside the door. We shrieked with terror and sat with palpitating hearts, and in marched George [Neville], who had been instructed by Bert to create the pandemonium at the critical moment, and who, strange to say, had not been missed. Mother sat in the kitchen alone, but content because we were happy.[9]

In these amateur performances, then, the young Lawrence showed himself capable of preparing a stage set, conceiving and performing a spoken narrative, and organizing the necessary offstage effects with the help of his willing stagehand.

However, Lawrence was scarcely the only thespian in the neighbourhood at Christmas time. Enid Hopkin Hilton remembered that:

Early attempts at local drama had also included the mummers. They performed plays during the Christmas season, going from house to house, offering to give performances before the assembled family. Father always invited them in and we listened with rapt attention. Sometimes the recital was in the local dialect, not too easy to understand, but the acting was often superb. When the plays were over the performers were fed Christmas fare and sent away with a little money. The travelling players ceased to visit in the early part of the century, but the mummers were with us until the First World War.[10]

Lawrence's knowledge of such performance shaped the very first work he ever published, written at the age of 22 when he was attending University College Nottingham. This was the pseudonymous short story, 'A Prelude', which the *Nottingham Guardian* printed in December 1907, and which revolves around a play being acted on Christmas Eve by members of a farming and mining family. Here, Lawrence captured the excitement of the performance preparations: the brothers in the story are readying a play about St George and Beelzebub, and are discovered applying makeup and 'roaring with laughter before the mirror'.[11] From a biographical point of view, there is undoubtedly an element of wish-fulfilment here: Lawrence scripted this story about *three* brothers who spent their Christmas having fun in playmaking, when in real life he was now one of only *two* brothers after the death of Ernest. In addition, the mother in the short story does begin the piece alone in the kitchen, but she quickly joins in with the preparations, and finishes the story sitting hand-in-hand with her husband.

'A Prelude' went missing from the Lawrence canon until 1949, and remains little known, but illustrates the way in which, from the very start, Lawrence's prose fiction had been shaped by acting and performance. Furthermore, he repeatedly revisited the same theatrical scenario in his more mature work. That short story of 1907 revolves around the 'guysers' (a dialect word meaning masqueraders) producing a drama about St George and Beelzebub, 'the ludicrous old Christmas play that everyone knows so well', which involves 'much horseplay, stabbing, falling on the floor, bangings of dripping-pans'.[12] In *The Rainbow* (published 1915), Lawrence reimagines exactly the same scenario when describing the Christmastide marriage of William and Anna Brangwen. After the ceremony, 'the guysers came' to perform 'the old mystery play of St George' in which 'every man present had acted as a boy', and which features 'banging and thumping of club and dripping pan'.[13] Of course, *The Rainbow* includes a darker note than the original short story: that theatrical moment in the 1915 novel foreshadows the grisly death of Tom Brangwen.[14] And Lawrence would also write similarly pessimistic narratives about such Christmas acting games in *The White Peacock* and 'Delilah and Mr Bircumshaw'.[15]

Yet in the original 1907 story of 'A Prelude', Lawrence had written a festive piece that ends happily, with reconciliation between the characters, and he had described a connection between personal sexual satisfaction and theatrical experience that would continue to inspire his later novels and short stories. 'A Prelude' tells of the farmer-actor's desire to impress a female friend, and the piece accordingly ends with those characters embracing, as the narrative gives an indication that the two will soon be married. In Lawrence's subsequent fictions, as we shall see, that sexual aspect which he associated with drama became increasingly dominant, even if the author's later work offers a challenge to the uncomplicated ideas about heterosexual fulfilment that are conveyed in his first published story.

The White Peacock

Just as Lawrence's first published story manifests his concern with drama, so his first novel, *The White Peacock* (written 1906–1910, published 1911), also looks to the theatrical realm, and particularly to performed opera. Since the time of Lawrence's birth, the Carl Rosa opera company had regularly toured to Nottingham with Bizet's *Carmen*. These productions proved exceptionally popular, and the 17-year-old Lawrence may have seen the performance given at the Nottingham Theatre Royal in December 1902.[16] By 1908 he was certainly expressing his preference for a lover who would be 'a little devil – a Carmen – I like not things passive' (*Letters* I, 103). And after he moved to Croydon in the autumn of 1909, Lawrence watched Carl Rosa, at a time when the critic for the *Observer* praised the company's *Carmen* as 'inspiriting'.[17] Thus, in Lawrence's earliest novel, *The White Peacock*, he dramatized the Carl Rosa *Carmen*, and his characters feel something similar to the *Observer* critic: they are left 'shaken with a tumult of wild feeling. When it was all over they rose bewildered, stunned, she with tears in her eyes, he with a strange wild beating of his heart'.[18]

In *The White Peacock* the characters who watch the Carl Rosa show are a male and female who are about to marry, but who are accompanied by a third figure – the novel's narrator Cyril – who has already expressed a strong homosexual attraction towards the potential bridegroom. When these three arrive at the theatre, they find their sexual feelings entwined with their appreciation of the playhouse performance. The betrothed couple cling to one another and find that the opera fills them 'full of the roaring passion of life'.[19] But at the same time as they watch the stage, the narrator Cyril observes them, and the fact that the three characters are experiencing the tragic love story of *Carmen* gives an indication that their own relationship will end badly, as indeed it does. Similarly to 'A Prelude', Lawrence connected theatrical art with the realm of sexual desire, although this time heterosexual union cannot provide a straightforwardly happy ending.

The Trespasser

Lawrence began his second novel, *The Trespasser* (1912), shortly after finishing his first, and made still more extensive use of opera. Again, the theatrical form is connected to the book's eroticism, although this time Lawrence took his cue from Wagner rather than Bizet.

Lawrence knew about Wagner, as he knew of Bizet, from performances by the Carl Rosa company. Lawrence had probably seen the Carl Rosa *Tannhäuser* in Nottingham's Theatre Royal during the first decade of the twentieth century.[20] *Tannhäuser* was the company's dependable 'Monday night battlehorse' in Nottingham, although Lawrence remained unimpressed when he saw it there, according to one source, and he reacted against 'the stridency of the Venusberg music'.[21] He later watched Carl Rosa playing Wagner's *Tristan and Isolde* in Croydon on 15 October 1909, and again observed that he was 'very disappointed', describing the piece as 'long, feeble, a bit hysterical, without grip or force. I was frankly sick of it' (*Letters* I, 140).

Nonetheless, when originally writing *The Trespasser* between April and August 1910, Lawrence showed an interest in Siegmund, the doomed hero of Wagner's opera *The Valkyrie*, to such an extent that the novel's early title was 'The Saga of Siegmund'.[22] In actual fact, Lawrence had not seen *The Valkyrie* at this point. Rather, he felt inspired by this Wagnerian character because of one of his own personal acquaintances. By the winter of 1908 he had left Eastwood for Croydon, and met a fellow teacher, Helen Corke, for whom he developed a strong sexual attraction. Corke meanwhile had been enjoying a love affair with a violinist from the Covent Garden Opera: she called him 'Siegmund' (although his real name was Herbert Macartney) and the romance ended in tragedy when he committed suicide.[23] Lawrence then provided friendship and support to the grieving Corke, but also read her diary and realized that her story had the potential to form his second novel.

As indicated by the original title for *The Trespasser*, the novel involves a sustained engagment with Wagner, although there exist a number of telling slips in *The Trespasser* that indicate just how much Lawrence relied on second-hand knowledge about Wagnerian performance (Helen Corke had seen two parts of Wagner's *Ring* at Covent Garden in 1909, with her own 'Siegmund' playing in the orchestra, so she provided Lawrence with valuable insights).[24] However, to give Lawrence himself some credit, he used what he knew about Wagner to create a number of intriguing formal effects. For example, the repetitive style of some of Lawrence's writing, which critics such as Roger Sale have found so irksome, may also, according to Hugh Stevens, constitute an attempt at producing a kind of Wagnerian leitmotif in textual form, with Lawrence developing an interlocking set of tropes that emulate the erotic conjoinings of the main characters in his novels.[25] Furthermore, most of *The Trespasser* is spent with very little actually happening in terms of plot development. After the two main characters run away together, the novel largely consists of a reflective piece about longing and desire until the final pages. Indeed, this structure parallels that of Wagner's *Tristan and Isolde*, where moments of action (such as the sudden arrival in Cornwall, or Tristan's duel with Melot) are displaced to the end of the acts. In addition, throughout this second of Lawrence's novels, the self-conscious Wagnerian parallels provide an ominous indication of where the central relationship is heading, with the novelist including numerous references to both *The Valkyrie* and to *Tristan and Isolde*, two works in which married women are taken from their husbands into liaisons that culminate with death.

The Trespasser also relies upon the kind of theatrical understanding that Lawrence had developed through non-operatic, spoken-word drama. According to Elizabeth Mansfield, after hearing about the disastrous end of Corke's love affair, Lawrence may 'have shown her [Corke] his play *A Collier's Friday Night*, and suggested that she try to dramatize her own experiences, using it as a model'.[26] Lawrence and Corke also spent time reading Greek tragedies together: she said that he 'tried to show me there was a way out. For instance, he read [Gilbert Murray's translation of Euripides'] *The Trojan Women*, and that tragedy in a sense came into line with the personal tragedy. Somehow he'd brought the personal tragedy in line with the universal tragedy'.[27] They also read Euripides' death-obsessed plays *Alcestis* and *The Bacchae*, and when Lawrence then began to draft a version of Corke's story as a fiction, he studied Gerhart Hauptmann's play, *Einsame Menschen* ('Solitary People'), which ends with the apparent suicide of a man who is torn between his wife and another woman.[28] Of course, all of this theatricality constituted a rather unorthodox way of helping her to cope with her trauma, but did assist Lawrence with structuring his novel.

Playhouse activities therefore take a central place in the plot of *The Trespasser*, most notably the musical performances that cause the love affair to commence between the main characters. The reader learns that Helena and Louisa 'went occasionally to whatever hall or theatre had Siegmund in the orchestra, so that shortly the three formed the habit of coming home together. Then Helena had invited Siegmund to her home: then the three friends went walks together; then the two went walks together'.[29]

In this passage, Lawrence's repeated use of 'then' as a conjunctive adverb presents the realm of performance as almost inevitably leading to the intimacy between the two main characters, who end up running away together for a liaison on the Isle of Wight. Indeed, on the eve of their adulterous escape, Siegmund is so excited during an operatic performance that he holds his violin and 'seemed to have his fingers on the strings of his heart, and on the heart of Helena'.[30]

Thus, in his first published story, 'A Prelude', Lawrence had shown how a potential marriage might come about through the realm of festive amateur performance, but he complicated this simple narrative in both of his earliest novels, *The White Peacock* and *The Trespasser*, by using the realm of opera – and particularly what he knew of the Carl Rosa company at the Nottingham Theatre Royal – in order to develop the ideas for which his fiction would become most famous: complicated sexual passions, doomed romantic relationships and sensual excess. Of course, such a connection between sex and theatre would continue to appear in Lawrence's fiction beyond the publication of *The Trespasser* in 1912, and, from that year, one of the writers who further inspired Lawrence in these ideas was G.B. Shaw.

G.B. Shaw

The connection with Shaw might, at first glance, seem counter-intuitive, as Lawrence repeatedly contrasted his own writing, with its celebration of the physical world, against a dry Shavian mode of intellectual theorizing. For more than twenty years, Lawrence intermittently grumbled over Shaw, complaining about the Irishman's 'rather bony, bloodless drama' (*Letters* I, 509), and wondering if 'Shaw ever felt one hot blood-pulse of love for the working man'.[31] Lawrence protested that some of Shaw's writing was 'too boring' and 'Too much gas-bag' (*Letters* VI, 472), and included a particularly vicious attack in 'A Propos of "Lady Chatterley's Lover"' (1929), complaining that Shaw 'has a curious blank in his make-up. To him, all sex is infidelity and only infidelity is sex. Marriage is sexless, null'.[32] In the 1950s this last quotation was highlighted by F.R. Leavis in a well-known book review, entitled 'Shaw against Lawrence', which furthered the notion of Lawrence and Shaw as oppositional.[33]

Yet Shaw often functioned as a contrarian inspiration for Lawrence. Although Lawrence animadverted, he also declared, 'Do not think because I rave at Bernard Shaw I don't like him. He is one of those delightful people who give one the exquisite pleasure of falling out with him wholesomely' (*Letters* I, 103). In any case, Lawrence was not always 'falling out': he openly admired Shaw's anti-militaristic pamphlet of 1914, 'Common Sense about the War', and felt pleased to received £5 from the Irishman in 1915 (*Letters* II, 236, 449). In turn, Shaw watched *The Widowing of Mrs Holroyd* in 1926 and proclaimed that it 'rushed through in such a torrent of profuse yet vividly effective dialogue, making my own seem archaic in comparison', a comment that made Lawrence feel 'vastly pleased'. Lawrence declared, 'He ought to know about dialogue, it's very generous of him'.[34] After Lawrence's death, Frieda accepted a lunch invitation from the Shaws, and commented on the 'wonderfully free atmosphere' where 'nothing you said or did would shock or surprise them. If you had suddenly turned a somersault they would have taken it along with the rest. Because of this freedom Shaw and Lawrence might have liked each other, I am sorry they never met.'[35]

One of the Shavian works that Lawrence most admired was *Man and Superman*. He watched this at Nottingham's Theatre Royal in March 1912, and felt enthusiastic enough to read the play in advance, allude to it in letters, and circulate the script amongst his Eastwood friends (*Letters* I, 373, 376). Of course, this particular show was no run-of-the-mill theatre trip for Lawrence. The production arrived at one of the most momentous points in Lawrence's personal life, as he visited the playhouse along with the married mother he had met for the first time earlier that month, Frieda Weekley. In fact, these lovers had already discovered a mutual interest in drama: Frieda remembered that, on first meeting, 'We talked about Oedipus and understanding leaped through our words.'[36] Subsequently, Lawrence and Frieda found it difficult to rendezvous, but, given their shared fascination with theatre, did conspire to see G.B. Shaw's *Man and Superman* together.[37]

In March 1912, Shaw's play was a supremely appropriate piece for Lawrence and Frieda to watch. *Man and Superman* was presented for performance in a way that focused the attention upon a central romantic relationship: the character of Jack Tanner being successfully pursued by Ann Whitefield. Tanner himself is a revolutionary writer whose words upset and provoke others, his method is to get 'into intimate relations with them [women] to study them', and he feels that, 'Of all human struggles there is none so treacherous and remorseless as the struggle between the artist man and the mother woman.'[38] In his literary writings, Lawrence had already drawn extensively upon his own acquaintances and particularly upon his relationship with his mother, so must have recognized an affinity. By the end of Shaw's play, Tanner and Ann have travelled to continental Europe and agreed to get married, while the main subplot revolves around a character 'Makin love [*sic*] to a married woman!'[39] There was much to ponder here for Lawrence and Frieda, who would themselves leave for Germany together within the following two months.

Sons and Lovers

At the time of watching Shaw's *Man and Superman*, Lawrence was writing *Sons and Lovers* (published 1913). As Jessie Chambers emphasizes, he had almost finished the novel by that point, so Frieda could have had little effect upon most of it, but: 'There is one incident, however, that may refer to her – where Paul Morel goes to the theatre with Clara. From the description of her dress I guessed at once Mrs. Weekley, and they actually did see *Man and Superman* here at Nottingham, together'.[40] In the passage from *Sons and Lovers* that Chambers mentions, Lawrence describes the overwhelming feelings of erotic desire for Clara that Paul experiences in the theatre:

> All the time his blood kept sweeping up in great white-hot waves that killed his consciousness momentarily [...] The play went on. But he was obsessed by the desire to kiss the tiny blue vein that nestled in the bend of her arm. He could feel it. His whole face seemed suspended till he had put his lips there. It must be done. And the other people! At last he bent quickly forward and touched it with his lips.[41]

After the applause dies down at the show's end, Paul Morel realizes that he has missed his train, and so Clara invites him back to her house. Clara is, like the real-life Frieda, a married woman: but that scarcely deters Paul. At her house, he goes upstairs and dresses in her clothes:

> He sat up and looked at the room in the darkness. Then he realised that there was a pair of stockings on a chair. He got up stealthily, and put them on himself. Then he sat still, and knew he would have to have her. After that he sat erect on the bed, his feet doubled under him, perfectly motionless, listening.[42]

This part of the novel was cut away by Edward Garnett, who no doubt realized that it would be too racy for the original publication.[43] Yet the unprinted passage provides a key example of how theatre and sex interconnect in Lawrence's fiction, with Paul, after becoming excited at the theatre, engaging in a spell of secretive cross-dressing that arouses him further, before finally sneaking downstairs, kissing Clara, and making love to her. In *Sons and Lovers*, the role-playing world of the theatre therefore leads directly to Paul Morel's sexual exploration of both Clara's most intimate costume and her body. In such descriptions, Lawrence pointed to the materiality of the theatre and to the fact that, unlike other kinds of literature, drama often relies on warm human bodies and titivating costumes, as well as the clustering of men and women in close proximity to one another.

The Rainbow

In his first books, *The White Peacock* (1911), *The Trespasser* (1912) and *Sons and Lovers* (1913), Lawrence thus developed his ideas about the erotics of the theatre audience and, in each case, as we have seen, the characters experience overwhelming sexual feelings as a result of fictionalized versions of what Lawrence himself had discovered at Nottingham's Theatre Royal. In *The White Peacock*, a heterosexual couple leaves the performance of *Carmen* at that venue 'in a tumult of confused emotion'.[44] In *Sons and Lovers*, Paul Morel attends the same Nottingham auditorium with Clara and identifies so thoroughly with the stage-world that the play continues 'somewhere, he did not know where, but it seemed far away inside him'.[45] And in *The Trespasser*, we find an operatic performance like those Lawrence had first seen in Nottingham, where Siegmund (who is shortly about to embark on an adulterous affair) feels a 'spattering roar of applause quicken[ing] his pulse. It was hoarse, and savage, and startling on his inflamed soul, making him shiver with anticipation, as if something had brushed his hot nakedness'.[46]

In Lawrence's next period of work – the writings produced during and shortly after the First World War – he continued to link sex and theatre. But, by contrast with his earlier depictions, he now drew upon a wider array of dramatic entertainments, including the variety hall, the circus and the cinema. Such popular theatricals facilitate, in Lawrence's texts, a far more shallow and superficial set of sexual liaisons and desires than the overwhelming sensuality of the early novels. In the subsequent works, the characters do not feel that they have internalized a dramatic spectacle, but feel removed from it and seek to exploit its erotic potential in a more cynical way.

For example, in *The Rainbow* (1915) William Brangwen looks for an adulterous sexual adventure after finding his wife Anna increasingly remote from him. He travels to a music hall, the Nottingham Empire, and sits next to 'two girls', one of whom displays a vulnerability that greatly excites him. He surmises that 'Probably she was a warehouse-lass. He was glad she was a common girl'; and then he expresses disconcerting paedophilic feelings, thinking that she would 'be small, almost like a child, and pretty. Her childishness whetted him keenly. She would be helpless between his hands [. . .] she was so young and palpitating'.[47] As he watches her, he imagines her being violated, 'Her open mouth, showing the small, irregular, white teeth, appealed to him. It was open and ready. It was so vulnerable. Why should he not go in and enjoy what was there?'[48] Brangwen then accompanies this woman outside but, although the two initially experience some mutual sensual pleasure, she soon escapes his clutches, and Brangwen instead returns to his wife, with whom he experiences a newfound discovery of anal sex. Ultimately, Brangwen remains unconcerned about who exactly he has met at the music hall, he does not even know her name at the end of the encounter, and has simply wanted to reinvigorate his own erotic life: 'About the girl herself, who or what she was, he cared nothing, he was quite unaware that she was anybody. She was just the sensual object of his attention.'[49]

The theatrical form that Lawrence relies upon here is worth some consideration. In *The Rainbow* Lawrence depicts Brangwen attending the Empire music hall, one of a cluster of theatrical buildings that – in real life – neighboured the Theatre Royal and dominated the entertainment district in the centre of Nottingham from the late 1890s.[50] In reality, the 3,000-seat Empire would not have been open at the time when it appears in *The Rainbow* (where it appears, anachronistically, in the 1880s), but – with its pagoda domes, grinning idols of Krishna and kitsch elephant-heads – Lawrence had found here a venue in which to imagine a cheap and cynical sexual encounter.[51] Here, the rotating bill of fare, and permission of laughter, chatting and applause, facilitates a quite different kind of sexual dynamic from the performances of the Theatre Royal that informed Lawrence's earlier fiction. At times, the characters of those previous novels feel overwhelmed by, and subsumed into, the stage world. But in *The Rainbow* William Brangwen sees himself, rather than any onstage performer, becoming the central focus of the show: 'He was himself, the absolute, the rest of the world was the object that should contribute to his being.'[52] Indeed, so self-absorbed is Brangwen that at no point do we, as readers, learn precisely what is going on onstage. In order to seduce the object of his desire, Brangwen compares the programme with that of previous weeks, and notes the 'best turn', but the text never specifies the name, genre or anything else about those acts. The theatrical performance, just like the woman herself, remains anonymous, and is simply used by Brangwen in order to satisfy his own personal appetites.

Popular theatricals

When Lawrence wrote his pre-war novels, he had described how the relatively highbrow playhouse encourages a heightened erotic dynamic by trapping spectators in a state of longing where escape becomes awkward, if not impossible. But this is not the case with *The Rainbow*, where the popular dramatic form of the music hall provides much opportunity for talking, flirting and other contact amongst members of the audience.[53] And *The Rainbow* was not a one-off. In some of his ensuing stories, Lawrence again used popular entertainment venues to depict scenarios in which there is sexual pursuit, but where at least one member of a couple is trying to avoid any meaningful personal relationship with a potential partner.

When Lawrence wrote *Women in Love* in 1916, he described Gudrun, when looking for a 'boy', as sitting 'among the louts in the cinema'. Her romantic quest in this venue is an unfulfilling one: she finds an electrician, Palmer, a cold egoist who really prefers her sister, and when Gudrun attends the cinema with him, his 'face flickered as he made his sarcastic remarks'. She feels 'filled with a fury of contempt and anger' and soon realizes she needs another man to take her 'out of the mud'.[54]

In 'Tickets Please', which Lawrence wrote two years afterwards, he developed these ideas about the dynamics of the cinema. Here, the male protagonist, who goes by the resonant name of John Thomas (and is also nicknamed 'Coddy', or testicles) is a serial philanderer who has an entire 'flock' of 'old flames'.[55] He accompanies Annie to the pictures, as a prelude to the 'dark, damp fields' where he can display 'all the arts of love-making'.[56] But afterwards, when she seeks to 'take an intelligent interest in him and his life and his character, he sheered off', and wants little more to do with her.[57] Ultimately, the couple prove so ill-suited that the story concludes with the characters enacting an updated version of Euripides' sanguinary play, *The Bacchae*.

The performance venue described in 'Tickets Please' is an Eastwood cinema-tent at the town's annual autumn fair, and this location is scarcely conducive to intimacy. The projector periodically fails and so 'pitch darkness falls from time to time, when the machine goes wrong. Then there is a wild whooping, and a loud smacking of simulated kisses'. In those moments of darkness, Annie feels her potential lover's breath on her hair and longs for his touch on her lips, but suddenly the projector's 'light sprang up, she also started electrically, and put her hat straight'.[58] Thus, just as the personal relationship between these two characters will – for Annie – be unexpectedly terminated, so the cinema showing itself is subject to jolting interruption.

Similarly, in the story that Lawrence penned in 1919, 'Monkey Nuts', the circus tent is presented as another performance venue that is connected with an anticlimactic sexual pursuit. Here, a lusty land-girl trails the character of Joe, even though he appears to her as almost a generic type rather than a discrete individual: 'She had seen also a good many Joes, quiet, good-looking young soldiers with half-averted faces'.[59] He in turn feels intimidated by her: she is a 'strong' woman who gives Joe a 'summons' to meet her, and who has first appeared to him 'at the head of her two great horses'.[60] Having refused a date with her, Joe prefers to go to the circus with his male friend, Albert. But during the show, Joe finds himself watching a female circus performer whose dexterity with horses parallels the intimidating land-girl. Joe then gazes around the audience and then feels 'electrified' by the sight of the very land-girl he has been trying to avoid.[61] Her presence in the circus tent threatens to spoil the male intimacy that he is enjoying with Albert, and although Joe spends the show trying to avoid her gaze, she embraces him afterwards and 'made all his bones rotten'.[62] Thus, again, the popular form of dramatic entertainment does not facilitate a profound form of sexual feeling, as in the early novels, but triggers an unwelcome and underwhelming erotic display.

Esther Andrews

During the war, the sexuality of the playhouse had once more intruded upon Lawrence's real-life experiences as well as upon his fiction. By the end of 1916, he and Frieda had moved to Cornwall, where they were cold, isolated and suspected of being spies. Into this situation materialized the strikingly beautiful Iowa-born actor, Esther Andrews. According to her nephew, she was 'glamorous, slim, fairly tall, around 5'7" and usually dressed in slacks and a shirt of painter's colors. Her voice was somewhat husky but clearly articulated, in a sort of international accent clearly influenced by her dramatic training'.[63]

According to Jeffrey Myers, Esther Andrews arrived on Lawrence's doorstep along with her lover, Robert Mountsier, having made the pilgrimage to Cornwall because both she and Mountsier admired the writer. Nevertheless, these lovers soon quarreled and Mountsier left for London, abandoning Andrews with the Lawrences until halfway through January. Three months afterwards, she returned again to stay – once more by herself – with the Lawrences from mid-April to mid-May.[64] Leading up to this encounter, at his base in Cornwall, D.H. Lawrence had already been dwelling on the sex-life of female actors. One letter of spring 1916 describes him 'often' considering the Italian Eleonora Duse 'with her lovers' (*Letters* II, 595), and when he wrote his first version of *Women in Love* during that year he referred to 'Duse, panting with her lovers after the theatre'.[65] He now took sufficient pleasure in the company of the actor Esther Andrews to base his future plans around her, writing in January 1917 that, 'She makes me feel that America is really the next move' (*Letters* III, 72). But how exactly the matronly Frieda felt about this visitor is less clear. When Andrews returned to stay with them in the spring of 1917, Frieda was suffering from ptomaine poisoning and diarrhoea, and recovering by drinking fermented milk (*Letters* III, 122). Lawrence escaped the sickness and smells by spending more time with Andrews (see *Letters* III, 119), and Catherine Carswell later described Andrews competing with Frieda: apparently Andrews 'could not resist attaching herself to Lawrence and trying to match her strength against Frieda's'.[66] According to Mabel Dodge Luhan, Frieda later admitted that, in Cornwall, Lawrence had an affair with Esther Andrews as well as with the farmer William Henry Hocking:

> Frieda told me about the two times Lawrence had evaded her. One time was with the American girl in Cornwall when she was absent for a visit to her mother, I think. She had returned to the little house and found a feeling in the air that she had not left there. She forced Lawrence to tell her about it and then showed the girl the door. It had, or at least so he told her, been a miserable failure, anyway. The other one had been a young farmer, also in Cornwall.[67]

Lawrence's recent biographers think this account unlikely, but whatever about the physical reality of these relationships, Esther Andrews and Lawrence clearly enjoyed one another's company. After all, Andrews first arrived on Lawrence's doorstep on Christmas Eve, 1917, the time of the year that, as we have seen, Lawrence associated with the excitement of acting games, and she was ideally suited to such festivities, being, according to Mark Kinkead-Weekes, 'a wonderful mimic', just like Lawrence himself.[68] In addition, Lawrence took the opportunity to share his dramatic ideas with Andrews, because she had professional onstage experience and had toured with US repertory companies before the war. An insight into Lawrence's theatrical discussions with Andrews comes from a letter that he sent to her in August 1917, in which he describes a charity 'Concert-Play' called *East and West* that had been organized in St Ives by one of his local acquaintances. According to Lawrence, the highlights of this amateur performance included a poetry recital, some violin music and an elderly busker who had been dragged in at the last moment and who 'yowled a street song' to general audience discomfort. As Lawrence described it, the show also involved a series of dramatic scenes, including a 'Spanish Gypsy' sequence that featured some of Frieda's donated frocks and shawls. There then followed African, Indian and Greek dancing, and Lawrence observed that – although the evening had raised funds for the Red Cross – the show had been so terrible that 'I want my money back'. Nonetheless, Lawrence explained with irony that 'I had to give you this [lengthy description] in full, as it is the greatest event in Zennor for some time' (*Letters* III, 26–27).

Lawrence may thus have viewed the performances with a cynical detachment, but he felt sufficiently moved to write an extended account to a woman for whom he clearly felt an attraction. And a concern with such small-scale provincial variety shows lies at the heart of his major forthcoming book, *The Lost Girl*, which was published in 1920, and which once again connects the theatrical with the erotic.

The Lost Girl

The Lost Girl concerns a woman, Alvina, based in a fictional version of Lawrence's Eastwood (named 'Woodhouse'), and whose narrative intertwines theatrical and sexual discovery. Initially, Alvina leaves home for London, where the playhouse looks like it might be a route to erotic awakening for her. When she revisits her home in the Midlands she 'was always speaking of the doctors: Doctor Young and Doctor Headley and Doctor James. She spoke of theatres and music-halls with these young men, and the jolly good time she had with them', which leaves one acquaintance in Woodhouse 'shocked' and worrying over the unasked question, 'Alvina, have you betrayed yourself with any of these young men?'[69] In fact, at this point Alvina remains a virgin, but those worries prove prescient. When she returns to live at home, her father buys a portable theatre, which provides ample opportunity for her to realize her erotic desires. At first, there are rumours that 'She was supposed to be "carrying on"' with one of the theatre managers; she then has a 'serious flirtation with a man who played a flute'; and she is drawn to the exotic appearance of a Japanese acrobat, admiring 'the serpent of his loins'.[70] A Southern Italian performer called Ciccio then arrives as part of a five-person 'Red Indian troupe', and whose body (and phallic spear) Alvina again happily admires:

> Ciccio was without his blanket, naked to the waist, in war-paint, and brandishing a long spear. He dashed up from the rear, saluted the chieftain with his arm and his spear on high as he swept past, suddenly

drew up his rearing steed, and trotted slowly back again, making his horse perform its paces. He was extraordinarily velvety and alive on horseback.[71]

Eventually, such charms coax Alvina to run away with this velvety equestrian to Naples, as Lawrence puts it – in a passage that he worked hard to revise – she was 'bewitched' because 'he seemed so beautiful, so beautiful. And this left her numb, submissive. Why must she see him beautiful? Why was she will-less? She felt herself like one of the old sacred prostitutes'.[72]

Alvina's journey, from daughter and virginal nurse to 'sacred prostitute', is entirely facilitated by the theatre, and so we are faced with the familiar Lawrentian idea of the playhouse enabling an erotic relationship to develop, much as he had shown in his novels since *The White Peacock*. Like the characters of the earliest novels, Alvina is overwhelmed by the sensual possibility of live performance. Indeed, at one point in the novel, when one of Ciccio's Red Indian troupe, Louis, performs a satirical mime it reduces Alvina to a sexualized moment of helplessness:

> At moments Alvina caught her lip between her teeth, it was so screamingly funny, and so annihilating. She laughed in spite of herself. In spite of herself she was shaken into a convulsion of laughter. Louis was masterful – he mastered her psyche. She laughed till her head lay helpless on the chair, she could not move. Helpless, inert she lay, in her orgasm of laughter [...] poor weak Alvina lay back in her chair in a new weak convulsion.[73]

Alvina, then, is physically dominated by the theatre that extends the way in which earlier male characters such as Paul Morel in *Sons and Lovers*, George Saxton in *The White Peacock*, and Siegmund in *The Trespasser* had felt overwhelmed by the sensual passion of live performance. But in *The Lost Girl* Lawrence also contrasts the overwhelming erotic sensations of dramatic performance with the notion, which he had explored in his wartime fiction, of the popular theatre being cheapened and debased. In *The Lost Girl*, Alvina's engagement with the theatre leads her to experience a profound (although scarcely unproblematic) journey of sexual self-discovery which recalls that described in *The Trespasser* or *Sons and Lovers*. But this intense engagement with theatre is contrasted with the other audience members who seek only a shallow form of dramatic sensation. When the collier-audience turns up for the opening of Alvina's family theatre, the spectators spend their time shouting, stamping their feet and making 'gurglings and kissings'.[74]

Thus, as Alvina reclines in a kind of post-coital helplessness after her 'orgasm of laughter', her visceral, bodily reaction is immediately counterpointed with lamentable 'Popular taste' described by one of the performers, who complains that most spectators now seek out cinematic shows that 'cost the audience nothing, no feeling of the heart, no appreciation of the spirit [. . .] they don't like us, because they must *feel* the things we do, from the heart, and appreciate them from the spirit'.[75] This contrast between Alvina, who experiences a deep, bodily connection with the live performers, and the film-desiring spectators who only engage superficially with the realm of drama, allows Lawrence to make a broader point about how, in the early years of the twentieth century, performance culture was moving away from the sensual realm of live theatre and towards the incorporeal imagery of the cinema.[76]

Portable theatre and cinema

In fact, the fictional playhouse of Alvina Houghton was a conflation of two real-life portable theatres that had set up outside the Sun Inn in Eastwood during the early years of the twentieth century. The first, 'Belmore's Pavilion Theatre', arrived at the start of July 1903, when Lawrence was 17, and remained *in situ* until the autumn, although the proprietor of this theatre, Charles Belmore, struggled to suit his approach to the town, largely because Belmore staged morally improving plays with titles such as *The Christian's Cross* and *The Wages of Sin*: quite a contrast with the blood-and-guts approach of the older, and commercially cannier Teddy Rayner operation, which had staged performances on the same spot in the 1890s.[77] In response, Belmore won praise from the town's newspaper but attracted vanishingly small audiences, and eventually a group of local businessmen took pity on him and arranged a more popular programme of songs, gramophone recordings and a 'highly-amusing comedy entitled "The Deaf Milkman"'.[78] Having been forced to adjust to commercial pressure in this way, Charles Belmore abandoned the town shortly afterwards.

Then, eight years after Belmore quit, the same site at Sun Inn Croft was occupied by another dramatic enterprise, a wooden hut called 'Parker's Picture Pavilion'. Unlike Belmore's venture, the Picture Pavilion was primarily a cinema and enjoyed immediate success, as the owner gave a number of charity performances in 1911 that won him a reputation for 'extreme generosity'.[79] But the Picture Pavilion soon ran into trouble when, in December 1912, another local man, Frederick Stubbs, opened Eastwood's first permanent theatrical venue, the 'Eastwood Empire', nearby on the corner of Nottingham Road and King Street. The wooden Picture Pavilion could scarcely compete with this new, centrally heated auditorium, where 800 spectators could sit in turquoise-blue armchairs before a large proscenium arch, and Lawrence must have felt intrigued by the contrast between these venues when visiting his hometown in August 1913. Predictably, of course, the owner of Parker's Picture Pavilion went out of business within the year.[80]

In *The Lost Girl* Lawrence conflated those two failing pavilion theatres that he knew from real-life Eastwood in order to create his portrait of Alvina's ill-starred theatrical enterprise. In the novel, the portable theatre only makes a small margin of profit, and remains a second-rate, stop-gap venue for those who would prefer, but are unable, to see entertainment elsewhere.[81] But in *The Lost Girl* the main reason for the unpopularity of the portable theatre is the competition posed by the nearby cinema, something that had not been the reason for the failure of either of Eastwood's real-life portable theatres.[82] Instead, Lawrence changed the historical details in order to illustrate a wider truth. As Philip Auslander puts it 'the relationship between the live and the mediatized is one of competitive opposition at the level of cultural economy', and he points out that 'film had thoroughly routed the theatre by 1926, so there was little left to pillage when television arrived in force some twenty years later'.[83] Lawrence probably knew that other theatres close to his hometown had capitulated in the face of the new threat, with the emergence of Heanor's 'Empire Palace' cinema (formerly St James Theatre until 1910), and 'Vint's Picturedome' in Ilkeston (formerly the Theatre Royal until 1911). Indeed, although the Eastwood Empire had been established in 1912 as a venue for live variety shows, 'all picture weeks' had become the norm at the venue by mid-1916.[84] Thus, in *The Lost Girl*, Alvina regrets the advent of the cinema age, which means that audiences 'only come [to her father's portable theatre] because they can't get to the Empire [...] They crowd the Empire – and the Empire is only pictures now: and it's much cheaper to run'.[85] This shift in performance culture leaves the members of the old touring theatrical troupes as 'Odd, extraneous creatures, often a little depressed, feeling life slip away from them. The cinema was killing them'.[86]

In this way, *The Lost Girl* describes the sexual awakening of Alvina Houghton, but also charts the way that popular culture was awakening to the seductions of the cinematic age, and laments the loss of an older world of performance.[87] As Lawrence explained in his non-fictional writings, one of the things he hated about the cinema was its tendency to atomize the viewing experience. Rather than encouraging the individual viewer to join the 'experience of the human bloodstream', the cinema presents only 'shadows' and the 'thinkings' of the spectator's mind, rather than tangible, touchable human bodies: thus, as Lawrence put it, 'the individual watching the shadow-spectacle sits a very god, in an orgy of abstraction'.[88] Lawrence's earlier novels had repeatedly examined the eroticism that might be involved in watching the live body of the theatrical performer. But in *The Lost Girl*, Alvina argues that cinema caters for those who do not wish to inhabit this dramatic realm of other people, theorizing that, whilst the admirer of live theatre 'like[s] things which aren't yourself', cinema audiences 'hate anything that isn't themselves. And that's why they like pictures. It's all themselves to them, all the time'.[89]

Elsewhere, Lawrence praised live performance because it enabled audience members to transcend their own isolated physical condition. For example, in 1913 he described Italian drama by writing: 'The people of the audience are a joy for ever [...] the men lounge and lean on one another, talk and laugh and stroll, or stare in utter childish absorption, so that the place seems full of pleasure for everybody, and everybody shares with everybody else. It gives a warm feeling of life'.[90] Similarly, his 1921 writing about Italian theatre describes the 'physical sympathy' that might be felt by members of a communal audience.[91] But by contrast, in *The Lost Girl*, Alvina make the case that cinematic audiences lack such fellow feeling, with onanistic viewers focusing only upon their own personal reactions. The mechanized moving pictures are therefore, in her view, more suited to the 'conceited'.[92] Readers may disagree with Alvina's analysis, but it is difficult to avoid the conclusion that *The Lost Girl* shows Lawrence as knowledgeable about a form of working-class entertainment – the portable pavilion theatre – that is seldom remembered by historians. And the novel also reveals an author who wrote with a brilliant sense of melancholy about the major changes that were taking place in Western performance culture during the early decades of the twentieth century.

Interestingly, Lawrence would develop a closer knowledge of the movie industry in later years, although he scarcely grew any more impressed by it. In 1922–1923, he lived on a Taos ranch with the Danish painter Kai Götzsche, who had previously worked at the film studios of Goldwyn and Louis B. Mayer. Lawrence even travelled to Hollywood with Götzsche in 1923, and during this trip the Nottingham writer was invited for tea at the house of an unnamed movie star. Lawrence later gave satirical re-enactments of this meeting for his friends, telling them about being given an 'appalling pint of whiskey and soda' by the celebrity, who was 'wearing white riding breeches and carrying a riding crop'.[93] *The Lost Girl* had been written before that unlikely Hollywood encounter, but the novel nonetheless engages with cinematic culture, and mourns the change in the erotic dynamic of audiences that occurred as popular drama shifted from predominantly 3D to 2D entertainment.

Aaron's Rod

In his next major novel, *Aaron's Rod* (written 1918–1921, published 1922), Lawrence further interrogated the communal feeling that might be felt by theatre audiences. As we have seen, *The Lost Girl* expresses dislike for the sensual changes underway in performance culture, lamenting that the cinema might draw the spectator back to himself rather than into a sense of shared experience with the live bodies of others. But in *Aaron's Rod*, Lawrence added a more political aspect to his thinking about such theatrical immersion into the communal.

In a number of ways, *Aaron's Rod* recycles many of Lawrence's earlier ideas about the connections between theatre and sex. This novel describes the adultery of its main character, the miner's checkweighman Aaron Sisson, who performs as a musician in various concerts and dances. The text begins on Christmas Eve, which, as we have seen in Lawrence's earlier work, tended to be connected with the festive mumming and mimicry that he had experienced since his youth. But Aaron's seasonal performance of music annoys his family, and he escapes this disapproval by abandoning his wife and three children in a fictionalized version of Eastwood, and taking up instead a career as a musician in operatic shows at Covent Garden. In this, of course, he echoes the work of the doomed violinist Siegmund in *The Trespasser* – another musician of Covent Garden – and just as that earlier work relied upon a set of Wagnerian motifs, so *Aaron's Rod* includes references to operas by Wagner, Debussy and Rimsky-Korsakov.[94] Indeed, *Aaron's Rod* is peppered with a wider range of playhouse allusions, from late-Victorian comedy to an extensive use of Shakespeare.[95]

Aaron's Rod also reprises Lawrence's interest in describing the erotic dynamic of the live theatre auditorium. The most extensive description of a playhouse audience in the book is based on a real operatic production that

Lawrence saw in November 1917, when he and Frieda were taken to the Drury Lane Theatre Royal as guests of Lady Cynthia Asquith, who felt she had brought with her 'the most comic concentration of human beings ever seen'.[96] The production they witnessed, an English version of Verdi's *Aida*, was impressive, at least according to both the newspaper reviews and the glowing report of Lady Cynthia.[97] But Lawrence's fictional version presents an 'interminable' evening, attended by a group of London bohemians whose main entertainment comes from making tactless comments about one another's love lives during the intervals.[98] In particular, one couple, whose marriage has lasted for six years, have their relationship so thoroughly probed that the woman ends up admitting that she craves a lover 'so *badly*'.[99] One of that bohemian group, a playhouse scene-painter called Josephine, then notices Aaron playing his flute in the orchestra, goes to speak to him, and (following a description that closely echoes the opening of Shaw's *Pygmalion*) begins a sexual relationship with him.[100]

So far, so familiar. As with Lawrence's earlier fiction, the live operatic auditorium is figured as a site that enables an erotic encounter. Josephine and her companions, whilst they watch *Aida*, are filled with sexual thoughts and longings, and the episode in which Josephine notices Aaron blowing his phallic flute leads directly to their physical relationship. But Josephine expresses a further thought at this point, about the nature of watching theatre itself. She reflects:

> The curtain rose, the opera wound its slow length along. The audience loved it. They cheered with mad enthusiasm. Josephine looked down on the choppy sea of applause, white gloves clapping, heads shaking. The noise was strange and rattling. What a curious multiple object a theatre-audience was! It seemed to have a million heads, a million hands, and one monstrous, unnatural consciousness.[101]

In *The Lost Girl*, Lawrence's characters express a set of worries – which Lawrence shared in real life – about the way that cinema might lead to an insular and abstracted version of spectatorship. But here, in *Aaron's Rod*, Lawrence also showed that it might also be problematic for an individual to become subsumed into the broader audience at a live theatre show. Josephine is troubled that such a dramatic event has the potential to make a disparate group of people think and feel as one, and that diverse spectators can be so led and guided by a small cadre of skilled actors, director and playwright.

Josephine's worries echo the kind of thinking outlined in 1895 by Gustave Le Bon's influential study *The Crowd*, in which he made the case that: 'Nothing has a greater effect on the imagination of crowds of every category than theatrical representations. The entire audience experiences at the same time the same emotions'.[102] Le Bon thus challenged the autonomous and rational actor of liberal political theory, showing how the individual's own thought might blur and disintegrate into the larger and less reasoning mind of the group. According to Le Bon, leaders could control this group mind of the masses, particularly by using theatrical techniques, and his ideas proved deeply attractive to fascist thinkers. Mussolini, for example, inspired by Le Bon, considered theatre 'one of the most direct means of getting through to the hearts of the people', and in 1933 gave a speech in which he declared that:

> The art work of the stage has to possess the wide-ranging appeal that people are asking for. It must stir great collective passions and must be imbued with a sense of vivid and deep humanity [...] Allow the collective passions to find dramatic representation, and you'll see the stalls crowded with people.[103]

In *Aaron's Rod* Josephine feels deeply troubled by this 'monstrous' phenomenon of playhouse spectators who all experience the same emotion at the same time.[104] And Lawrence developed this point through the character of Rawdon Lilly, who, when in the theatre, is able to draw a distinction between his elite friends, 'us in this box', and 'the crew out there' in the rest of the auditorium, 'the infinite crowds of howling savages outside there in the unspeakable, all you've got to do is mind they don't scalp you'.[105] Josephine and Lilly feel contempt for the masses and for shared popular emotion, but Lilly – who is, tellingly, a playwright – believes that the elite might be able to escape from that mass, and can potentially guide it. He does, after all, end the novel in its final pages by urging a submission to the 'greater' kind of man.[106]

Such a discussion about theatre in *Aaron's Rod* shows how Lawrence continued to use the connection between theatre and sex to explore some of the most pressing dramatic issues of the day. In *The Lost Girl* he had thought about that major transition from live to filmic drama; and now in *Aaron's Rod* he showed his prescience in thinking about the nature of the audience in an era of crowd theory, something that would take on a major political significance in the years ahead. Lawrence of course died in 1930, shortly before the early Nazi victories in the Reichstag, but soon afterwards Europe would see a fascist *Gesamtkunstwerk* emerge in those carefully orchestrated mass rallies that were, as Hans Ulrich Thamer puts it, 'not forums for discussion' but instead events designed to replace 'rational forms of discourse with vague and emotional appeals to the audience's fears and aspirations'.[107] In *Aaron's Rod*, the thoughts of Josephine, and the declarations of Lilly, show that Lawrence perceived something of the dangerous road that European dramatic thinking might take. In his previous novels he had described the way that audience members might feel 'mastered' by the overwhelming feelings generated by live theatrical performance, but now he described how such absorption might be freighted with a more politically troubling impulse.

Towards a theatre of cruelty

On Easter Sunday 1923, Lawrence and Frieda watched a very different type of performance. They saw a bullfight in Mexico City, and Lawrence felt so appalled by the brutal treatment of the animals that he spent his time screaming 'Stop it!' towards the arena, berating the bemused spectators around him as 'cowards and madmen', and then demonstrably storming from the arena.[108]

Nonetheless, in October 1923 Lawrence attended a second bullfight, accompanied by Kai Götzsche. This time the event occurred near Tepic, with two bulls being slaughtered and Götzsche feeling as outraged as Lawrence had originally been, although on this occasion Lawrence refrained from raging.[109] Perhaps Lawrence was now enduring such tauricide as useful research, as he employed such a setting both in his novel *The Plumed Serpent*, which he started writing a month after watching the first bullfight, and in his later short story 'None of That!', which he drafted in May 1927.[110]

In both stories, the carnage of the arena is connected with a disturbing kind of sexuality. *The Plumed Serpent* begins with a gruesome bullfight based on the Mexico City event that Lawrence had witnessed, and much of the disgust that Lawrence had felt in real life is expressed by the novel's main character, the Irishwoman Kate Forrester. In the Mexican arena, Kate loathes the sexual dynamic on display. She initially fears that she will be mauled by a steward who rolls 'his eyes with pleased excitement'.[111] She then witnesses a horrible act of penetration, as the bull 'lowered his head and pushed his sharp, flourishing horns in the horse's belly, working them up and down inside there with a sort of vague satisfaction'.[112] Then 'his rear was still heaved up, with the bull's horn working vigorously up and down inside him [...]

And the cries of pleased amusement among the crowd'.[113] Lawrence also describes the 'almost sexual' gaze of the onlookers, and how, after the fight, the chief toreador reclines 'on his bed all dressed up, smoking a fat cigar. Rather like a male Venus [...] like Venus with a fat cigar, listening to her lovers'.[114]

In the 1927 short story 'None of That!' the main female character, an American called Ethel Cane, sits in a more expensive part of the auditorium, high in the shade rather than in the cheap seats described in *The Plumed Serpent*, but, from this elevated height, her abasement is more complete. In *The Plumed Serpent*, Kate has to endure watching the sexualized murder of a bull and fears sexual assault in the auditorium but in 'None of That!' Ethel personally experiences physical brutality that puts her in an analogous position to the tormented animal. Ethel loves European theatre, and finds herself fascinated by the Toreador's 'dramatic sort of power'. She watches as he kills a bull with sensuous passion:

[H]e held his arms out to the bull, with love. And that was what fascinated the women. They screamed and they fainted, longing to go into the arms of Cuesta, against his soft, round body, that was more yearning than a fico ['fig']. But the bull, of course, rushed past him, and only got two darts sticking in his shoulder. That was the love. Then Ethel shouted, *Bravo! Bravo!* and I saw that she too had gone mad.[115]

The death of the bull is, however, a dangerously prophetic act. The bullfighter himself (based on the notorious real-life Mexican bull-fighter, Rodolfo Gano) is a violent misogynist who, when pursued by amorous women, spits at them, and speaks to them with 'terrible obscene language', wanting to 'whip them, or kill them, for pursuing him'.[116] At one point he speaks with a kind of peculiarly Lawrentian *vagina dentate* when he describes one woman whose 'gate is a beak. What man would put his finger into that beak? She is all soft with cruelty towards a man's member'.[117] By the end of the story, Ethel herself has died after pursuing Cuesta: he has arranged for her to be the victim of an implied gang rape that leaves her corpse with 'deep, strange bruises'.[118]

In the same 1928 volume in which Lawrence published 'None of That!', he also included the story of 'The Woman Who Rode Away', which, as we shall see in the following chapter, describes the ritual slaughter of a white woman by Native Americans. In 1970, Kate Millett quite rightly drew attention to the anti-female violence of this volume (labelling the writing 'sadistic pornography', 'a formula for sexual cannibalism' and 'demented fantasy') and made this book central to her critique of Lawrence's retrograde view of women.[119] Yet, from a performance perspective, what is also noticeable is that Lawrence, in writing this 1928 volume, was coming close to the kinds of ideas that were expressed during the following decade by the actor and theatrical pioneer Antonin Artaud, who gave a lecture in 1933 (published 1934) on 'Theatre and the Plague' in which he linked theatre with a 'mood of slaughter, torture and bloodshed'.[120] Like Lawrence, Artaud had come to believe that European theatre had lost much of its potency, which could be recovered by looking to the ritualized dance and music drama of other societies, particularly Mexico. Artaud felt affected by the Balinese performances he saw in Paris in 1931. Then, in 1933, he drew up an outline for a four-act play about Mexico (*The Conquest of Mexico*) that revolved around severed heads and ritualized violence in which Europeans are 'squashed like blood'. And later, in 1935, he travelled to reside in Mexico City and then in a community of Tarahumara Indians where he tried the psychoactive peyote, and witnessed a sacred dance during which he was 'aroused and staggering'.[121] Lawrence, of course, had been here more than a decade earlier, feeling deeply moved by the Mexican bullfights he saw in 1923, as well as by the Puebloan Indian dance and music performances he witnessed in New Mexico during 1924.

By contrast with the vitality of such traditional performances, Lawrence and Artaud thought that modern Western drama had reached its nadir in the degraded form of the cinema. As Artaud explained in an article on 'Theatre and Cruelty' (published 1933):

> The damage wrought by psychological theatre, derived from Racine, has rendered us unaccustomed to the direct, violent action theatre must have. Cinema, in its turn, murders us with reflected, filtered and projected images that no longer *connect* with our sensibility, and for ten years has maintained us and our faculties in an intellectual stupour.[122]

For both Artaud and Lawrence, then, the Western world of dramatic performance – which culminated in the flickering abstractions of the cinema – needed to be innervated by emulating the ritualized modes of drama found outside Europe. Like Lawrence, Artaud turned from the abstract world of the movies towards the physical world of sensation, recommending a theatre of 'cruelty', which meant, as Günter Ahrends puts it, 'confronting the audience with the primeval, anarchic and cruel components of their lives' in order to 'set free the elemental, uncheckable and uncontrollable manifestations of vitality which have been entombed in the course of Western civilization'.[123] Artaud's theatre offered the possibility of reviving Western art by recognizing, as he wrote in 'Theatre and Cruelty', that 'the masses think with their senses first and foremost', and that theatre must release the 'magic freedom of daydreams, only recognizable when imprinted with terror and cruelty'.[124]

If Artaud spoke in favour of 'terror and cruelty', Lawrence praised ritual theatre for including the 'unspeakably terrifying', and accepting the fact that life involves 'cutting the throats'.[125] This, then, is the furthest extreme of Lawrence's theatrical thinking, but is also the logical extension of his earlier writing. As we have seen, he had consistently explored the way that the theatrical auditorium might allow spectators to feel life in vibrant, physical terms. This sensory effect of the theatre was something that he characteristically described in his fiction through an exploration of the erotic, with the characters of his novels repeatedly feeling aroused or embarking on sexual relationships as a direct result of experiences at the playhouse. Yet as Lawrence moved into his late period of writing, he figured the auditorium as the realm of a more bloodthirsty kind of eroticized and sensory performance. In *The Woman Who Rode Away* and *The Plumed Serpent* he had moved away from opera singers and variety artistes to think about the sanguineous outdoor performance of slaughter. Such a manoeuvre took Lawrence's writing into the avant-garde territory of Artaud, who also advocated, in his 'Theatre of Cruelty', a kind of theatre that would use sensation and physical shock in order to awaken the ossified Western realm of performance. Lawrence, the writer of plays that have been characterized as 'determined naturalism', is not usually associated with the formally challenging work of Artaud, but as we shall see in the following chapter, Lawrence remained aware of contemporary developments in theatrical thinking, and consistently showed an affinity with, and fascination towards, the dramatically experimental and avant garde.[126]

Lawrence's final story

The very last story that Lawrence ever completed was 'The Blue Moccasins', which he drafted in the summer of 1928, less than two years before his death. This piece tells the story of a provincial English bank manager, Percy Barlow, who takes the lead role in a festive play and who finds himself drawn to the woman who plays his lover in the show. Meanwhile, Percy's own wife sits in the audience and watches as 'the love-scenes between Percy and the young woman were becoming nakedly shameful'.[127] The wife eventually confronts her husband during the interval and angrily asks him to take her home, but he decides to continue his performance, sends her away with another driver, and is 'softly' invited back to the actress's house instead.[128]

The Lawrence who wrote this story had returned to Europe from New Mexico, and so includes here a heightened awareness of cultural difference. In 'The Blue Moccasins' the English actors are performing an orientalist fantasy called *The Shoes of Shagpat*, in which the main character of Percy has a 'blackened face', and is 'dressed as a Moor [. . . with] dark-green sash, and negro boy's red fez'.[129] But one of the things that enrages Percy's wife is the falseness of the vision being presented by the actors. She is particularly maddened by seeing onstage her own pair of blue moccasins, which she had acquired before her marriage when travelling in New Mexico, but which Percy has sneaked from the house in order to use in this Arabian Nights-style fantasy. During the performance, the blue footwear plays a central role in the plot: the character played by Percy can only approach his lover when she is not wearing them. But in the audience, Percy's wife feels enraged by the presence of this footwear, at least in part because she originally obtained the shoes during her own independent days in New Mexico, and knows that 'Moccasins are male footwear, among the Indians, not female'.[130] When she sees the shoes in the production – during which they are kicked across the stage by someone in Turkish dress – 'a little bomb of rage exploded in her. This, of all places! the blue moccasins that she had bought in the western deserts!'[131] She knows just how incongruous is the appearance of the New Mexican moccasins in such a pseudo-Arabian setting, and she interrupts the performance in order to demand, 'Will you hand me my moccasins!'[132]

This New-Mexican performance dynamic would scarcely have been included in Lawrence's early writings about English drama. Yet, despite such novel elements, when this last completed story of 'The Blue Moccasins' first appeared in December 1928, Lawrence had clearly continued to manifest a similar set of theatrical interests to those he had expressed in his very first published story 'A Prelude' (1907). Essentially, both tales revolve around an amateur theatrical show being staged on Christmas Eve by face-painted characters in the English midlands, and both tell a story of sexual desire. Ultimately, just like his counterpart in 'A Prelude', Percy Barlow in 'The Blue Moccasins' uses acting and performance in order to attract the woman he wants. Of course, it is true that, during the twenty-one years between the writing of those two pieces, Lawrence's awareness of international performance had affected and adjusted his dramatic thinking. Yet his fiction-writing career is nonetheless bookended by these two short works that reveal that, no matter how far Lawrence had journeyed, there persisted in his work an abiding interest in expounding, explaining and exploring the connection that might exist between drama and sex. Although Lawrence failed to make his name as a playwright during his own lifetime, his prose fictions nonetheless rely on theatre and drama in order to develop the erotic ideas for which his writing is still best known.

CHAPTER 4
LAWRENCE'S THEATRICAL DEVELOPMENT: REALIST AND EXPERIMENTALIST CROSSCURRENTS

Lawrence the realist?

When Anaïs Nin reviewed Lawrence's overall dramatic output in 1966 she said, 'these plays remind one of the perfect rendering of the illusion of reality by the Moscow Art Theater'.[1] The critics who watched Lawrence's plays at the Royal Court Theatre in 1968 tended towards a similar conclusion, with Michael Billington, for example, praising *The Daughter-in-Law* by writing:

> [T]his production depends heavily on its fidelity to the details of ordinary domestic life: the dramatic crises gain enormously in credibility from being set in such a solidly believable context. When a pie is scooped out of a dish, you can hear the crust being broken and the miner washing himself at the end of his day's work becomes a fascinating ritual in itself: first he cleans out the kitchen sink, then crosses to the stove where he takes the hot water and slowly empties it into a pail and then takes the pail back again to the sink.[2]

As one of the actors in the Royal Court's productions of Lawrence, Edward Peel, put it, 'Water steamed when it came from the hob, meals steamed and there was a wonderful smell of freshly baked bread and Yorkshire pudding'.[3]

There might appear a bewildering gulf between such representations of reality, and the way in which the mature Lawrence moved towards a mode of theatrical thinking which resembled that of Antonin Artaud. What had caused Lawrence's theatrical thinking to shift so fundamentally from the realism that characterizes his early playwriting?

As we will see in this chapter, that question is framed somewhat incorrectly. Lawrence in fact remained aware of theatrical innovation throughout his writing career, and from his earliest dramatic work an experimentalist current was a fundamental part of his realism. As Toril Moi points out, stage technique is often inadequately described by a formalist distinction 'between realistic "illusion" or "representation", on the one hand, and self-conscious modernist explorations of the relevant artistic medium'.[4] But Lawrence's writings reveal the crudeness of such divisions, and this chapter will examine his drama alongside his novels, short stories and essays to see how notions of theatrical experiment repeatedly affect his work.

Lawrence's very first play, *A Collier's Friday Night*, comes closest of any of his dramas to being a photographic reflection of real experience, portraying many features that connect directly with life in Eastwood. Yet even here, that link between the fictive stage world and the real world is scarcely straightforward. For example, the opening stage direction specifies that the mother '*is reading the "New Age"*' (6), and as Andrew Thacker emphasizes, we should not understand this direction to reveal that the real-life women of Eastwood were typically reading this modernist and socialist magazine: rather, the direction has a symbolic purpose, showing 'Lawrence's view of the maternal feminine as the bearer of culture in working-class homes'.[5] Situated behind her is a selection of other suggestive texts, including a copy of Richard Garnett's *International Library of Famous Literature*, which Lawrence had relied upon when writing his play, and which, when put onstage, gives an indication of the constructed nature of the drama. As Hiran Malani puts it, 'Though realistic in its details, *A Collier's Friday Night* develops certain images into symbols'.[6] After all, even the play's title self-consciously points back to Robert Burns's poem 'The Cotter's Saturday Night', encouraging us to contrast the volatility of pay-night in Lawrence's Eastwood against the prayerful joy of family life described by Burns. Right from the start, then, Lawrence's playwriting combined the symbolic with the realistic, and in 1926 Desmond MacCarthy tellingly described Lawrence's theatrical technique as 'A Poet's Realism'.[7]

Lawrence's second play, *The Widowing of Mrs Holroyd*, continues to manifest this 'poet's realism', most notably in the body-washing of the final scene, which, as Catherine Carswell put it, leaves 'the whole production lifted into a plane beyond realism'.[8] But by the time of his third play, *The Merry-go-Round*, Lawrence had abandoned realistic narrative altogether in favour of a schematic comedy that resolves with the simultaneous decision of multiple couples to get married. Indeed, the opening scene of *The Merry-go-Round* – in which an old lady hallucinates about a 'little fat chap as stands there laughing at me' (113) – offers a warning that we should not necessarily expect to see reality on the stage. Accordingly, the script goes on to include pantomimic Polish aristocrats, some melodramatic lumber about a hidden will, and the fancifully coincidental appearance of the nurse's former lover. Such incorporation of fantasy means that, if we approach *The Merry-go-Round* expecting to find a life-like depiction of what Lawrence actually experienced in his early years, then we are likely to feel disappointed.

In fact, by the time that Lawrence wrote this third play, he set about including features that would be very difficult to achieve within the bounds of the contemporary realistic stage. The directions of *The Merry-go-Round* specify that, '*The goose flaps and squarks and attacks him*' (123), and later require that the same creature '*walks mildly*' (176). Lawrence's detractors have asserted that this is simply bad writing. In 1965, for example, W.A. Darlington described the goose by remarking that Lawrence's 'naïvity about the stage must have been formidable indeed'.[9] For sure, *The Merry-go-Round* will inevitable prove a headache for any theatre director who is determined to see Lawrence as simply a photographic realist. But Sylvia Sklar suggests that one way of bringing the play into production might be to highlight the fantastic elements of Lawrence's script by casting Patty as 'A larger-than-life-size bird', a technique specified by Seán O'Casey in the 1949 play *Cock-A-Doodle Dandy*.[10] For modern readers, perhaps, Lawrence appears to have been issuing a theatrical challenge comparable to that of Sarah Kane, who included the famously difficult stage direction in *Cleansed* (1998): '*The rats carry Carl's feet away*'.[11] Indeed, Lawrence himself specified in *The Widowing of Mrs Holroyd* that '*a rat careers out of the scullery*' (72).

Lawrence's best-known director, Peter Gill, simply removed the goose from the Royal Court's 1973 production of *The Merry-go-Round*. But nonetheless, as Gill highlights in Chapter 5 of this book, the celebrated 1968 performances of the 'Eastwood Trilogy' never involved a straightforward realism in any case. As Gill describes it, some of his stagings involved: 'An intense hyper-realism on the one hand, but staged on sets that were selective of what was presented, with a designed rig of lights hanging above the action and very much in sight' (p.151). He remembers his assistant-director Jane Howell observing that 'the realism we obtained had a hallucinogenic quality', and Barney Norris has commented elsewhere that Gill's productions 'never sought to persuade their audience [members] to forget they were in a theatre'.[12]

Una Chaudhuri observes that, as playwrights attempted to recreate actual environments in the theatre, what actually emerged was 'an attempted closure of fictionality, a will to close the gap between the world of the stage and the world of the spectator', which placed the audience member 'in an impossible displacement, where s/he was asked to play the role of ultimate hermeneutic authority while being reminded simultaneously of the authorizing but invisible presence of the omnipotent puppet master/ playwright, creator of all meaning'.[13] That is to say, during any realistic theatre production, the material conditions of the playhouse building – lighting equipment, stage blocks, ticket office and so forth – serve as a continual reminder that the event is being carefully orchestrated and controlled by the dramatist and various assistants, at the same time as the onstage space itself seeks to short-circuit the connection between stage realm and the world outside. Rather than ignoring that dynamic, Lawrence's drama repeatedly seeks to exploit it, and to emphasize, as Anne Ubersfeld puts it, that '*What is given in the theatrical space is never an image of the world, but the image of an image. That which is "initiated" is not the world, but the world recast according to the fiction and in the frame of a culture and a code*'.[14] Lawrence's dramas may have drawn on real-life people and locations, but often prompt us to remember that the theatrical event is constructed, and that onstage action should not be mistaken for external reality.

By the time Lawrence wrote his fourth play, *The Married Man*, he had created a piece that, as Sylvia Sklar puts it, 'makes no attempt to reproduce the forms of "actual" life. Against a very generalised background the constantly changing partnerships in *The Married Man* are presented as kinetic elements'.[15] Similarly, Susan Carlson has argued that the play which Lawrence wrote soon afterwards, *The Fight for Barbara*, is so stylized that it ought to be viewed as an extension of the seventeenth-century comedy of manners.[16] In 1913, he did move back towards the artistry of his very first plays, when he scripted the realistic dialect-play *The Daughter-in-Law*: but even here, the breakneck speed with which the final act apparently reconciles the main characters begins to look rather suspect if considered simply as an example of 'what actually happens in real life'.

Five years later, when Lawrence wrote his next play *Touch and Go*, he created characters that can scarcely be understood as people who might exist in the real world, but are instead embodiments of abstract ideas and principles. For example, Job Arthur represents embittered Labour, and Gerald Barlow embodies an unfettered Capital. Accordingly, as the play continues, Gerald and Job Arthur have difficulty in seeing their opponents as discrete individuals at all: Gerald views Job Arthur as 'the voice of the people [. . .] the epitome' (408), while Job Arthur sees Gerald straightforwardly as 'Vermin' (421). On the stage, as Sylvia Sklar observes, 'What is required here is something more in the Brechtian style: the kind of performance in which the actor "narrates" his character's part rather than becoming identified with the character whom he is portraying'.[17]

Touch and Go is also the most metatheatrical of Lawrence's plays, with the characters pointing to the fact that they are creating a fiction: declaring 'You're making a scene here in this filthy market-place, just for the fun of it', 'we *are* making a scene', 'We'll make an end of the scene' (377–378). In a similarly unrealistic vein, the play moves towards a Shavian-style discussion in which contrasting political opinions are aired, and ends with a scene showing murderous miners being stopped in their tracks by a chanted declaration of shared humanity.

It is not, then, that Lawrence avoided writing theatrical realism. But, as David Krasner argues, 'The theatrical procedure of realism is based on the optical fallacy of "seeing" the truth', and Lawrence's plays tend to question how far that artifice can be pushed.[18] Indeed, one of the characters of his 1911 novel *The White Peacock* comments upon the paintings of George Clausen by saying: 'he is a real realist; he makes common things beautiful, he sees the mystery and magnificent that envelops us even when we work menially'.[19] According to such a viewpoint, the job of the genuine realist is not simply to reflect common things as they are, but to make those common things the subject of aesthetic pleasure, as Lawrence's plays about both everyday mining communities and personal relationships undoubtedly sought to do.

By the end of his career, Lawrence's thinking had developed further, and he declared in a non-fictional essay of 1927 that realism 'has no more to do with reality than romanticism has. Realism is just one of the arbitrary views man takes of man'. By this point, Lawrence felt he had identified 'the defects of the realistic method', which mainly revolved around it 'choosing *ordinary* people as the vehicles of an extraordinary passionate feeling of bitterness', when in fact, 'Ordinary people don't have much sense of heroic effort in life'.[20] He had probably heard about the Birmingham Repertory Theatre's celebrated modern-dress version of Shakespeare, the 1925 'Hamlet in plus fours' and bemoaned the attempt to combine the heroic and the day-to-day, saying: 'The public only wants foolish realism: Hamlet in a smoking jacket' (*Letters* VI, 204). Hence, towards the end of his life, Lawrence came to see that in order to depict heroism on the stage, dramatic scripts should revolve around figures who could scarcely be mistaken for workaday modern figures, and so he set about writing scripts about the mythic characters of the distant past: King Saul, King David and Noah.

Ibsen and Strindberg

Lawrence's thinking about realism reflected a similar process that can be identified in the work of a number of other dramatists. At the end of the nineteenth century, the best-known writers who had recently proposed a realist stage space begun to toy with the kind of contradictions discussed above, abandoning any idea that their brand of playwriting could be classified as purely illusionistic realism. Ibsen, for one, might often be considered as the creator of archetypical drawing-room realism, but when he wrote his final play, *When We Dead Waken*, he spent time drafting and redrafting the ending so that it finished with a moment that would be almost impossible for a director to realize in performance: the characters of Ibsen's play become '*lost amid the lower clouds*' of a mountain that then envelops them in an avalanche, leaving them '*obscurely glimpsed, swirled about in the masses of snow, and buried*'.[21]

There can be little doubt that Ibsen provided a key model for Lawrence's early plays. Jessie Chambers remembered that Lawrence 'admired Ibsen tremendously', and he repeatedly gave copies of Ibsen's work as gifts both to her and to his other girlfriend, Louie Burrows (*Letters* I, 112–113).[22] Indeed, Lawrence's very first play, *A Collier's Friday Night*, begins in the same way as Ibsen's best-known script, *A Doll's House* (1879). Both plays start with a mother who is preparing for Christmas – with a fir-tree amongst other things – and whose initial secrecy about those festive preparations indicates something deeply amiss within her marriage. In fact, in 1972, the Nottingham Playhouse made a suggestive link between the two plays by advertising and producing them together on its summer programme.[23]

But Lawrence had read widely enough in Ibsen's work to realize that the style of *A Doll's House* was only one of the ways in which the Norwegian master had scripted plays. The young Lawrence noted Ibsen's aesthetic development and declared that *The Lady from the Sea* (1888) showed Ibsen being 'most poetical'.[24] The latter play is set entirely outside, compares the main female character to a mermaid, and shows her yearning for a mysterious man who arrives onstage and is simply labelled 'stranger'.

In 1912, Lawrence noticed a similar progression away from illusionistic realism in the work of another great writer. That year, he read Strindberg's early and realistic play *Miss Julie* (1888) as well as Strindberg's very different later play, *There are Crimes and Crimes* (1899), which Hans-Göran Ekman suggests contains elements of 'expressionist drama'.[25] The latter play includes a particularly notable scene in which the main character's troubled mind is echoed by a pianist playing Beethoven's Sonata no.17 *'sometimes pianissimo, sometimes wildly fortissimo'.*[26] This scene prefigures Strindberg's proto-surrealist play of 1907, *Ghost Sonata*, which is named after the same Beethoven piece. In this way, Strindberg's progression as a playwright, like Ibsen's, reveals a writer who increasingly resists being defined by a restrictive view of his early work. Lawrence certainly noticed the affinity between Strindberg and Ibsen, and in 1912–1913 repeatedly described those two playwrights – in unflattering terms – as writing in a similar way.[27] At this time Lawrence pronounced himself profoundly unimpressed by 'that rotten Strindberg' (*Letters* I, 467), although that may have been because of the way in which he received copies of these plays from Edward Garnett. The Strindberg scripts arrived with ludicrous incongruity after Lawrence told Garnett that 'I want to read something romanticky' (*Letters* I, 462). In addition, we may suspect an element of professional jealousy here. Strindberg's *There are Crimes and Crimes* had, after all, accomplished something for which Lawrence himself had strived. Strindberg's play is subtitled a 'comedy', but begins in a graveyard, where a child is scolded for playing with flowers, and the drama then goes on to report that child's death, allegations of murder and an autopsy. Similarly, Lawrence had recently completed his play *The Merry-go-Round* as a 'comedy' (*Letters* I, 200), even though that drama begins with a woman on her deathbed complaining of loneliness, and then goes on to feature grieving, accusations of child and animal abuse, and a moment when Harry ties his girlfriend to a chair and tells her, 'Scream, an' I'll squeeze thy head again that chair back till it cracks like a nut' (140).

Hauptmann

A second dramatist with whom the young Lawrence compared Ibsen was the German playwright Gerhardt Hauptmann. In 1910 Lawrence read Hauptmann's early 1891 play, *Einsame Menschen* ('Solitary People'), a story of extra-marital desire and apparent suicide, which helped Lawrence to structure his own novel *The Trespasser*. Indeed, in *The Trespasser* Lawrence pictures Helena, in the year after her lover's death, being accompanied by her new beau who is holding 'a yellow backed copy of "Einsame Menschen"'.[28] But when Lawrence wrote *The Trespasser* in 1910, he was also reading Hauptmann's subsequent plays, *Die Versunkene Glocke* ('The Sunken Bell', 1897) and *Elga* (1905), and therefore knew that Hauptmann, just like Ibsen and Strindberg, had journeyed away from a relatively straightened version of theatrical realism and towards a broader imagining of the possibilities of the stage. After all, Hauptmann dedicated his early work *Einsame Menschen* to 'those who have lived it', and presented what Leroy R. Shaw calls 'a familiar world delineated by the things of everyday life'.[29] But Hauptmann's later work aims for something quite different: *Elga* presents a dream play about adultery, seen through the eyes of a sleeping knight; and *Die Versunkene Glocke* discusses potential infidelity by alternating everyday domestic scenes with those featuring elves, a witch and a wood-sprite.

Thus, in 1910–1912, Lawrence's reading of Ibsen, Strindberg and Hauptmann made him aware of the way that some of the best-known writers of the realistic stage had experimented with a wide range of theatrical possibilities, and could scarcely be characterized as simply presenting a photographic impression of real life. Lawrence, of course, proved incapable of bringing his own work to production in the playhouse, so his own theatrical experiments remained largely unknown. But the playscripts were not his only outlet for such thinking, and he also manifested a concern for the innovations of European theatre in his short stories.

For example, in both the short story 'The Prussian Officer' (started in 1913 and first published in 1914) and in the short story 'Autobiographical Fragment' (composed in October 1927 but unpublished until 1936), Lawrence's narratives rely on the same formal device that is characteristic of Hauptmann's best-known plays. As in Hauptmann's *Elga* and *Hannele* (1893), Lawrence presented relatively realistic narratives that are transformed when a key character falls into a dream state and encounters a fairy-tale environment that is luminous and defamiliarized.[30] Similarly, when Lawrence wrote the 1921 short story, 'The Captain's Doll', he created a potentially wife-murdering army captain who resembles the stepfather of Hauptmann's *Hannele*: and Lawrence even used the name 'Hannele' here for one of the characters, drawing the reader's attention to this parallel by including in his story the question, 'There's a play called *Hannele*, isn't there?'[31]

Maeterlinck

In the influential study, *Theory of the Modern Drama*, Peter Szondi identifies a 'crisis' that happened in drama in around 1880. At this point, he argues, the alienated subjects of modernity and their social ideas could not be adequately contained by the Aristotelian form, and so writers including Ibsen, Strindberg and Hauptmann unknowingly introduced epic elements to their works. One of the key figures in Szondi's argument is the Belgian playwright Maurice Maeterlinck. Szondi argues that Maeterlinck's work is dominated by death, but that:

> [N]o action brings on death, no one is responsible for it. From the dramatic point of view, this means that the category 'action' is replaced by 'situation' [. . .] It is this distinction that lies behind the rather paradoxical term *drame statique*, which Maeterlinck coined for his work.[32]

Lawrence, of course, knew about Maeterlinck's work for many years. The full version of Maeterlinck's play *The Sightless* (as translated by Lawrence Alma-Tadema) was on the Lawrence family bookshelves at the start of the twentieth century, and Lawrence had certainly read the play by 1909, when he spent time discussing it with Jessie Chambers.[33] He promised to pass some of Maeterlinck's other work to Louie Burrows in 1911 because, 'It will help you to understand yourself and me' (*Letters* I, 237–238), and repeatedly alludes to Maeterlinck in *The White Peacock* of 1911, *The Trespasser* of 1912 and in private correspondence of 1914 (*Letters* II, 181).[34]

The Lawrence text that comes closest to Maeterlinck's style is not, however, a play, but a short story called 'The Blind Man', written during the closing days of World War One.[35] This work revolves around the central character of 'Maurice', and like Maeterlinck's *The Sightless*, is set at night during bad weather. Both narratives feature a woman who is either mad (in Maeterlinck's play) or fearing that she is going mad (in Lawrence's story) who is carrying or bearing a symbolic baby; and both revolve around that central image of sightlessness. Furthermore, Lawrence's story and Maeterlinck's script both involve very little happening in terms of plot development, other than a moment of emotional intensity and facial touching towards the end. A deathly inaction and stasis therefore become central to both works.

In 'The Blind Man', Lawrence pictures a soldier who has been blinded in Flanders, but rather than showing the battle or the heroism of conflict, the story is set during the following year, when the invalid is now adjusting to life at home with his heavily pregnant wife Isabel, as both of them struggle to resist despair. Here, then, Lawrence's fiction works towards an effect that Szondi identifies as the key idea of Maeterlinck's drama, the presentation of characters as 'suffering objects in the hands of death' rather than as 'speaking, active subjects'.[36] Patrick McGuinness, amongst others, describes how this tendency in Maeterlinck foreshadows Beckett:

> Like Beckett's, Maeterlinck's characters are *tied* to the place in which we find them, the 'en attendant' of theatre, whose dual function is to promise change, while binding them to the boredom and uncertainty of the interim. Boredom, anguish, extemporization, and 'second degree dialogue' are all responses to time as it emerges through the magnifying lens of the wait.[37]

In a similar way, Lawrence's 'The Blind Man' revolves around the married characters who remain in their house: the husband is affected by 'devastating fits of depression, which seemed to lay waste to his whole being [...] when his own life was torture to him', and the wife is affected by 'a weariness, a terrible *ennui*' and moments when 'She felt she would scream with the strain, and would give anything, anything, to escape'.[38] Ever since his first play, Lawrence's drama had depicted the troubles of those who yearned to escape from the terrible confinement of particular domestic environments, but, as his inability to produce his work on the stage became increasingly apparent, he explored this idea in prose fiction rather than play-scripts, culminating, as we shall see, with the domestic situation described at the start of *Lady Chatterley's Lover*.

Italy and Germany

By the time that Lawrence travelled to Germany with Frieda in 1912, then, he had already accumulated a considerable knowledge of the leading European theatrical luminaries of the age, having absorbed the influence of Ibsen, Strindberg, Hauptmann and Maeterlinck. But Lawrence's sense of dramatic possibility was broadened still further when he began to travel abroad himself, and increasingly absorbed experimental impulses from Germany, Italy and North America.

For example, his travels to Italy and Germany brought Lawrence into contact with puppet drama. In January 1921 he wrote in praise of a marionette theatre in Palermo, where, despite struggling to make sense of what was being said, he felt fascinated by the movements of the characters. Similarly, in October 1927 Lawrence went to watch marionettes in Baden-Baden, even though he admitted that attempting to understand the German being spoken there 'nearly cracked my brains' (*Letters* VI, 178). After seeing the show in Palermo he wrote about the emotional effect that the puppets had upon him:

> The dragon was splendid: I have seen dragons in Wagner, at Covent Garden and at the Prinz-Regenten Theater in Munich, and they were ridiculous. But this dragon simply frightened me, with his leaping and twisting. And when he seized the knight by the leg, my blood ran cold.[39]

Lawrence's attempt to find the emotional seriousness in such drama echoed some of the most advanced theatrical modernists, who were also, in the early years of the twentieth century, taking inspiration from puppet theatre. A number of thinkers looked to Heinrich von Kleist's 1810 essay 'Über das Marionettentheater', and foremost amongst them was the British dramaturg, Edward Gordon Craig. Craig edited the influential journal *The Mask* (1908–29), in which he published his essay 'The Actor and the Übermarionette', arguing that the word 'Puppet' often proved 'a term of contempt', but that in fact marionettes 'are the descendants of a great and noble family of Images, Images which were made in the likeness of God'.[40]

Such thinking also features in Lawrence's writing, which has a longstanding fascination with such puppets. Marionettes are evoked, for example, in *The Trespasser* (1912), 'The Mortal Coil' (1917) and *Women in Love* (1920).[41] But he probably discovered a personal connection with Craig in the summer of 1918, when striking up a friendship with the wife of Craig's music director, Leigh Henry. Leigh Henry had worked with Craig in Florence, and in 1918 Henry's life and work became deeply interesting to Lawrence (see *Letters* III, 262). Furthermore, when Lawrence was in Italy the following year, he developed such a friendship with Gordon Craig's business manager, Maurice Magnus, that Lawrence later wrote a memoir of Magnus. Maurice Magnus had worked as the German translator of Craig's work ('badly, I am told', said Craig), and so although Lawrence may not have subscribed to *The Mask*, he had the chance to absorb Craig's views through both Magnus and Henry.[42]

Unsurprisingly, then, in the wake of these friendships, Lawrence wanted to express the power of mannequins, as well as their superiority to human performers, and he used an essay of 1921 to assert that:

At first one is all engaged watching the figures: their brilliance, their blank, martial stare, their sudden, angular gestures. There is something extremely suggestive in them. How much better they fit the old legend-tales than living people would do. Nay, if we are going to have human beings on the stage, they should be masked and disguised. For in fact drama is enacted by symbolic creatures formed out of human consciousness: puppets if you like: but not human *individuals*.[43]

Such thinking obviously brought Lawrence close to the theatrical theorizing of Gordon Craig, who had, in the first edition of the journal *The Mask*, praised the superior 'conviction' of the masked face over the 'fleeting expression' of the 'frail, restless' human visage.[44]

Lawrence also knew about Alfred Jarry's *Ubu Roi*, a play that famously featured actors moving like marionettes. Jarry's play triggered a Parisian riot when the character of Père Ubu addressed the audience with his opening word 'Merdre!', and Lawrence included a reference to this disturbance in *Aaron's Rod*, where the character Josephine feels so disgusted by the crowd in the theatre that she wishes to act like Ubu:

It was not till the scene was ended that she lifted her head as if breaking a spell, sent the point of her tongue rapidly over her dried lips, and looked round into the box. Her brown eyes expressed shame, fear, and disgust. A curious grimace went over her face – a grimace only to be expressed by the exclamation *Merde!*[45]

Lawrence's drama had long aimed to challenge the assumptions of a complacent and shallow bourgeois audience, and so perhaps it could be expected that, after travelling to Germany and Italy, he would find an artistic affinity with figures like Craig and Jarry, as well as with the futurist experiments of Marinetti.[46] After all, Craig sought to redefine how audiences might understand the movement of actors and stage space by thinking about how marionettes might perform before experimentally lit and abstract monumental places. Lawrence, by the time that he travelled from England, had already written plays that relied upon a very different theatrical technique, but which also sought to make spectators reconsider their preconceived ideas about actors and the geographies of the stage, particularly by presenting the socially and regionally unfamiliar. If *Ubu Roi* threw a 'merdre' at the spectators, then Lawrence's drama launched at least a 'clat-fart' or two.

Puebloan ritual

By January 1921, when his attempt to get his work staged at the Nottingham Repertory Theatre had stalled, Lawrence asserted that, by contrast with the vibrant Italian drama, the English 'stage is all wrong, so boring in its personality'.[47] The marionette theatre of Italy had impressed him, and shortly afterwards he looked further afield, and felt even more enthusiastic about the performances of the Native Americans of the south-western United States. In 1924 he wrote three essays based on what he saw in the USA:

1. 'Indians and Entertainment', about the Easter ceremonials he saw at the Taos Pueblo.

2. 'The Dance of the Sprouting Corn', probably a composite of Easter dances at Santo Domingo Pueblo and at the Taos Pueblo.

3. 'The Hopi Snake Dance', based on a summer ceremony he saw in Hotevilla, Arizona.

Lawrence published these essays specifically in order to make an intervention into contemporary debates about drama.[48] Indeed, one of the essays – 'The Dance of the Sprouting Corn' – was considered so significant by the editor of *Theatre Arts Monthly*, Edith Isaacs, that she included it in her 1927 collection *Theatre: Essays in the Arts of the Theatre*, a volume that sought to present the thinking of those who 'make the best approach yet made to a formulation of the American theatre idea'.[49] His own essays on ritual drama also meant a great deal to Lawrence himself: when they were included in *Mornings in Mexico* he commented on the volume, 'I like "Indians and Entertainment" and "Hopi Snake Dance" best' (*Letters* VI, 91); and he admitted elsewhere that he felt 'rather deeply' about 'The Hopi Snake Dance' (*Letters* V, 116).

Lawrence intended these dramatic essays to have a political as well as an aesthetic impact. At Easter 1924, he had seen Pueblo-Indian performances in New Mexico, and then learned of a threat, made by the white officials of the Bureau of Indian Affairs, to ban such dances.[50] He felt outraged by this meddlesome bullying, and wrote the poem 'O! Americans' to issue a reminder that the Native Americans had a prior claim on the land, and that the white population should now 'draw a line around the Indians, beyond which line you abstain from further interference'.[51] If such a course of action proved impossible, Lawrence advised, then the Native communities ought to be destroyed altogether rather than left as a political plaything, although he added that such destruction would 'damage once more the frail quick of the future/ America, that is in you'.[52] His three admiring articles about Puebloan performances were therefore written in order to defend such practices, and to claim their superiority over Western theatrical norms.

Ballets russes

Nonetheless, Lawrence's view of Puebloan ritual had itself been shaped by his earlier experience of European performance, with Lawrence having long felt intrigued by the possibilities of modernist dance. Indeed, dancing and rhythmic movement had affected Lawrence's stagecraft for some time. We might remember that in *The Widowing of Mrs Holroyd* (written 1910) the father dances in the pub to signify his liberation from the constraints of family and sobriety, in *The Married Man* (written 1912) a group of dancing partners change and rotate in order to reveal the fickleness of personal relationships, and in *Touch and Go* (written 1918) the characters dance a '*free little ballet-manner*' that transforms into a more militaristic march in order to indicate the inevitability of future conflict (381–382). From at least 1912, Lawrence was familiar with the *ballets russes*, and after those dancers premiered the experimental *Rite of Spring* (in which a young girl is selected as a sacrificial victim and dances herself to death) in Paris in 1913, Lawrence's fiction repeatedly evoked the work of the company.[53] He began working on *The Rainbow* in the year after the riotous premiere of *The Rite of Spring* and, as Hugh Stevens suggests, 'Ursula at times is like a dancer in the *ballets russes*, dancing madly to the powerful wild colours and smells of nature'.[54] Similarly, in *Women in Love* (1920), Gudrun and Ursula perform 'a little ballet, in the style of the Russian Ballet'; and *The Lost Girl* (1920) evokes *The Rite of Spring* by describing routines such as the 'squaw's fire dance'.[55]

When Lawrence looked at the Puebloan rituals in 1924, then, he could scarcely help thinking about those European dances with which he was already familiar. Although he mocked other tourists for arriving at the pueblos in order to find the kind of cultural experience that might be had 'while Anna Pavlova dances with the Russian Ballet', the charge can certainly be levelled at Lawrence himself.[56] As Susan Jones points out, Lawrence's own 'imaginative reconstruction of primitive ritual' in the south-western USA 'uncannily suggests (even if unconsciously) the performance strategies of Diaghilev's *Rite*'.[57] Diaghilev's choreography had, after all, featured dancers in squaw-like costumes, with the dancers emphasizing the dead weight of their contorted bodies in order to suggest a radical break with traditional European conceptions of ballet.[58] Lawrence's articles about Puebloan ritual focus upon similarly costumed participants, who stamp and thump their way through dances that likewise affront Western expectations of performance. The parallels would have been particularly apparent to Lawrence's original readers, as his article 'The Hopi Snake Dance' appeared in *Theatre Arts Monthly* during December 1924, at the same time as a number of reviews of a revived version of *The Rite of Spring*, and soon after an article published in the March issue about 'The Russian Ballet of 1923'.[59]

Sumurûn

Lawrence's view of Native-American performance had also been shaped by Max Reinhardt's orientalist fantasy, *Sumurûn*, which Lawrence had seen at London's Savoy Theatre in October 1911.[60] That play retold – without using words – a story from the *Arabian Nights*, in which a carpet seller falls in love with the favourite wife of an old sheik. The production featured a number of scantily clad women wearing little more than scarves, and British critics hailed the work as 'sensational'.[61] According to J.L. Styan, it made Reinhardt's name outside of Germany, representing 'a peak in Reinhardt's early work in the symbolist vein: it was dramatic symbolism at its most dazzling and charming'.[62] At the time of the show, Lawrence had himself been helping to prepare another of the *Arabian Nights* stories for performance, readying *Ali Baba and the Forty Thieves* for production in the hall of Croydon's Davidson Road School.[63] When Lawrence saw Reinhardt's drama, then, he predictably commented that he 'liked it very much' (*Letters* I, 310), and clearly remembered this experience when writing about North America many years later, because he mentioned Reinhardt's work both in a Mexican short story of May 1927, and in the very first sentence of his 1924 essay 'Indians and Entertainment'.[64]

Furthermore, Reinhardt's influence can be found in Lawrence's fictional recreations of Native-American ritual. For example, the short story 'The Woman Who Rode Away' (published 1925) imagines a traditional ceremony taking place in the cave near Arroyo Seco in Mexico that Lawrence had visited in May 1924 (a 'vast, pelvic-shaped aperture [that] faces the west and yawns upward to the sky').[65] But the ritual itself – a procession that culminates in the ceremonial sacrifice of a white woman – resembles little that Lawrence had seen amongst the Native Americans. The fictional ceremony looks much more like a theatrical composite in which the sacrifice of the virgin in *The Rite of Spring* is melded with *Sumurûn*'s much-praised processional section, which, in Reinhardt's famous production, preceded a murderous finale of stabbing and strangulation.[66]

Bertolt Brecht

There can be little doubt, then, that when Lawrence saw Native-American ritual he was strongly swayed by his own earlier knowledge of European modernist performance. Yet paradoxically, at the same time, he proved keenly aware of the dangers of viewing Puebloan performances through European eyes. In this regard, Lawrence's thinking really recalls the way in which Bertolt Brecht considered Chinese theatre, with Brecht's ideas both deeply embedded within a set of European discourses, yet determined to disrupt and destabilize those very attitudes and norms. As Brecht put it in 1936:

> Above all, the Chinese artist never acts as if there were a fourth wall besides the three surrounding him. *He expresses that he knows he is being watched.* This immediately removes one of the European stage's characteristic illusions. The audience can no longer have the illusion of being the unseen spectator at an event that is really taking place.[67]

In the 1924 essay 'Indians and Entertainment', Lawrence applies a similar mode of examination to Native-American rituals, and sees that such events fundamentally disrupt the Cartesian assumptions of Western performance. He felt that European drama, because it evolved with the Greeks, always posits a divide between spectator and actor, because at the heart of Attic theatre there existed the notion of a god looking on: a god who, over time, has had his position usurped by European audience members. But, by contrast:

> There is absolutely none of this in the Indian dance. There is no God. There is no Onlooker. There is no Mind. There is no dominant idea. And finally, there is no judgement: absolutely no judgement.

> The Indian is completely embedded in the wonder of his own drama. It is a drama that has no beginning and no end, it is all-inclusive. It can't be judged, because there is nothing outside it, to judge it.[68]

As a result, Lawrence warned, those in the West ought to 'leave off trying, with fulsome sentimentalism, to render the Indian in our own terms'. Instead, white men and women need to acknowledge that the 'Indian way of consciousness is different from and fatal to our way of consciousness'.[69] For Lawrence, these observations did not simply remain a set of admonishments for those who would judge Native-American thought by the norms of the West. Rather, he felt that Puebloan performances charted a more enlightened way forward. In his article 'Indians and Entertainment', Lawrence describes how, in white performances:

> We lean down from the plush seats like little gods in a democratic heaven, and see ourselves away below there, on the world of the stage, in a brilliant artificial sunlight, behaving comically absurdly, like Pa Potter [in J.P. McEvoy's 1923 comedy *The Potters*], yet getting away with it, or behaving tragically absurdly, like King Lear, and not getting away with it.[70]

By contrast, Lawrence felt that, on the Native-American stage, 'There is no spectacle, no spectator' and 'There is no division between actor and audience. It is all one'.[71] As Amit Chaudhuri puts it, both Brecht and Lawrence therefore sought 'to disrupt the structure of power around which the actor-spectator equation is built into Western theatre, and, as Lawrence would no doubt see it, into Western consciousness itself'.[72] In a letter of 1925, Lawrence wrote:

> I hate the actor and audience business. An author should be in among the crowd, kicking their shins or cheering them on to some mischief or merriment – That rather cheap seat in the gods where one sits with fellows like [French novelist] Anatole France and benignly looks down on the foibles, follies, and frenzies of so-called fellow-men, just annoys me [...] whoever reads me will be in the thick of the scrimmage, and if he doesn't like it – if he wants a safe seat in the audience – let him read someone else (*Letters* V, 201).

In his fiction, Lawrence also indicated that such an approach to performance might eventually come to dominate in Europe itself: his 1927 short story 'Autobiographical Fragment' is set in a version of Eastwood in AD 2927, and shows that the dances of the near-naked Puebloans in the USA of 1924 have become the norm in a futuristic reimagining of Nottinghamshire.[73] In reality, of course, Lawrence's thoughts about the actor–spectator division were a refiguring of something that had long concerned him since his days in Eastwood: as we saw in Chapter 1, when Lawrence was a student in 1906–1908 he had preferred the lively participation in practical drama that he had found in Jessie Chambers's farm rather than the remote position of 'gods in the window seat' that he had found at the university.[74] In 1913 he had then read Jane Harrison's *Ancient Art and Ritual*, which explains that in ancient Athens 'A god presides over the theatre', and points out that modern drama is characterized by 'differentiation, by the severance of artists and actors and spectators'.[75] By the 1920s, then, his discoveries about theatrical participation in North America were framed in new ways, but actually confirmed Lawrence's longstanding dramatic interests and inclinations.

The final play

Although Lawrence articulated a proto-Brechtian formulation about the relationship between spectator and actor, he had little of Brecht's engagement with professional theatre-making and so explored this performer/spectator relationship largely through texts that were not intended for performance. However, the inspiration that Lawrence derived from contact with the Puebloan peoples did also affect his dramatic writing. His restricted production of theatrical scripts in the years after 1913 meant that he largely failed to engage with experimental dramatic ideas through practical theatre work of his own, but he nonetheless wrote the 1925 play *David* in order to bring the energy of Native-American performance into the realm of the playhouse. *David* may be set in the Kingdom of Israel in about 1000 BC, but suggests that the energies of Puebloan ritual may have affected this distant past. Hence the chanting that Lawrence described hearing in Puebloan ritual ('Ay-a! Ay-a! Ay-a!') has its theatrical counterpart in the continual chanting of scene nine of *David* ('Ai-li-lu-lu! A-li-lu-lu-lu!' (478–479)); the rhythmic drum-playing that Lawrence saw and described in Arizona is recycled into the tambourine-playing character of Michal; and the kind of god that Lawrence believed was worshipped in Puebloan performance also affects the animist versions of the deity that he included in his final complete play.[76] In his writing about Puebloan ritual, Lawrence described how the Native Americans had no Western conception of God, but that, 'Behind us lies only the terrific, terrible, crude Source, the mystic Sun, the well-head of all things'.[77] The end of *David* makes clear that such a deity is also honoured by King Saul's prophets: as he arrives for his final appearance in the play they chant, 'Fire within fire is the presence of the Lord! Sun within the sun is our god' (518).

By that last point in Lawrence's final completed play, the actions of King Saul merge with those of a broader group of performers. As Saul comes to greet his chanting chorus of prophets in the final scene, he begins '*to come under the influence of the chant, and to take the rhythm in his voice*' (517). The prophets make '*wild music and rough, ragged chanting*', and Saul strips off by removing his weapons, his mantle, his tunic and then finally his sleeveless shirt; until he '*is seen, a dark-skinned man in a leathern loin-girdle*' (518–519). The ending of Lawrence's *David* therefore offers a kind of male counterpoint to the ending of 'The Woman Who Rode Away', the story that presents a woman who, to dancing and musical accompaniment, is willingly stripped and taken to her death on an outdoor altar. At the conclusion of *David*, Saul undresses and moves towards a rock altar, declaring:

> Surely I feel my death upon me! Surely the sleep of sleeps descends (*Casts himself down.*) I cast myself down, night and day, as in death, lie I naked before God [...] I feel my death upon me, even in the glory of the Lord. Yea! Leave me in peace before my death, let me retreat into the flame (520).

Thus, as in 'The Woman Who Rode Away', where the one figure who might have kept separate and distinct from the religious ritual ends up being central to the rite that is enacted; in *David* the figure whose kingship might have been thought to mark his separateness similarly ends up, as the music continues, in a kind of personal annihilation and embrace of the communal spirit. In both cases, Lawrence's text draws upon Native-American ritual but also veers towards *The Rite of Spring*, that radical European dance-drama which showed how, according to the original programme notes of the *ballets russes*, 'The one who has been chosen to be delivered to the gods is exalted and acclaimed. The Ancestors are invoked as venerable witnesses. And the wise ancestors of man watch the sacrifice. It is thus that the sacrifice is made to Yarilo, the magnificent one, the flaming one'.[78] In addition, the conclusions of *David* and 'The Woman Who Rode Away' may carry a hint of the willing sacrifice of Aida in the Temple of Vulcan at the end of Verdi's opera, which Lawrence had watched with Cynthia Asquith in 1917, and again, 'in a half-devilish mood', at the Hollywood Bowl in 1923, when he had made jokes that kept his companions hooting with laughter until late in the evening.[79]

If Lawrence had consistently been writing playscripts in his mature period, then he may have explored some of these cross-cultural and proto-Brechtian ideas more extensively (with the implications of such an intercultural engagement being teased out by Soudabeh Ananisarab in Chapter 8 of this volume). As it is, *David* includes some anomalous features when compared with his other complete theatre scripts. Yet, as we have seen throughout this chapter, even if Lawrence had rarely been writing for the stage after 1913, the fiction that he wrote did repeatedly engage with the most advanced theatrical thinking of the age, and this aspect of his work can be observed right up until the end of his career.

Lady Chatterley's Lover

Lawrence's very last novel, *Lady Chatterley's Lover* (1928), exemplifies the way in which his prose fiction incorporated the dramatic ideas that a successful playwright might have explored in his scripts, and reveals the influence of various experimental theatrical ideas. Indeed, we need only look at the opening line of *Lady Chatterley* – 'Ours is essentially a tragic age, so we refuse to take it tragically' – to see how notions of theatrical form might pervade the work.[80] This chapter therefore concludes with *Lady Chatterley*, revealing how Lawrence utilized the various dramatic influences traced in this chapter in that most famous of novels.

As we have seen, Lawrence knew and felt influenced by the developing theatrical work of the European dramatists who proposed a realistic stage space but who swiftly moved beyond narrow definitions of realism. He had been particularly influenced by Gerhart Hauptmann, whose name accordingly appears at the start of the first draft of *Lady Chatterley*. The opening sentences of the novel originally pictured Clifford Chatterley, when uninjured and on leave from the war, reading aloud to Connie from the work of Hauptmann.[81] The German playwright disappeared from subsequent revisions, but his early inclusion reveals how Lawrence, when beginning the text, felt influenced by the dramatist who had so often created formally experimental work about adultery. Subsequent filmmakers who create cinematic or television adaptions of *Lady Chatterley* have often portrayed the sex of the novel with a quasi-pornographic literalism, yet Lawrence's debt to Hauptmann suggests that some of these descriptions may always have been intended to involve a dreamlike and fantastic element.

When Lawrence himself first set about reading Hauptmann between 1910 and 1912, the Eastwood man was also studying Maurice Maeterlinck, whose influence can similarly be discerned in *Lady Chatterley*. As Patrick McGuinness observes, Maeterlinck's drama creates settings where 'safety becomes entrapment, familiarity gives way to disorientation, and the domestic interior is transformed into a place of terror and disquiet', something akin to the situation in which Connie and Clifford find themselves at the start of *Lady Chatterley*.[82] The novel's opening describes how, after the First World War, 'there is now no smooth road into the future', and the characters are consequently marooned in a world of oppressive stasis.[83] Indeed, if the book had stopped at the point just before Connie has her first adulterous affair then the work would have remained, like Lawrence's 1918 short story 'The Blind Man', singularly bleak and static. Maeterlinck is often thought to prefigure Beckett, and the Maeterlinckian relationship between Connie and the disabled Clifford at the start of *Lady Chatterley* does offer a premonition of the antagonistic and damaged couples that populate Beckett's stage world:

[H]e was absolutely dependent on her – he needed her every moment. Big and strong as he was, he was helpless. He could wheel himself about in a wheeled chair, and he had a sort of bath-chair with a motor attachment, in which he could puff slowly round the park. But alone he was like a lost thing. He needed Connie to be there, to assure him that he existed at all.

Still he was ambitious. He had taken to writing stories, curious, very personal stories about people he had known, clever, rather spiteful, and yet in some mysterious way, meaningless. The observation was extraordinary and peculiar. But there was no touch, no actual contact. It was as if the whole thing took place on an artificial earth. – And since the field of life is largely an artificially-lighted stage today, the stories were curiously true to modern life.[84]

Thus Connie's life, at the start of the novel, is spent in telling empty fictions to pass the time, 'this life with Clifford, this endless spinning of webs of yarn, of the minutiae of consciousness, these stories, of which Sir Malcolm said there was nothing in them and they wouldn't last'.[85] In this way, although Lawrence's narrative does move in a different direction, the novel initially presents itself as a distant cousin of *Endgame* and *Krapp's Last Tape*. Indeed, Beckett's play *Happy Days* (1961) presents a woman who is trapped in the ground, has an unfulfilling relationship with her husband, and remains aware of her erotic capabilities: and Jacqueline Thomas has convincingly detailed how this drama 'is a rescript of Lawrence's *Lady Chatterley's Lover*'.[86]

Connie, of course, does not remain in this situation for the rest of the novel. She escapes by finding a different kind of theatre. The affair with Mellors might provide the novel's most memorable sex, but Connie Chatterley's first adulterous relationship in the novel actually takes place with an Irish playwright, Michaelis, who is portrayed in deeply unflattering terms and in whom she sees 'that ancient motionless of a race that can't be disillusioned any more'.[87] The character of Michaelis was no doubt partly based on the wealthy Michael Arlen, a Bulgarian writer with a tubucular testicle who had earned incredible sums of money, and roused Lawrence's jealousy in 1927, by writing a novel *The Green Hat*, which enjoyed tremendous box-office success in adapted form on Broadway.[88] Lawrence, who could only dream of such a theatrical triumph, felt vexed by the accomplishment of an acquaintance who remained ten years his junior, and the decision to make Arlen into a fictional *Irish* playwright had been most likely triggered by Lawrence's post-1916 political feelings about the country that had once exerted such a key influence upon his own playwriting. Accordingly, Michaelis proves a thoroughly disappointing lover, 'sneering' at Connie after sex for taking so long to achieve orgasm, and thus providing 'one of the crucial blows of Connie's life. It killed something in her'.[89]

It is of course with Mellors that Connie finds greater fulfilment, and the world of the gamekeeper – by contrast with the stifling and anti-climatic world of the Irish dramatist – offers the liberating possibilities of avant-garde performance. At one point, before having sex with Mellors, Connie strips naked and then: 'She slipped on her rubber shoes again and ran out with a wild little laugh, holding up her breasts to the heavy rain and spreading her arms, and running blurred in the rain with the eurhythmic dance-movements she had learned so long ago in Dresden'.[90]

Here Lawrence connects Connie with the world of experimental dance through her knowledge of the German-based Émile Jaques-Dalcroze, who had, from 1910, been promoting the physical practice of Eurhythmics, an uninhibited, movement-focused way of learning and appreciating music.[91] In *Women in Love* (1920), Lawrence had already imagined Gudrun engaging in a similar set of movements, and now in *Lady Chatterley's Lover*, Connie's performance is profoundly liberating, connecting her with her teenage memories of having lived in Germany, where she first discovered both her sexuality and her independence of mind. This Eurhythmic dance therefore becomes a bodily expression of such freedom, and helps Connie to escape the despairing stasis with which she begins the novel. Furthermore, we might note that, as Connie dances, she is not entirely naked. She still wears rubber tennis shoes, a symbol of modernity famously sported by Diaghilev's *ballets russes* when staging *Le Train bleu* as a celebrated collaboration between Picasso, Henri Laurens and Coco Chanel in June 1924.[92]

When Connie has sex with Mellors, she describes some of Lawrence's most advanced thoughts about the relationship between performer and spectator. We have already seen how Lawrence, in his late career, expressed ideas that came close to those of Bertolt Brecht, who, when writing about Chinese theatre, tried to disrupt Western drama's conventional division between actor and onlooker. Lawrence similarly felt that European drama, since the Greeks, had sundered the performer from the audience member, and he discerned something quite different in Native-American ritual. In his 1924 essay 'Indians and Entertainment' he argued that, in Puebloan drama 'There is no Onlooker' and 'there is no judgement' because 'The Indian is completely embedded in the wonder of his own drama': and in *Lady Chatterley's Lover*, Connie moves from the European to the Native-American perspective through her experience of sex.[93] At one point, she has a moment of viewing her own sexual activity with the same distance as those European audience members at the theatre: whilst she is *in flagrante*, 'her spirit seemed to look on from the top of her head, and the butting of his haunches seemed ridiculous to her, and the sort of anxiety of his penis to come to its little evacuating crisis seemed farcical [...] it was a performance'. During that performance, 'Cold and derisive her queer female mind stood apart', and she weeps after the deed is done.[94] But by contrast, shortly afterwards, when Connie experiences a more complete feeling of sexual satisfaction, Lawrence does not picture her as a distant, European spectator, but instead imagines her as being: 'like the sea, nothing but dark waves rising and heaving'.[95] In this rhythmic sexual encounter, when Connie is more attuned to the fecund natural world and her place within it, she comes closer to the experience described by Lawrence in 'Indians and Entertainment', where he observes that, with a 'surging, crowing, gurgling, aah-h-h-ing!' the participants 'are giving themselves again to the pulsing, incalculable fall of the blood'.[96] Lawrence felt that the Pueblo Indians had, in their ceremonies, discovered a way of achieving what Virginia Crosswhite Hyde calls an 'enactment of pure "being" and of taking part in the cycles of nature and the animate universe', and Connie makes a similar discovery during the course of her relationship with Mellors.[97]

Finally, at the end of the *Lady Chatterley*, Connie and Mellors are undone by their relationship being revealed, something that is again described in tellingly theatrical terms. The affair is uncovered by the discovery of one crucial piece of evidence: Mellors' estranged wife 'broke into the hut, and found one of your books, an autobiography of the actress Judith, with your name, Constance Stewart Reid, on the front page'.[98] Thus, what ultimately betrays Connie, and offers tangible proof of her infidelity, is her affinity with the actor Julie Bernat, a beauty who acted at the Comédie-Française from 1846 onwards, and whose gossipy memoir focuses on love affairs and theatrical performances in nineteenth-century France.[99] Connie's need to inscribe her own name onto that particular volume is revealing about the way that her own life has involved a similar imbrication of role play, sex and hearsay. But the presence of Bernat's volume at the end of *Lady Chatterley* also points back to Lawrence's own long-standing theatrical concerns. Bernat was, after all, one of the first to play the main part in *La Dame aux Camélias*, and she used her memoir to boast of how she had brought that play to provincial locations where 'people are always more prudish'.[100] In 1908, the young Lawrence had encountered that very same play onstage in the English East Midlands, and had felt so moved by the drama's sexual power that he had beaten on the doors of the theatre until he was released. Consequently, when he came to write *Lady Chatterley* as the ultimate antidote to provincial prudery, he evoked one of the most famous actors of *La Dame aux Camélias*, and showed that he continued to be concerned by the intersection of the theatrical and the erotic that had so fascinated him for two decades. Perhaps, then, we should not be surprised that *Lady Chatterley* has tended to appeal to later playwrights, and that the novel has enjoyed such a proliferating afterlife in stage, television and film adaptations.[101]

Joycean parallels

In tracing these realist and experimentalist currents, we can see that Lawrence, for all of his dislike of James Joyce, had ultimately travelled a similar journey. As a young man, Joyce felt so attracted by Ibsen's drama that he had learned Dano-Norwegian, had corresponded with Ibsen, and had penned an Ibsenite play called *Exiles*. When Joyce completed *Exiles* in 1915 he felt determined to see the piece performed in the theatre and declared that he 'would prefer the publication in book to come after its eventual production on the stage'.[102] But the play failed to reach the footlights for four years after it was written, and on that occasion in Munich, it flopped and Joyce described the staging as 'A fiasco'.[103] Yeats also rejected Joyce's script at the Abbey, and although the Stage Society did produce a version in 1926 (the same year that the organization first staged Lawrence's work) *Exiles* never achieved any significant recognition in performance until the 1970s. This difficulty that Joyce encountered in trying to get his work before the limelight contributed to the fact that, after *Exiles*, he abandoned writing dramatic scripts altogether, and instead developed his theatrical interests through his novels, particularly in the madcap brilliance of his 'Circe' chapter in *Ulysses*, which provides an impossible and hallucinogenic version of a theatre playscript, set in a brothel of Dublin's red-light district.

Lawrence went through a similar process to the Irishman. Like Joyce, Lawrence had been influenced by Ibsen and European drama, wrote his own plays that he desperately wanted to see performed, but encountered little other than frustration and disappointment in the attempt at staging. Instead, Lawrence turned to the novel and short story, and here continued to explore his ideas about theatre as he pushed the boundaries of what it might be permissible for fiction to say, with *Lady Chatterley's Lover* relying on various kinds of theatrical performance in order to illustrate the changing dynamics of Connie's sex life. Both Joyce and Lawrence, then, were schooled in the methods of realistic drama. But after their own playwriting failed to generate the kinds of production that they had hoped for, they continued to explore the possibilities of theatre – often in increasingly experimental ways – through fictions that were primarily intended to be encountered by readers in textual form. Both Joyce and Lawrence were capable of leading the Anglophone playhouse into a more adventurous era, but each man found his theatrical ambitions stymied and so his dramatic experiments often occurred instead in writings that were not written for actors. In neither instance, of course, should we mistake the skilled realism of their dramas for the work of formally conservative literary figures. They may not have liked one another, but Joyce and Lawrence were more similar than they liked to think, and both brought dramatic realism into contact with an expansive range of experimental theatrical influences in the first decades of the twentieth century.

CHAPTER 5
A DIRECTOR'S PERSPECTIVE: PETER GILL, IN CONVERSATION WITH JAMES MORAN

Peter Gill was born in 1939 in Cardiff and has worked as an actor, director and playwright. He became assistant director at the Royal Court Theatre in 1964, where he was responsible for introducing D.H. Lawrence's plays to the playhouse. He staged *A Collier's Friday Night* in 1965, *The Daughter-in-Law* in 1967 and the 'Eastwood Trilogy' in 1968, which has been described by Richard Eyre as 'one of the landmarks of post-war theatre'.[1] Gill then became associate director at the Royal Court, after which he directed a version of Lawrence's *The Merry-go-Round* at the theatre in 1973, prompting Michael Billington to write in the *Guardian* that 'Our debt to Peter Gill increases with each new production'.[2] Between 1976 and 1980 Gill worked as the founding director of Riverside Studios at Hammersmith, then became an associate director of the National Theatre of Great Britain (1980–1997) and founding director of the National Theatre Studio (1984–1990). His extensive work as a playwright ranges from *The Sleepers Den* at the Royal Court in 1965 to *Versailles* at the Donmar Warehouse in 2014.

JM Peter, your career is now very much associated with D.H. Lawrence, but when did you first become aware of the writer?

PG I first read *The White Peacock* when I was about seventeen, and I remember being greatly taken with it. I suppose when you are young you are looking for identity and I remember finding that Lawrence was, as I was, born in September and in *The White Peacock* there is a paragraph beginning 'I was born in September, and I love it best of all the months' – that is Lawrence at his most typical.[3] I read it and read it at the time, but did so reluctantly for fear of being disappointed. I read *Sons and Lovers* soon afterwards, when I was doing my first job as an Assistant Stage Manager on a tour of theatreless areas sponsored by the Arts Council. Thinking of *Sons and Lovers* brings back that time of travelling in mid-Wales and the northeast. Those two books are still my favourites of his novels, in spite of the obvious claims of others. Of course, at that time, he was part of a broader cultural discussion than he is now, still then a controversial figure. This was before the *Lady Chatterley* case.

JM   It seems almost obligatory that critics who discuss your work have to spend some time mentioning your working-class family background and the fact that your father was a docker. So can you tell me what kind of perspective on Lawrence that gave you?

PG   *Sons and Lovers* perhaps more than *The White Peacock* was about things that I knew about first-hand. So that – although what Lawrence is writing about is different from my wartime and post-war council-estate experience – there was much in the novels that I could identify with. But it's more than documentary realism and my having access to much of what it is about, there's the poetry of it. There is a heightened mythic aspect to the relationship of Paul Morel and his mother, which suited a boy of the age I was when I first read it. Most working-class boys, perhaps all boys, want to rescue their mothers. I think many of the novels and plays after Lawrence written by lower-middle and working-class authors about their confused relationships with women have that reparatory element. And *Sons and Lovers* is a beautiful book in all its aspects. And I knew some of Lawrence's poems too at that time, as I had a little Penguin edition of a selection of them. All that reading coincides with my going into a very different world to learn my trade.

JM   When you went into that trade you encountered lots of people from a very different background to yourself. You would perhaps have met some of Leavis's former English students for example, who viewed Lawrence in a different way than you did.

PG   Well the Court Theatre was very Oxford. And the RSC of the time was very Cambridge. I don't know how that contributed to the differences in the two companies but they were strikingly different. So the Leavisite thing was not perhaps as a big deal at the Court where I spent much of my time, although Leavis was still an influence everywhere that English was taught. Certainly I realize now at my school. I think Leavis very much appealed to the Catholic educationalists of the time because I suppose of his moral stance, and I think two of the brothers at my school who taught English had been taught or influenced by him, or anyhow had been at Cambridge at the time of his greatest influence. I remember later reading Leavis's comparison and evaluation of Lawrence's education in relation to Eliot's. When we did the plays, the Court seemed to be Lawrence's home. And I think the Court then reflected something of the contentiousness we associate with Lawrence.

JM   Why exactly was the Royal Court so well suited for Lawrence?

PG   Well it was part of a movement in the theatre concerned to reflect a world that had not been much represented in the theatre until after the war. There had been a longing for a serious British theatre from Tom Robertson to George Devine. But, except for a few notable exceptions, the British theatre was, until the setting up of the Arts Council after the war, principally a commercial business restricted by censorship and the star system. The Royal Court had been at the centre of that struggle both in the days of Granville Barker in the early twentieth century, and later under the artistic directorship of George Devine in 1956.

JM   Does that battle between star vehicle and serious drama explain why Lawrence's plays go missing from the stage between the 1940s and 1960s?

PG   The problem was the star system rather than stars. Stars in the wrong parts and the type of stars, with a narrow range, who were cast simply because of box-office appeal rather than their suitability for the part. And the tension between the need for a charismatic actor to bring a certain kind of a leading part to life and the desire for ensemble, which was very much a concern of the time. Lawrence's plays didn't fit the commercial criteria of the day. There would have been a limited number of available actors suited to the characters he was writing about. The theatre then was still influenced by the Scribe idea of the well-made play. And the, admittedly small, number of managements who should have promoted Lawrence simply didn't. So Lawrence just got lost amidst the other novelists or poets who wrote unperformed plays. No great writer, up until the modern period, has failed to write a play, as far as I can make out. Wordsworth, Shelley, Byron, Conrad, Henry James. They all wrote plays. Perhaps the women less so, though Fanny Burney wrote plays. So for many years Lawrence's plays were simply left in the dark, part of a catalogue of scripts by writers who were famous for other reasons. And many of those plays were written for an imaginary literary theatre, not for the living theatre. Joyce and Lawrence were the writers of the modern period who did write good plays. Why did Henry James not manage it, considering his love of theatre and his admiration for Ibsen?

JM   So when did you first know that Lawrence had written plays?

PG   Somewhere along the line, by word of mouth. Actors are good at passing things on at the Court Theatre. Gwen Ffrangcon-Davies, who was well-known at the Court, was the partner of Marda Vanne, who had performed in Esmé Percy's 1926 version of *The Widowing of Mrs Holroyd*. And I remember the dramatist Donald Howarth talking about what must have been the 1961 Granada-television version of *The Widowing of Mrs Holroyd*.

JM   And when you heard about that Granada production, you then read the plays and decided to stage them.

PG   I was an assistant director at the Court at the time, and anxious at the prospect of doing my first production, since I had never done even a student production. My friend Desmond O'Donovan directed the first play I'd written, *The Sleepers Den*, on a Sunday night, and when it became clear that I would have to face up to directing a play, I sent to the British Drama League for a Lawrence play. I think I'd actually sent off for a copy of *The Widowing of Mrs Holroyd*. But a little first edition, in green covers, of *A Collier's Friday Night* came. And I read it and thought it was beautiful, but thought perhaps no-one else would like it. I could see that the play was in fact a dramatization of one the chapters called 'Lad-and-Girl Love' in *Sons and Lovers*, and was excited to find a version of the story in dramatic form. I asked George Devine if he would read it, which he did. And he encouraged me to stage it. He said he liked it or rather, I think, he liked that I liked it. Despite its awkwardness, the Court was a collegiate theatre then. There was solidarity necessary to offset Arts Council opinion and the often less-than-enthusiastic response of the critics. So I directed *A Collier's Friday Night* on a Sunday night.

JM   Tell me about that 1965 production of *A Collier's Friday Night*.

PG   It was a Sunday night production, without décor. Different perhaps because those Sunday night productions were intended principally to promote new work and though *A Collier's Friday Night* hadn't been much produced before, it wasn't new in the sense intended. I think it chimed with the spirit of the Court Theatre of the time, strange as that may sound, and the play's apparent slightness of form stood up and it came alive in performance, and the quality of the writing lifted it out of documentary realism. The play comes suddenly to a peculiarly vivid life, as when Ernest, the character who is clearly a self-portrait by Lawrence, describes the French language to his girlfriend: 'That's what they can do in France, it is so heavy and full and voluptuous: like oranges falling and rolling a little way upon a dark-blue carpet; like twilight outside when the lamp's lighted; you get a sense of rich, heavy things, as if you smelt them, and felt them about you in the dusk: isn't it?' (33). And the production had lots of good actors. Victor Henry gave a revelatory performance as Ernest Lambert. I was rather over-obsessive when casting the part and I think I auditioned Victor six times. He was later marvellous as Joe in *The Daughter-in-Law*, and quickly established himself as one of the most interesting actors of his generation. But he had an ungovernable nature and it was always on the cards that he would die young, though in the event through no fault of his own. He was knocked down waiting to cross the road and died, having survived in a vegetative state for some time. He was a marvellous actor.

JM   During that Sunday night production, you reportedly managed to find great beauty in day-to-day things. What were you doing?

PG   I realized that the physical life, the accumulation of the everyday actions during the course of the play was an essential to its meaning. The commercial theatre of the time still afforded a very short rehearsal period, when there was time only to get the lines under your belt. Any refinement came on a pre-London tour. We still relied on the efficiencies of the repertory theatre, full of short cuts, where a property box of matches had a match partly sticking out of the box ready for you to strike, so you avoided the chance that if you opened the box hurriedly, the matches would spill everywhere. So there was a superficial gloss over things. Demonstration rather than realization, and though *A Collier's Friday Night* had a very short rehearsal period, as did all the plays at the Court then, I realized that making short cuts to the physical life of the play was not the way.

JM   Did you also feel that you were part of a broader movement in terms of Lawrence? After all, *The Complete Plays* was published by Heinemann four months after your production, and there was a production of *The Widowing of Mrs Holroyd* by Clive Perry in Leicester at the start of 1965.

PG   No. Though I think I must have realized that the theatre I was part of was involved in a change.

JM   Did you know about Gordon McDougall's production of *The Daughter-in-Law*, which opened at the Traverse in 1967?

PG   The plays were on a shelf in our office when Gordon worked at the Court – I didn't see the Traverse production.

JM   That 1913 play, *The Daughter-in-Law*, was pretty unknown when you started directing. It had only been printed for the first time in 1965, and yet you produced this play in 1967.

PG   About the time that we did *A Collier's Friday Night*, Heinemann published the complete plays so I read them and was particularly taken with

The Daughter-in-Law. It was not an easy read, written, as it were, phonetically as Robbie Burns wrote. It was more common to write anything not expressed in Standard English in this way then. Very few writers do that now. Writers tend to assume that the actors will have the skill required as far as accents are concerned. In the case of *The Daughter-in-Law* Lawrence was also at pains, it seems to me, to show he was portraying a class lower than the one he wrote about in *A Collier's Friday Night* – with *A Collier's Friday Night* he was in fact writing about his own family.

JM   Was it a reasonably straightforward decision to do *The Daughter-in-Law* after *A Collier's Friday Night*?

PG   I think that it was in part because Bill Gaskill, who was now artistic director at the Royal Court, had liked the first play, which was done under Anthony Page's artistic directorship. So when a gap appeared in the programme, needing an inexpensive production, it was more or less straightforward to plan a production of *The Daughter-in-Law*.

JM   What had you learned from the first Lawrence play that affected your approach to *The Daughter-in-Law*?

PG   I understood, retrospectively, how important my attempt to realize the physical life of *A Collier's Friday Night* had been. So because of this, when I was preparing *The Daughter-in-Law*, I could see it was important for of us to see Luther washing, after work, rather than had happened on the Sunday night production of *A Collier's Friday Night*, when the father went offstage to wash. It seemed to me that seeing this essential part of a collier's life – the ritual of it if you like – the completion of his return to his life above ground, was vital. The conventions of the plays at the time of Lawrence writing them, the decorum, meant that Lawrence wrote for what is known as a box set, which enclosed the action in one place. I felt the need to counterpoint what was going on, in the principal action, by revealing the action of the father (or Luther in the case of *The Daughter-in-Law*). Action against action. This of course produced its own difficulties. In a box set you can, as it were, shrink the offstage life at will. I remember Luther's washing took place while Victor Henry, the actor playing Joe, delivered just one line, sat in a rocking chair eating Yorkshire pudding with jam on it, and then fell asleep. Victor had to fall asleep while waiting until he sensed Mike Pratt, in the part of Luther, was finishing. It was a long, long pause, and relied on the audience being intent on watching two very different actions coming out of the flow of the play up until then. One brother washing, the other sleeping, but both in tune with one another. John Gunter devised a set, putting the two houses in *The Daughter-in-Law* on two angles, so we could see the main action and the counter action.

JM You visited Eastwood as part of the rehearsal process for *The Daughter-in-Law* – what did you learn there?

PG John Gunter and Deirdre Clancy, who were designing the sets and clothes respectively, went with me to Eastwood, and we found Lawrence's house at the Breach, 28 Garden Road, which was still inhabited. And then we found the family's subsequent and grander house on Walker Street, which was up for sale and which is described in *Sons and Lovers* and in *A Collier's Friday Night*. I had also read Lawrence's short story 'Fanny and Annie', which is a version of *The Daughter-in-Law*, and which specifies that the events are set in Princes Street – the street that is next to the street on which Lawrence was born – so we found Princes Street, and located an empty house, which we explored. And that is the house upon which we based the designs for *The Daughter-in-Law*, and subsequently elements of the other two plays. I also happened upon the setting of *The Widowing of Mrs Holroyd*: I walked down the old railway line next to Brinsley Colliery and found what I subsequently realized was Vine Cottage, which today sadly exists in a terrible state of dilapidation but which had once been home to Lawrence's Aunt Polly, whose husband was killed in a mining accident. It was clear to me from the opening of *The Widowing of Mrs Holroyd* that Lawrence had set the play in this exact location as I could see here precisely what he had described in the stage direction: '*the colliery rail can be seen not far from the threshold, and, away back, the headstocks of a pit*' (63).

JM In early 1968 you revived productions of *The Daughter-in-Law* and *A Collier's Friday Night*, and added a new production of *The Widowing of Mrs Holroyd*. At what point had you decided to stage the works as a trilogy?

PG *The Daughter-in-Law* was in many ways a sleeping success. The play seemed to stay in the minds of people, and having done *A Collier's Friday Night* and now knowing the other plays, and liking *The Widowing of Mrs Holroyd* – which had some reputation of its own – the three seemed to make a natural trilogy. So we got a company together, and we designed sets based on the solutions we had found when doing *The Daughter-in-Law*. The three plays shared many of the same elements while answering the needs of each play. So there was a coherent style. And we did them in rep, in a season with all three performed on one or two Saturdays. And we cross-cast as best we could. It was a tight rehearsal period. I can remember that Bernard Gallagher, an actor friend of mine who lived locally to me, used to meet with me at Hammersmith station every morning during the rehearsal period. He was going off to be in Peter Brook's production of *Oedipus* by Seneca, at the Old Vic, and I was going to the Court to rehearse the trilogy. And the *Oedipus* company had, for one play, more than our complete rehearsal period for three. So the work was hard. And we had to have understudies at the Court in those days. But I did have two assistants.

JM   Was it always a trilogy? Did you ever consider putting together a different number of plays?

PG   No, I didn't. I suppose there could be different ways of looking at putting the plays together. *The Daughter-in-Law* with *The Fight for Barbara*, say. But doing the trilogy seemed to be the perfect way to put Lawrence's plays together.

JM   Did the actors cope well with being in more than one play at the same time?

PG   Well not everyone was in more than one play. Only Anne Dyson was in all of them. But certainly having a company, most of whom were in two of the plays, gave the project an identity. The cross-casting had the effect of underlining the themes common to the three, as well as providing the enjoyment that audiences find in seeing talented actors in different parts.

JM   I've heard that you were quite a stickler for not allowing the cast to change Lawrence's words at all.

PG   Yes it's a matter of commitment. I have rarely asked a writer for alterations once I have committed myself to the play.

JM   Was this because you had read so much of Lawrence by this point that you had developed a kind of reverence for the writer?

PG   It is not that I object to dramaturgical intervention, but am perhaps wary of it as a matter of course. All productions and performances are, of their nature, interpretive. Part of the success of the plays perhaps lay in my determination to do them on their own terms. As well as expressing my feeling for them, this approach was perhaps at variance with many of the directorial concerns of the internationalist theatre of the time, with the director seen as auteur. In late '68 we did a tour of *The Daughter-in-Law*, including to an international festival in Belgrade, where we won a first prize.

Any realism of the time tended to be seen through the prism of American psychological realism. But what we were doing was different. I suppose we were operating with two ideas of theatre, which the Belgrade audience in particular found intriguing and found different. An intense hyper-realism on the one hand, but staged on sets that were selective of what was presented, with a designed rig of lights hanging above the action and very much in sight.

JM You always felt that there was something more than realism going on?

PG The plays are – not perfumed exactly – but heightened certainly. And there is an exquisiteness in the writing. I remember Jane Howell thinking they were not, as we did them, realistic in the accepted sense of the word, they were more pre-Raphaelite: the realism we obtained had a hallucinogenic quality, she thought.

JM The working-class Nottinghamshire dynamic is potentially pretty tricky for actors. How did your company cope with the Eastwood dialect?

PG Well, they did fine. I didn't exaggerate the need for accuracy in the accent, since we concentrated with how Lawrence had written in the dialect from the characters' point as well as from his own. We were not seeking anything anthropological. Tony Douse had a natural Nottinghamshire-Derbyshire accent, many of the company either came from, or had access to, the North or the Midlands. Judy Parfitt's from Sheffield, which has got something of the same softness, and Anne Dyson from Manchester.

JM In British theatrical history, you are famed for having directed with incredible precision during those performances. Even the movement of a hand or the twitch of an eye was painstakingly rehearsed.

PG I'm a bit less exacting nowadays.

JM Why was that sense of precision so important for you at the time?

PG I don't know. I'd been an actor, which means you are often at the mercy of short cuts and lack of investigation. And you must remember that in other productions there wasn't the time often to rehearse in depth – not that our rehearsal period was very long. And that was all part of the discussion about the nature of realism, I suppose, that comes after *Madame Bovary*: what realism is, what it stands for, and what its poetics might be.

JM We perhaps shouldn't ignore the fact that this production nearly killed you.

PG   I have had a wonky digestive system since childhood. I did a technical rehearsal of *A Collier's Friday Night* in which everything went unusually well, in fact it was more like a dress rehearsal because we were so well prepared. All the plays had had full run-through on consecutive days, so I was exhausted I suppose and didn't know it, and I was very sick after that rehearsal. And I got home, and I found I could barely crawl up the stairs to my flat. And the next morning I was due at a photo call and could barely move, and I realized that I must be ill. The doctor came and sent for an ambulance, and I went to Bart's hospital, and I was lying in bed, and a young doctor came in and to tell me that they would have to operate. He was called Michael Perry and I'd been in school with him: that's the Butler Act for you. Anyway, as a result I was in hospital for a few months.

JM   And you were visited by Bill Gaskill in your hospital bed, from where you still managed to give some instructions about the production.

PG   Jane Howell looked after *The Daughter-in-Law* and Bill Gaskill did the others. And I remember him coming to the hospital to ask whether he could move an onstage cup. I wouldn't be so apparently controlling like that now.

JM   The trilogy of plays was highly praised. But it was *The Widowing of Mrs Holroyd* that drew the attention of audiences and critics. Stephen Lowe has written in this volume that *The Widowing* 'shaped everything that I've done since'. Why was it so affecting?

PG   I think he's referring in particular to the last scene, when the two women wash the dead body of the man – dead husband and son – after a pit accident. Well, it was made affecting by the work of two actresses: Judy Parfitt played the dead miner's wife and Anne Dyson was his mother. This was the 1960s, and Stephen comes from working-class Nottinghamshire. For the whole company, perhaps for everyone at the Court, those productions had a special meaning.

JM   Did you worry that the actors' affinity for the characters would overwhelm the production?

PG   I saw our job was to articulate the tragedy not for us to feel it. I was very concerned in rehearsal to curb easy tears. I looked at washing the body very much as a technical matter, concerned with what the actresses were doing if you like. As the women, no matter what they felt, they had to get the job done before the body set. Rehearsing tragedy of this kind, which is rooted in reality, in a physical action that is not rhetorical, is not unlike farcical comedy. You have to remove yourself – in farce from the humour, and in tragedy from the feeling – in order to get to the truth on behalf of the audience, so things are not fudged and generalized. It's not about your feelings, but about realizing the thing that is tragic itself. And the actresses didn't turn on the tap as readily as some seem to now. I remember Judy, in another production that we did together, apologizing for crying in a rehearsal – she thought that was inappropriate and said she would not be doing that in performance. She felt it wasn't suited to the scene. Somewhere Athene Seyler writes about playing Ranevsky in *The Cherry Orchard* with Charles Laughton at the old Vic, and finding, when she rehearsed a particular scene without him for some reason, that she was moved to tears, but when they rehearsed it together and she found that he also was moved to tears, she stopped. She didn't think it would do – the two of them weeping. Of course the two actresses in *The Widowing of Mrs Holroyd* wept, as the characters would have done when it came to a run, but had channelled their feelings to the service of the scene, to the expression of tragedy. And their expression of grief then was palpable.

JM How long did that washing of the body actually go on for?

PG As long as it took.

JM The production had an extraordinary printed programme – full of photographs of miners, dialect poems and essay writing. Was that framing important for the audience?

PG Shirley Matthew, who was one of the management secretaries at the Court Theatre, researched much of which was new. Many years later she did much similar research when I was at the National Theatre.

JM Were you pleased with the way the audiences understood the trilogy?

PG Yes it was very, very exciting for me. Although I never saw the productions, I only saw one performance at the end.

JM Simon Trussler's Oxford edition of the Lawrence plays includes a dedication to you. But what I find quite weird is that, in the earlier Penguin edition of the 'Eastwood Trilogy' in 1969, Raymond William makes no mention of your work, even though that edition clearly takes its cue from your production. What do you make of that?

PG Well, Trussler is a theatre man. For Williams it must have seemed that putting the three plays together was an obvious choice, forgetting that no-one had ever done it before. The academic attitude to the theatre, particularly the living British theatre, often takes an Olympian stance. I looked at the list of a big educational publisher recently and I couldn't find anything much of substance on the modern British theatre. There is very little investigation, for example, into what Granville Barker actually did as director.

JM After your productions had been staged, there was then a flowering of Lawrence in the theatre. In 1968 audiences could have watched *The Daughter-in-Law* in Lincoln, Harrogate and Nottingham. Did you feel you had released something?

PG I wish there were more productions of the plays. *The Daughter-in-Law* is still revived. But the plays are not particularly director's pieces. They don't offer much in the way of ostentation.

JM You returned to Lawrence in 1973 to do *The Merry-go-Round*. Was that a straightforward decision?

PG I don't know how or why that came about, except that I felt it deserved to be seen. But it is full of, again, beautiful writing. And there is a sexually ambiguous element to the writing of Harry Hemstock that marks it out. Only a certain sort of man could have written that character, I think. People were not so pleased with that production. But I loved doing the play.

JM Is it just a weaker play than the other three?

PG Well it's not so well formed, and I had to edit it for performance. But it's actually broader in its scope than the earlier plays I'd directed. Lawrence is writing about a wider social group, so it's not so nattily composed. And of course it has lots of different scenes.

JM But that wasn't altogether the last time you did a Lawrence play.

PG I did a rehearsed reading of *Touch and Go* at Riverside Studios in the late 1970s. I'm rereading *Women in Love* again at the moment, and those two works are connected. And that play is puzzling politically. But I think it's such an interesting play. I don't know why it hasn't been done. People enjoyed the reading that I did. It might benefit from some work.

JM You weren't tempted to move from that rehearsed reading to a full production?

PG Well I was, but at the time I felt I couldn't go back to Lawrence. Part of me was anxious that I wouldn't do it as well. I have thought about other plays too. *The Fight for Barbara*, for example, is never seen now, but is a lively play compared to lots of other plays of the period that do get revived. I remember Bill Gaskill saying if Lawrence had been alive in the 1960s and the plays had been presented to the Court at that point, then they would all have been performed. And I remember asking, 'do you even mean *Altitude*?' And he said 'yes, I do'. It's extraordinary that Lawrence couldn't find a place for his plays at the time of writing them. It's absolutely astonishing to me. Because he had a natural feel for the theatre.

JM   How does Lawrence influence your own playwriting? You haven't directed his plays since the 1970s, but some of your own works seem to be affected by a Lawrentian dynamic – I'm thinking here of scripts like *Small Change*, *The Sleepers Den* and *The York Realist*.

PG   Not consciously. I'm too concerned with getting things down to think of influences while working. But perhaps I find that Lawrence in the plays, and in some of the stories and poems, is remarkable because he doesn't see the working-class as a problem. He's not concerned with making the representation of working-class life serve any broader liberal agenda. He was simply trying to express the life he knew first hand as he'd observed it, and the plays aren't full of his own views to the extent that the novels are.

JM   You have said elsewhere that, onstage, the making of a real cup of tea is more shocking than an actor pretending to be stabbed.

PG   Well it is, because audiences are surprised by its obvious reality. Violence, no matter how skilfully done, is always a wonder of skill. Real things have a different effect.

CHAPTER 6
A PLAYWRIGHT'S PERSPECTIVE
Stephen Lowe

Stephen Lowe is a playwright and theatre director, who was born in Nottingham in 1947. He is the founder and co-artistic director of the experimental Meeting Ground Theatre. He has written more than fifty plays, including *Touched* (which was joint winner of the George Devine award and directed by Richard Eyre at the Nottingham Playhouse), *The Ragged Trousered Philanthropists* (for Joint Stock directed by Bill Gaskill, and then Stratford East directed by Stephen Daldry) and *Tibetan Inroads* (produced with assistant director Danny Boyle at the Royal Court). Lowe has written extensively for television, including the BBC Classic Serial *Scarlet and Black*, starring Ewan McGregor and Rachel Weisz, the BAFTA-nominated thriller *Tell-Tale Hearts*, the BBC2 film *Fleabites* staring Nigel Hawthorn and the eight-hour ABC serial *Greenstone* on the colonization of New Zealand. He has also scripted more than one hundred episodes of *Coronation Street*. Since 1985 he has been a director of Meeting Ground Theatre Company, and was chair of Arts Council East Midlands and council member of Arts Council England (2002–2007). He is also a senior fellow of the Institute of Mental Health. Many of his plays have been inspired by the work of D.H. Lawrence, including, between 2005 and 2012, a Lawrence trilogy of plays: *The Fox . . . and the Little Vixens* (Tangere Arts), *Empty Bed Blues* (Lakeside Arts Nottingham) and *Just a Gigolo* (Edinburgh Festival).

It's quite tricky to remember when I first heard the name of D.H. Lawrence. My background made me know about him pretty early because I'm a Nottingham working-class lad, and my family was very similar to his: my father wasn't a miner but was an itinerant labourer, and when he came back from the war there were great difficulties in my parents' relationship. I moved into other worlds as best I could. My family had no books, but I went to grammar school, by which point I knew a great deal about Lawrence, but hadn't really read much of his work. So then I was absolutely primed when I was 13 in 1961 for the *Lady Chatterley* trial. I can remember that in considerable detail, and the way that the first book arrived in the school and went round the tables at such speed while we read pages 237–238, not really understanding much of it, but it looked pretty exciting. It's a rare book that most people start in the middle.

Subsequent to that, I then read *Sons and Lovers*, which to this day still affects me, particularly the film: in fact I broke down the last time I saw it, as the relationship between child and mother is so moving. As a young teenager the novel had a profound effect on me, like so many of my generation. I was Paul Morel. It was my story. Morel had the painting. Lawrence himself had the writing. And me, I was an actor. That's what fascinated me. Writing didn't really appeal then. This was before the sixties had really kicked off – I was about 14 or 15 at this point – and I went to work on Saturdays in a 'continental' sex cinema. But funnily enough I had a girlfriend in that period, who was in a way my Jessie Chambers, a good Catholic who would not 'break through' with me, and it became crucial for me to see the parallels between Lawrence's life and my own. From then on I started reading everything of Lawrence's, and became obsessed – sexually obsessed I might say.

The next key development was that I became fascinated to discover that Lawrence had written plays. Nobody else seemed to know. Of course, I couldn't find any publications of the plays, so I went to the Nottingham central library. And by now I would be 16 or 17, it was 1965, and the librarians brought out a battered cardboard box, and in it there were some copies of plays. The scripts of the 'Eastwood Trilogy' were included in one volume, there was a separate copy of *David* from somewhere or other, and loads of press reports, all jumbled together. In fact there was also Walter Greenwood's adaptation of *The Daughter-in-Law* (*My Son's My Son*), which ended rather weirdly. I struggled with *David*, but by the time I got to *The Daughter-in-Law* I became convinced that something really remarkable was happening in my life. The Nottingham Playhouse had only opened just over a year before, in 1963, and I joined the youth group there, meeting on Saturday mornings, talking about plays and hanging around the bar to talk to actors. Anyway, the Nottingham central library wouldn't let me take the Lawrence plays out, so I went and spoke to the theatre's artistic director John Neville, in hushed tones, saying I thought these were wonderful plays by Lawrence, and asking why the Nottingham Playhouse was not doing them. John Neville probably didn't even hear what I was saying because of my appalling tendency to mumble like Jimmy Dean. Certainly my suggestion came to nothing. So what was fascinating for me was that I felt I was the only person who knew these plays existed, and was very excited by them, particularly *The Daughter-in-Law*. The class background, and the personal relationships that Lawrence describes, really grabbed me as a teenager. I had this sense that here was actually a new kind of theatre, a feeling which was only confirmed when I saw the plays onstage later in the decade.

I then went to university, to Birmingham, and again I was aware of the connection with Lawrence, in that he had attended a redbrick in the Midlands rather than Oxbridge. To be honest, at the time I was almost a bit over-the-top about the identification with him. And that identification was split between the character and the work. I read the quote where Lawrence writes of *Women in Love* that: 'The book frightens me; it is so end-of-the-world. But it is, it must be, the beginning of a new world too' (*Letters* III, 25). And the effects were cataclysmic on me. This was intensified by the fact that now there were people around me who know of, and some had even read, *Women in Love* and *The Rainbow*. Indeed, the star lecturer was Richard Hoggart, the key defence witness at the *Lady Chatterley* trial.

Meanwhile I continued working in that sex or 'continental' cinema, called the Moulin Rouge. And I'd also taken to going to Eastwood with my girlfriend (still dreaming of 'breaking through') to pay homage outside Lawrence's house. So, as a result of these influences, I decided to make a film. My uncle had a wind-up Bolex camera, which I nicked at weekends, and using Russian Technopan 8mm film, I tried to make the kind of film of Nottingham that I imagined Lawrence would have made if he were still around. He actually hated cinema and he would almost certainly have hated mine, rather ponderously entitled *Monochrome Summer Begun*. And the key scene was the love scene, which I was attempting to film in my family's council flat with my girlfriend. Unfortunately the shoot broke down after my dad came home early from the pub. His misunderstanding intensified by the fact he was deaf (as well as drunk) did little to help my conveying the serious artistic intent of our nudity. That incident became the basis of my second play at London's Royal Court, *Moving Pictures* (premiered as *Glasshouses* in 1981), which is a pretty accurate depiction of all of that happened on that occasion. The lad in the play is trying to film all this Lawrence stuff and doesn't realize the real Lawrentian story is what's going on with his parents. It's still one of my favourites actually, being mostly about my father and how he had returned from the war damaged and difficult and angry.

During my university years, I'd also joined a theatre company in Buxton, and they were doing a musical on Jimmy Dean, casting me in the main role. My mumbling paid off, and so my identification fused into Jimmy crossed with Paul Morel. One of the actors, Eddie Peel, got a job in the Peter Gill production of the Lawrence trilogy at the Royal Court, and with no money I hitched down from Birmingham to London, and slept on this actor's floor. He was just one of the extras, but he got me tickets for the gallery to see the three plays in 1968. And I was mesmerized. The washing of the body in *The Widowing of Mrs Holroyd* seemed to make time stand still for me. It felt like it had shifted the audience onto another planet. Those two women looked like they were enacting a kind of Greek ritual, cleansing a man all over, and converting him from black to white. Probably more than any other image, that shaped everything that I've done since. Lawrence finds a space between the line of realism and poetry, and I have been trying to do the same. In fact, at some points – such as in my play *Touched* (Nottingham Playhouse 1977, Royal Court 1981) – I have directly emulated Lawrence by including a bath scene. And more generally I guess I have been trying to do what Lawrence did in *The Widowing of Mrs Holroyd*, by getting at something that cannot be analysed away, something that can only be theatre.

After I saw the Lawrence trilogy at the Royal Court I went straight back to university for my third year, and I directed *The Daughter-in-Law*. That was the first time I got inside the kind of decisions that Lawrence was making and the nature of the theatrical language he was using. And it was probably the most joyous directing experience that I've ever had, because I was so close to the material.

Towards the end of my undergraduate degree, I decided to start doing my MA on Lawrence's plays. Now one of the reasons I'd gone to Birmingham, apart from the fact that it was near enough to bring my washing home at weekends, was Professor Hoggart. I knew him because of course of the *Lady Chatterley* trial, and he was the major English tutor at the university, and he had set up – which I didn't fully understand until I went there – the Birmingham Centre for Contemporary Cultural Studies with the brilliant Stuart Hall. But I had read, before I went to Birmingham, Hoggart's *The Uses of Literacy* (1957), which extended my awareness that working-class literature and art could be viewed with seriousness and rigour. So I went to Hoggart to do my MA, and we had one meeting, on Lawrence's plays. And a somewhat heated and interested discussion about Lawrence's poem 'The Ship of Death', which Hoggart correctly argued was about the fact that we are going to die and I was arguing, less correctly, was a metaphor for the artistic process. But in the second week I went in and he had disappeared to take over UNESCO. I don't think he was just trying to avoid me, but I was left with a tutor who was in a total panic about the thought of doing the plays, which he didn't know anything about. I'd fallen out with the theatre department, the professor there had tried to get me thrown out, so I did my MA in the English department, and it was suggested that I should focus on the poems, which, given that I could hardly name a handful of flora – mostly a simple catalogue of weeds/non weeds – wasn't particularly inspiring. So I switched the subject of my MA to Magic and Art – a study of Yeats, Aleister Crowley and the magic cult the Golden Dawn (it *was* 1969), but at the same time I began writing creatively for the first time. Lawrence of course was a major inspiration here, and it felt as if, by getting to know his plays, something had been released in me.

There was one particular drama that I wrote at the age of 23 called *Waste*, which was a very dangerous play, it was about confronting the white English with their worst fears, with exactly what they had inflicted on the rest of the world. So it was about the Afro-Caribbean black community taking over, and the whites being pushed out to the suburbs. I wrote that piece while I was a temporary assistant clerk at the Department of Health and Social Security, and sent it to the Royal Court. The playwright and literary manager, the wonderful Ann Jellicoe, called me in and said 'we are not going to do your play: half of the people here think you're a racist, and the other half think you're the divine light'. She said, 'however, it's been read by more people here than any other work, and I'm wavering on the good side'. She then employed me as a script reader and occasionally gave me tea on Sundays. The reaction of course got me blacklisted on two television channels, but she sent it to Richard Eyre, who had just taken over at Nottingham Playhouse. And Richard, being Richard, read it quickly, asked to see me, and said he wouldn't be able to do the play because nobody would understand it. It really was quite edgy. But he would commission another play from me.

In the meantime, I went to work in Scarborough with Alan Ayckbourn, first as an actor and then as a director. Richard Eyre came up to see me – he was very generous. He said – he was lying actually – that he was going to leave Nottingham quite soon, and asked whether I was ever going to write a play for him. So I made it up on the spot. I said, yes, it's about three sisters during the war (that thought was inspired by Chekhov), and it's about working-class women (that part was inspired by Lawrence). And he asked me to send it to him, so I started writing the play, and it became *Touched*, which Richard directed at the Nottingham Playhouse in 1977 and which became my breakthrough work.

Touched was immersed in the working-class world in a way I hadn't written before, indeed set right in the street that I grew up in. So much so that the designer went and did moulds of the backs of the houses where I had lived and put those moulds on the stage. But it contained a hint of *The Widowing of Mrs Holroyd* for me because, often, when you design a play you spend all your money on the last scene. You finish with a castle or something.

But *Touched* echoes *The Widowing of Mrs Holroyd* because by the end of it there is in a way no set – an almost ritual space. The characters are at the top of a hill looking down and they move into a kind of other world. I'd also begun to find that I could move the Lawrence material into the internal landscape – the play revolves around one crucial soliloquy. I was inspired by knowing that the lives of the working-class females that I was describing in the play were valid. To be honest, I had no idea that I had written a play that had women in it until much later. I'd started by asking a question about what had happened on the home front in the war, which at that point – the mid-seventies – hadn't really been explored much apart from a cockney musical called *Roll Out The Barrel*. After all, I knew what my father had done in the war, he'd been in the eighth army. There were films and documentaries aplenty. But I didn't know about my mother's life, even though it had happened on the very street of my own childhood. So that set me off on finding a voice. And I now see that there are parallels with the voice that Lawrence finds for his women. You have to say about Lawrence's plays, he may be accused of over-romanticizing women sometimes, but he's not sentimental. Women can sometimes be arrogant or over-the-top, just like men can, and that's often how they're portrayed by him, and I think he works very evenly. I've never really felt he was a misogynist.

After *Touched* I did the Lawrentian thing, whether consciously or not, and set off into a brief exploration of other worlds – to India and Ladhak. And the play that I wrote, *Tibetan Inroads* (premiered at the Royal Court, 1981), starts with the most working-class figure, Dorje, the blacksmith, having sex with the wife of the landlord. So it starts as *Lady Chatterley's Lover*, and I was very aware of that. I guess I was bringing Lawrence into contact with Tennessee Williams, and overall the play was strongly about the theme of personal and political oppression. I don't think anyone ever noticed that it was *Lady Chatterley's Lover*, although it was. All the critics slammed it when it was produced at the Royal Court. But I'm incredibly proud of that play.

After I'd written *Touched* I was awarded the George Devine prize, and was approached by Joint Stock, one of the leading experimental companies. I wasn't actually too bothered about that particular company at first, so I went back to Scarborough to do pantomime. But Bill Gaskill of Joint Stock phoned and said let's meet, and as a starting point he wanted me to pick a book that had changed my life. And he would do the same. We met and slid the name across the table and amazingly it was the same novel, and it wasn't by Lawrence! It was Robert Tressell's novel *The Ragged Trousered Philanthropists*

(1914), and my version is now the most performed of my plays. But Lawrence was never far away.

Bill Gaskill and I had also tried to do a staged version of Lawrence's novel *The Plumed Serpent*, which we both found really problematic. It was not explored for personal reasons as my marriage broke up, and the new love of my life was pregnant and vanished into the women's camps at Greenham Common. In fact, during the time she was there I wrote a film, one of the first commissioned films for Channel 4, called *Embrace*, a most Lawrentian film that was perhaps fortunate never to see the light of day.

My third play at the Royal Court was the comedy *Glasshouses* (later renamed *Moving Pictures*), which followed the life of a young would-be artist in 1965 trying to make a Lawrentian film with his girlfriend. Years later, I treated this autobiographical subject in a very different way in *Glamour* (Nottingham Playhouse 2009). But professionally, in the mid-1980s, I wasn't really getting to the audience that I wanted to, and that sense of dissatisfaction culminated in me leaving the Royal Court and my residency at Riverside Studios. I've never felt part of the London scene. We were supposed to be some kind of left-wing group – writers like me, Churchill, Edgar, Kureishi, Hare et al. – but I felt increasingly trapped in the London theatre scene. Time to move.

And writers can live in two places – Anywhere and Home.

So I made the decision to head back to Nottingham. To the town that Lawrence described as: 'that dismal town/where I went to school and college'.[1]

I needed a re-centring, and part of that involved finding different places to perform. So I came back to Nottingham and co-founded the experimental Meeting Ground Theatre Company with my partner Tanya Myers, which we've been running ever since.

But that move did leave one question up in the air. I had been commissioned to do a play by the RSC, which was eventually performed by them in 1988 under the title *Divine Gossip*. The advantage with the RSC was that I could write a play with more people in it and a full orchestra. So I went for something of epic scale, which included a large selection of my favourite songs of the period. Set in Paris it revolved around 1929 when both Lawrence and George Orwell were there (but never meeting). Lawrence was trying to get a rich and wild American, Harry Crosby, to publish *Lady Chatterley,* so that Frieda's future might be secured, but at that time she was also having an affair with the Italian Angelo Ravagli. And Lawrence was coming to the end of his game – and he knew it. I found that play very moving to do, and it was the first time I'd given words to Lawrence himself. And the key to it was the discovery of a secret. Or so it seemed to me.

I felt that *Lady Chatterley's Lover* was being misread. It's often seen as a covert autobiography with himself as the potent gamekeeper Mellors and Lady Chatterley as Frieda. It's actually more painful and poetic than that. Lawrence is the castrated man. He is not Mellors, but the impotent husband Clifford. The big secret is that Lawrence knew of the affair, and Ravagli, who worked as their gardener in Italy, was of course the gamekeeper.

Ultimately, I think *Divine Gossip* was too complex, too many stories. Years later Annie Castledine phoned me up, when I was broke as normal, and said she was doing some radio work. She had directed my play *Touched* for the Derby Playhouse and she said – 'why don't you write a 60-minute radio play based on *Gossip*?' Until that point my only radio work had been a radio production of *Touched*, so the Lawrence radio-play took some doing, taking only a few scenes from the original and extending that and transforming the whole language of the piece. It was re-named as *Empty Bed Blues* – the Bessie Smith record that Lawrence smashed over Frieda's head at a wild evening with the Crosbys. So I did a forty-five minute radio play.

It was fun.

But still I couldn't leave these two couples alone, and now I returned to the theatre again for a new two-act version. The characters were still demanding more space.

I wanted to strip it back from a play that had been grand and symphonic to one that was a close chamber piece quartet. That was the intention, to look at the way that just the four characters – Lawrence, Frieda and the Crosbys – were overcome by the sheer force of art. So I wrote a quiet play *Empty Bed Blues* (premiered at Lakeside Arts Nottingham, 2009), which is really pared down: even the radio play had started in Paris whereas the stage version is simply set in one place. And the four characters, the two couples, provide a classic Lawrentian form – it could be Birkin and Gerald, one is heading towards suicide, and the other is heading to who knows where. So the gang is there, you look at it and say, if Lawrence had had more time he would have seen that, he would have started writing the play himself.

But he didn't.

Shortly before I returned to the stage *Empty Bed Blues*, my old friends at Tangere Arts came to me, and wanted me to do a small-scale show, preferably by Lawrence.

I looked at his story 'The Fox', which of course had been a remarkable film in the 1960s (with Kier Dullea). I read it again, and thought the setup was both controversial and confrontational – indeed it is a darkly prejudiced piece in its notions of man/woman power games in the way it treats the lesbian couple and their final defeat. I looked at what Lawrence had done, and I thought, you've made such an argument that I have to react. So that got me going really. And the other thing that happened while I was working on the play was that I discovered an opera about the fox, *The Cunning Little Vixen*, which was written by the great Czech composer Janáček in the same year that Lawrence published his story (1923). So I played and played that music. And I saw films of the opera, which has such a different tone to the Lawrence piece, and I thought the more humanistic Janáček could be used alongside 'The Fox', so I decided to put the two together and make it a contemporary tale. Those two forces of Lawrence and Janáček fed into each other in narrative terms. My personal battle is of course to produce something that's watchable. More than that – something finally affirming.

I've never really felt inclined simply to adapt Lawrence. It seems to me that he demands you to 'respond', to enter into a kind of battle (almost a naked wrestling match) and to fight towards the discovery of your own values, the creation of your own profound vision.

And as you grow older the relationship with him changes as with siblings, parents, close friends. Sometimes you don't speak for years, sometimes you argue, sometimes you dance and he changes and you do too.

And I was left with one final play I needed to write – a play that would somehow encapsulate my own feelings – perhaps even love – for this difficult artist. It is the one-man show *Just a Gigolo* (premiered at the Edinburgh Festival, 2012), which starred the brilliant Maurice Roëves. I had been working on a three-part TV treatment centred, for once, on Frieda. And I wanted it to be a corrective to how maligned Frieda is, particularly by some sections of the academic world. She is often seen as dumpy, fat, oversexed and stupid, and more and more I felt that this was a terrible calumny. She was in fact an extraordinary character and far from hindering Lawrence on his journey, she was in many ways (including sexually) leading him, sometimes into places he didn't want to go. So I initially thought about a three-part television drama, with Frieda probably played by three different actresses. The first part would be about her, aged 18, meeting Professor Weekley and arriving in England; the second part would be the meeting with Lawrence; and the third part would be her life afterwards. At this time I was also speaking with the Lawrence scholar John Worthen, who had been very helpful with *Empty Bed Blues*, and is of course the leading expert on Frieda, and John and I talked about her and discussed our similar views. And of course he guided me to look at her lover Angelo Ravagli, who is the only character we see onstage in *Just a Gigolo*.

A great deal of what I do is based on what I call *the politics of the imagination*, and a lot of that is about very simply reclaiming voices that have either been insulted or oppressed; it could be the Luddites, it could be a gigolo, it could be Frieda Lawrence. What you do is, you look and see that things are more complicated, and that the simple narrative is inadequate. With Frieda and Angelo, for instance, he isn't simply a gigolo, because he stayed with her twenty-odd years, he looked after her. Cared for her. Theirs is a love story that lasted even longer than the one she had with Lawrence. In my play, he says he *is* just a gigolo in the song at the end, but by that point we think there is much more to him. And I wanted to create not simply a piece about his love for Frieda, but also about his and Lawrence's attraction to each other. And mine to all of them. It is a curious love song.

Frieda, Lawrence, Ravagli now seem to have become part of my family – sometimes I can't bear the thought of another Christmas dinner with them, at other times I can't wait to spend a holiday together. I play Bessie Smith just to wind up Lorenzo, I listen to Frieda singing *O Tannenbaum* like Lotte Lenya. And Angelo's pasta . . .

Recently I came face to face with a snake at my house in the Pyrenees. Locked in stillness I instinctively recited Lawrence's poem to it.

'A snake came to my water-trough/ On a hot, hot day. . .'.[2]

And the snake seemed to like it.

What more can one hope for?

CHAPTER 7
A SCREENWRITER'S PERSPECTIVE
William Ivory

The screenwriter and playwright William Ivory was born in Nottinghamshire in 1963. He played the part of Eddie Ramsden in *Coronation Street*, and is now known as one of Britain's leading television and film writers. His breakthrough BBC script *Journey to Knock* starred John Hurt and David Thewlis (1991) and won the best drama, best screenplay and best actor awards at the New York TV Festival. Ivory has since written a number of drama serials for the BBC, including *Common as Muck* (1994–1997) and *Truckers* (2013). He also wrote the film *Made in Dagenham*, which starred Bob Hoskins and Miranda Richardson (2010). He spent six years writing a two-part adaptation of D.H. Lawrence's *Women in Love*, which was broadcast by the BBC in 2011, and which starred Rosamund Pike and Rory Kinnear. As a playwright, he has staged the first two of a planned 'Southwell Trilogy' of plays at the Lakeside Arts Centre's D.H. Lawrence Pavilion in Nottingham, *The Retirement of Tom Stevens* (2006) and *Bomber's Moon* (2010, later at London's Park Theatre in 2014); and his play *The Diary of a Football Nobody* was staged by the Nottingham Playhouse in 2012. He was patron of the D.H. Lawrence Festival in Eastwood in 2013 and 2014.

I knew Lawrence at first by reputation, because of my own Nottinghamshire connections. I was born in Southwell, and went to the Minster School there, and was really interested in anything about Nottingham from that point onwards. And I was particularly concerned with Lawrence because one of my schoolteachers at Southwell, Alan Cattermole, had been taught by Leavis at Cambridge, and of course as a result was mad keen on Lawrence. I had already read some of Lawrence's poetry when I was about 13 or 14, but then Alan gave me a copy of Graham Hough's book, *The Dark Sun: A Study of D.H. Lawrence*, which helped me to develop my critical thinking. Alan also recommended that I should read *Sons and Lovers*; he thought I'd love that, and I did think it was fantastic. Especially striking was the dialogue, because although Lawrentian dialect is usually associated with the Derbyshire border, you get a very similar effect in the speech patterns of the north of the county of Nottinghamshire as well – which is where I'm from, and to see that in a book was amazing.

I also discovered a personal connection with Lawrence's subject matter. When I read *Sons and Lovers* I found that the most powerful moment was when Paul Morel wins a prize in a children's paper, and he tells his father, who responds by saying, 'And how much is the prize, then, as you've got?'[1] And I can remember thinking that this was an amazing piece of writing, because it was brutal, and it was hard. My dad was from South Wales, and was quite a tough man, a hard man, although a brilliant man too, in lots of ways. And I just recognized something very familiar in that moment that Lawrence had described. The world of the working class was very powerful and very recognizable to me, partly because my mother also came from a working-class Nottinghamshire family, but was at pains to stress to me that I should read and study and get away from my roots. Along with her sisters, and I don't mean this unkindly, I think she had a belief that the emphasis was on leaving school and getting a trade and earning a living. Anyway, it meant that Lawrence spoke to me right from the off, because at the heart of his work there seemed always to be that conflict which obsesses me in my own writing, between lucre and poetry, mammon and words, and the idea that the working classes are not allowed to be lyrical in any way. That refusal to acknowledge the poetry of the working class is a very English thing I think – it's not true in Ireland, for example, where you have people like Patrick Kavanagh and Seán O'Casey being widely celebrated. But the English often seem to ignore the poetry of working-class life, which is something that I just love to explore. For example, when I wrote a six-part television series called *The Sins* (BBC, 2000), which is one of the things that I'm most proud of, I got flack from certain critics because the main character – played by Pete Postlethwaite – is Len Green, a former criminal and now an undertaker, who often expresses himself in relatively heightened, poetic language. Some commentators said snootily, 'well, he must have read a heck of a lot while he was in prison because he has an awful lot to say afterwards'. And I just thought, well why not? Why wouldn't he? I don't hold that only the language of a certain class, or a certain part of the country, can be expressive and poetic.

Anyway, I read *Sons and Lovers* when I was at school, and then I just started ploughing through all of Lawrence's work. I quickly read *Women in Love*, which I did find incredibly difficult at first. In fact, parts of it were almost unintelligible when I initially came to it. But even though I struggled with parts, overall I was overwhelmed by the sheer brilliance of the language and the intensity of it all. And I was reading this stuff at a time when I started to go to the theatre regularly, to Nottingham Playhouse where Richard Eyre was the artistic director. So at the very time I was discovering Lawrence in all his glory, I was also witnessing some groundbreaking theatre. I saw some wonderful dramas during Eyre's time in charge of the Playhouse: I saw David Storey's *The Contractors* there in 1974, and then Trevor Griffiths' *Comedians*, which premiered at the theatre in 1975, and shortly afterwards I watched Stephen Lowe's *Touched*, which appeared at the Nottingham Playhouse in 1977 and is a remarkable play about the city. And when I saw those plays I had a very similar feeling to what I found when I read Lawrence, the discovery of what Leavis would call 'felt life'. To me the plays achieved exactly what all great writing should – they connected viscerally and not purely cerebrally. And shortly after that, after starting to think in this way, I began attending classical concerts, too, because the new Royal Concert Hall had opened in Nottingham in 1982. Once there, I encountered composers like Beethoven and Tchaikovsky and I continued to develop the belief that for me, at least, the art which endures is the art which we feel rather than think. Subsequently I made a conscious effort to explore those artists who are considered easy to 'get', like Tchaikovsky rather than Schoenberg, Betjeman rather than Craig Raine, those who, as a result of their accessibility, are often dismissed by the cultural elite. Indeed, what fascinated me and what I loved about them, *was* that very accessibility; the fact that they spoke with a voice which was instantly understandable and which didn't need intellectual decoding. They brought art into the every day, the common, the communally felt – but *then* they elevated those feelings into something moving and profound. And that, despite the difficulty of his language, was how I had always felt about Lawrence. Sex, money, violence, cruelty, love; *I got him* because the themes he explored were instantly recognizable.

As I entered my teenage years, some of my friends were becoming quite overtly political, and at the time I didn't feel that I had a comparable bent, but on reflection I think perhaps I was moving in a similar direction. It was just that much of my political radicalization was coming from elsewhere. Writers like Alan Sillitoe, Francis Stuart, John Cooper Clarke, Linton Kwesi Johnson and of course Lawrence, were making me challenge and rethink my own views about issues like sex and gender and the capitalist society. The theatre was doing it, too, especially with left-wing companies like Red Ladder, 7:84 and the People Show being so active in this period. Of course, we were also heading towards the second wave of feminism and, with two older sisters, I was already well aware of the sexual/political explosion of the late sixties, so Lawrence's attitude to sex felt especially relevant to me. Admittedly, there is a lot of quite peculiar phallocentric stuff in Lawrence, and there is clearly much in that phallocentrism to disagree with, even to feel repelled by, but at the same time I've always felt quite strongly that Lawrence, for all of his faults, is struggling towards something admissible and significant. Whilst in the 1970s there were people like Erica Jong and Germaine Greer who helped to explore the idea of women's gender and sexual identity with seriousness and passion, there hadn't, to my mind, been a similar process whereby men had looked at their sexuality and tried to understand what that meant in anything like the same way. Maleness, in all its forms, was just accepted: it was what it was. And that felt wrong, because masculinity had been arrived at. What is more, what *had* been arrived at seemed ugly and confused and where it was examined formally, tended to be dismissed glibly and comfortably. Certainly it was a far from satisfactory examination of what it was to be human for half the world's population. And Lawrence had got into so much trouble over the years for trying to start a debate on that very situation; he had posited a set of questions about men and their sexual essence, about this 'Thing-Down-Here that I am attached to, which so defines me' and had been crucified for doing so ever since.

During my teenage reading of Lawrence, I also read the short stories, which astonished me because so many of them were so funny. There is one that begins with a local tram ride, 'Tickets Please', which is richly, darkly comic. And then the final Lawrence novel that I encountered was *Lady Chatterley*, read quite late in the day. I knew that there had been all this fuss about it, but once I did take a look I actually thought that the novel was rather beautiful. I have to admit though, that by that stage, I had become quite defensive of Lawrence; especially when I heard other people criticizing him. Because I felt he was ours, I suppose. Also, he risked so much as a writer, because his prose *was* purple and over-the-top at times, and he *did* misjudge it on occasion and his heart was *never* off his sleeve. On top of that visceral, localized response though, I was also reading plenty of Donne and Marvell around now, and I felt, quite passionately, that Lawrence was upholding a great and fascinating tradition of writing about sex and desire in beautiful and highly wrought language.

My interest in Lawrence and the theatre coincided when I went to see *The Daughter-in-Law* playing at the Derby Playhouse in September 1979, and I just thought it was the most brilliant experience. To see Lawrence's words and concerns rendered in such an immediate form and to see the way the production shocked the audience physically, was completely eye opening. And humbling. It seemed to me that Lawrence wrote well in every conceivable discipline. It was particularly interesting to witness the character of Mrs

Gascoyne, too, as I thought it was such a compelling and vital female role. Indeed, for all of the accusations of sexism that surround Lawrence, I find it remarkable that time and again he describes such extraordinarily strong women. After I saw *The Daughter-in-Law* I felt inspired to read *The Widowing of Mrs Holroyd* and I remember thinking again that at its core was a stunning and forensic portrayal of a hugely complex woman. In fact, a portrayal of *two* fascinating women by the end of the play. So my experiencing Lawrence as a dramatist, alongside the other work I'd seen at the Nottingham Playhouse, persuaded me to think about developing my own literary output in this direction – especially having seen the way that theatre could physically jolt people, even more, I believed, than poems or novels.

In 1982, though, I went to the University of London. But it didn't suit me very well at all, so I dropped out after a few months, and became a bin man in Nottinghamshire for the following two years. The lads who I worked with on the bins would say, 'What are you going to do? You're not stoppin' on this forever are you?' and I would say, 'No, I want to be a writer', and then they would ask, 'Well, what are you going to write about?' In other words, right from the outset, there was an acceptance of writing that I hadn't necessarily found with some of my university friends when I admitted the same ambition to them. Mind you, on the bins, we spent a massive amount of time telling all sorts of stories to each other and I have a feeling that the nature of the job bred an instinctive understanding of the medium I wanted to explore. The thing is, being a bin man gave you a terrific licence to play because there was no real hierarchy, you were all the same, you were all rock bottom. And that, in turn, engendered a great sense of 'We're all in this together ... we might as well have fun!' And with *that*, the sense of equality and frivolity, we felt happy to share things – including the stories we told. I loved it, too, hearing blokes – some of whom were really hard – telling their intricate tales. And ever since then, I've operated according to the belief that through brute bad luck or other uncontrollable circumstances, there are many people in working-class communities who are deeply creative but can't necessarily explore that creativity or find an outlet for it. And that causes me to collide quite often with those who want to portray the working classes in a purely negative way; or if not negative, at least as victims, struggling terribly against the odds. That strikes me as a form of misery porn, perpetuated by middle-class cultural commentators who want to display their solid liberal credentials by wringing their hands and wagging their fingers. For me, on the other hand, the aim should be to capture the complexity of life, wherever that may be, and to render characters that are described and understood as nuanced individuals rather than as types that are animated for the purpose of illustrating a point about the social divide. I think Lawrence was doing exactly that nuancing, and I think that's one of his greatest gifts to writers who follow him.

After a couple of years, I stopped working on the bins and picked up a job as a stagehand at the Nottingham Playhouse. In fact, I wrote my first play just prior to getting the job at the Playhouse, a piece called *Cause for Concern*, which is set around the Hyde Park bombings by the IRA in 1982. The script was very much influenced by my love of punk, and explores the relationships between three students, all very radical, all living together, who become embroiled in the attack. It was really a play about responsibility, and avowals of belief. The trouble was, initially, that I'd typed it on three different typewriters (loans which kept getting recalled) and it was full of mistakes, but I still sent it to Kenneth Alan Taylor who had just been appointed the new artistic director at the Playhouse in 1984. He sent me a really narky letter back, saying 'Send me something I can read. This is hopeless'. So I then had to pay to get it typed; it was a matter of honour! And back it went. This time he *could* read it and he said, 'I can't use this, but come and see me because I think you might be a writer'. In fact, he turned out to be very supportive, and while I was working as a stagehand at the Playhouse, he encouraged me to keep writing all the time. And finally *Cause for Concern* was actually performed: at the Perspectives Theatre Company space (now New Perspectives) in Mansfield in 1985.

So I was working at the Playhouse, just crewing there, but then I got a phone call from an actor-mate asking whether I could do a proper Nottingham accent, because there was a small D.H. Lawrence film being made for television and they wanted people who could speak with a native twang. I'd actually done a tiny bit of acting for Kenneth Alan Taylor in his production of Barry Heath's *Me Mam Sez* at the Playhouse – again because they needed a man with a Nottingham accent – so I had my Equity card, which meant I could go for the job. The film was a version of Lawrence's short story 'Strike Pay', about a miner called Radford who is out on strike and whose wife is struggling to get him to share his strike money. It was actually one I hadn't read, but it had been made into a TV film by Granada in 1966, and now the BBC wanted to make a new TV version, I think, as part of their schools' output. I got the job, anyway. And we actually managed to film in the D.H. Lawrence birthplace museum in Eastwood, as well as the countryside outside Cossall. This acting made me realize that in Lawrence's writing there is an absolute contrast between the dark and grimy world of the mines and the astonishingly beautiful rural landscape all around. Lawrence is writing about men who are dehumanized, working like pit ponies and who are then released into this totally boundless landscape, in a way which creates a real jolt in their psyches as they struggle to move between the beauty and the ugliness, and the space and the confinement. Even when I was working on the bins, in the pit villages, all around Ollerton, Blidworth and Rufford, you came across something similar in that you'd be emptying the bins on what was a crowded, built-up street and then the tarmac of the street would just stop, end. You'd come to the edge of the urban and the road would literally run into the fields, the grass, the countryside, immediately beyond it. In fact, some of the lads who worked on the bins with me had previously worked down the pits as well, especially on some of the heavier rounds in Ollerton, and they used to take me out in the evening and we would try to tickle trout, and these same men would suddenly become rural and of the country, glorying in its opportunities and space. In some ways the contrast in the lives of these individuals mirrors the contrast in Lawrence's writing, in that although he is often remembered for his depiction of heavy industry and the pits, he is really quite remarkable for his detailed descriptions of nature and the rural landscape. In *Women in Love*, for example, he describes the stile that was 'rubbed shiny by the moleskins of the passing miners', and I think you have to have quite a sharp eye for the outdoors if you are including that kind of detail.[2] It's funny because the first play I put on for longer than a couple of nights emulated something of this aspect of what I'd found in Lawrence. *The Truth About Eric*, which was staged at the Nottingham Playhouse Studio in 1986 and is about a man who undertakes to explode a VIP lounge at Heathrow Airport because he feels an acute sense of social injustice: he includes amongst his hostages a character who is yearning to get back to nature, to a simpler life, but who is trapped in the city, and so is doubly held against his will.

By 1989, as well as writing, I had started to act a bit more. I'd appeared at Manchester Royal Exchange, Derby Playhouse and York Theatre Royal, but I wasn't really having very much success. Then I heard that there was a job going on *Coronation Street*, and I got the part of Eddie Ramsden; largely because I was already friends with the actress who was going to play opposite me, a regular called Michelle Holmes (who played Tina Fowler) who contrived to be rubbish with every other auditionee but me. God bless her. It was a great break and I was really thrilled to get the part, not only because it was regular work but because I loved the *Street*. And that was mainly down to the quality of the writing but also because the show was attempting, in those days, to make central the kind of working-class life that Lawrence had attempted to describe in his plays and in his early work. *Coronation Street* has changed a lot now, but back then it was so different to all the other soaps because it was solely concerned with character, with working-class character and, particularly, the way in which community life revolved around and relied upon extremely powerful female figures. The writers gave an incredible sense of the hierarchies and the matriarchies that were set up in these places. And the working-class characters were always sufficiently interesting as people for us to be gripped by them and their dilemmas, rather than just seeing them as pawns to be moved about according to the plot needs of endlessly hysterical storylines – which was how the other shows functioned. The jeopardy in those early years of the *Street* was always to be found in the tiniest detail of the lives of working class people – just as it was in Lawrence.

I really enjoyed being in *Coronation Street*, and stayed in it for about six months. But of course while I was there I also saw, up close, the way TV worked for the first time. I particularly noticed the scripts and how short they were. I remember thinking: 'It wouldn't take me very long to write one of those', which was exactly what I wanted to do – because not too long before, in 1989, my mother had died and I was desperate to write a piece that celebrated her. So I wrote my first television drama *Journey to Knock*, which the BBC picked up and broadcast in 1991. The drama revolves around two terminally ill characters, one played by David Thewlis, and one played by John Hurt, as they journey to the Marian shrine in County Mayo. Thewlis's character is going because he hopes for a miracle, and Hurt's character is going along because he wants a piss up. And there is clearly an influence from Lawrence in this script. For one thing, the John Hurt character has been injured in a mine-working accident, just like the characters in Lawrence's plays *The Widowing of Mrs Holroyd* and *The Daughter-in-Law*. Additionally, there's a link in that the film is a love letter to my mum (who, like the Thewlis character, suffered from Motor Neurone disease) and it is well documented that Lawrence's close, sometimes troubled, relationship with his mother, underpinned much of what he wrote.

But when I look at that script now, though, I think perhaps the more profound connection between Lawrence's work and my first TV drama is in the way that I was trying to describe a particular way of *being* in the world; of thrusting yourself into everything and living with vigour. The key moment in *Journey to Knock* occurs when John Hurt and David Thewlis take a trip in the hospice van, and their driver gets drunk, and they crash and are stuck in the back of the vehicle, wedged in a ditch. Thewlis starts to despair; to feel the trip is wasted. And then he feels more generally that their situation is hopeless. John puts his hand over the mouth of the severely disabled Thewlis character and starts to smother him, and at first David's character thinks it's just a joke, but then he starts thrashing around, thinks he's going to suffocate. At the point of despair, John throws the van doors open and says 'breathe – breathe that in', and I suppose he's saying that none of us know how much time we've got on earth, but that is not the issue really; the issue is, that what time we do have, we must devour, we must gulp down, we must inhale deeply.

I can see that when I came to write *Common as Muck*, the BBC series about bin men that ran between 1994 and 1997, I was probably also showing an affinity with Lawrence. I loved my time on the bins. When I was doing that work, at that time and in that place, I couldn't help but feel part of that world that was still connected to the collieries (a world which, by the time my television career had taken off, Thatcher had completely obliterated – so much so that when the BBC came to do my drama *Faith* in 2004 we couldn't even find a place to film that still had the headstocks in situ). Anyway, what I remember most about being a bin man was that you became dirty and you stank. We would go into shops sometimes to buy a bottle of pop and the shopkeepers would ask us to wait outside. But there was something so clean about what we were doing as well. The money was honestly earned. There was nothing of the corrosiveness of the world of business or corporate life, or of earning a wage where you have to take advantage of people in some way. And I think there's an affinity with Lawrence, here, too; with the similarly straightforwardly clean dirt that needs to be washed off the miners in *A Collier's Friday Night*, *The Daughter-in-Law*, *The Widowing of Mrs Holroyd* and *The Merry-go-Round* before those characters can return to the day-to-day domestic life of the house.

The BBC has been very supportive of me ever since *Journey to Knock*. Thankfully, a lot of my work has been received very well, but I realize that it can be quite polarizing at times and what people don't like about my work, sometimes, is that it doesn't behave itself. It's not northern, for a start. Some viewers have this strange expectation – they think that if it's going to be a working-class drama then it ought to be properly of the North – so that they recognize it. And when it isn't, they are kind of affronted. The thing is, they aren't quite sure where this place is, the East Midlands, and I'm not prepared to make it generically Ooop North the way a lot of blue-collar drama is directed, because the East Midlands is *specifically* the place that I love and which I want to keep writing about. The thing is, viewers can be lazy at times, I'm afraid, but that's even more of a reason to stick to your guns if you ask me because the more we all agree to be herded one way, the more horizons will shrink still further.

Critics, too, need to work a bit harder, I believe. When I recently read the US reviews of my film *Burton & Taylor* (BBC America, 2013, starring Dominic West and Helena Bonham Carter) I was amazed at how detailed and proper these essays and critiques were. Not everyone liked what I had done, but I could see the clear process of thinking that lay behind the US critics' thoughts. It was joyous. By contrast, in the UK, so much criticism comes from people who want to show that they are liberal, metropolitan, right thinking and fashionable individuals. This regularly leads to problems when dealing with the working classes. Because if those working-class characters are being plucky and rising up against poverty and battling against the odds, or even just suffering in terrible squalor, then clearly it's easy and *proper* even, to support these depictions. What's more difficult is if the critic is asked to relate to the working classes as they genuinely are (and which would require an *actual* connection) because that takes him into unknown territory. And the unknown is frequently dismissed out of hand. Especially where it makes us feel uncomfortable or challenges our perceived views. For example, in *A Thing Called Love* (BBC, 2004) I portrayed a black, working-class Nottingham man, whose wife has become pregnant. She subsequently displays huge levels of self satisfaction, and I depicted this in a pretty bleak light. At one stage he says to her, 'You're having a baby, you haven't cured fucking cancer' – and some critics really objected to that. They wanted a much more positive rendering of a working-class character in this situation. But of course what they wanted wasn't necessarily any more truthful at all.

Anyway, I finally ended up doing my own version of a Lawrence script for broadcast by the BBC in 2011, when I adapted *Women in Love*, and I thoroughly enjoyed the process. It all came about because a number of years earlier, George Faber, who was at Company Pictures at the time, said to me that I should do a version of Lawrence's short story 'The Rocking-Horse Winner'. And I wasn't sure about that, partly because it had already been made as a film in 1949 (with a screenplay by Anthony Pélissier) and partly because I wasn't sure it was the Lawrence piece I'd choose anyway. George came back and mooted the idea of me writing a version of *Sons and Lovers* (which he eventually made with a different scriptwriter and broadcast on ITV in 2003) but again I said no because I thought if I was going to lock horns with Lawrence it would almost certainly be a one-off experience and in which case there were other books I'd rather do. Catherine Wearing, who was a producer and friend of mine, wanted me to try working on *The Lost Girl*, which I thought would have been fantastic. But we never had the chance to take it on before she sadly passed away in 2008. Essentially, I was holding out for *Women in Love*, which, although it had confused me when I was young, I had come to believe was the greatest modern novel written in English. And finally, George agreed it was the one we should do. He just said, 'You write it, I'll pay for it, and then we'll sell it once you've written it'. And so I wrote a ninety-minute film to start with and I was slightly despairing because I couldn't get in all that I wanted. But all the same, the BBC read it, and they loved it, and said they'd make it. However, the schedulers, who are so powerful, were convinced it should be a two-parter, and then we found we still couldn't get it into production because of changes in editorial direction. Then, out of the blue, I got a call telling me that BBC Four was doing a season on sexuality, and they were talking about maybe broadcasting *Women in Love* as a part of it. So I dashed down to see Richard Klein, who was then the controller of BBC Four, and he was amazing. He looked me in the eye and said, 'Tell me why I should make this then?' I rattled on for fifteen minutes and he said: 'Okay'. And that was that. But he was clear that he wanted *my* version of the novel rather than something that was slavishly faithful to Lawrence, or something that would simply repeat what Ken Russell had done with his famous film of 1969 (which thankfully I hadn't actually seen at that stage, so I wasn't as daunted as I might have been by that example). So I went back to the script again and added all the things I'd wanted to previously, but which I had held off doing for fear of upsetting the purists.

Then Mark Pybus, who produced the film for George, rang me up, and said 'We can't afford to make this. There's no way we can fund it, unless we go to four hours – and find some economy of scale'. And I said, 'I'm looking at it now, Mark and I can't possibly pad it out to last that long'. To which he replied, quite blithely, 'Well let's add *The Rainbow* in as well'. So I went off to ponder this and at first that idea – of putting together *Women in Love* and *The Rainbow* into a unified script – really frightened me, because I just thought there is no way we can extend the narrative link across both books when Gudrun is completely redundant in *The Rainbow*. But then I looked again at Lawrence's novel *The Trespasser* and what was interesting was that the artistic paradigm that is described in that book could just about be made to fit into *The Rainbow*'s narrative – as long as the Helena character, who loves the violinist in *The Trespasser*, could be rendered as the artist Gudrun in *The Rainbow*. So I borrowed from that novel too, and Gudrun gained a real presence in the second half of my script, which ended up combining material from *The Rainbow* and *The Trespasser*, as well as from *Women in Love*. Today I just think that the whole thing fits together beautifully. Of course, it isn't particularly faithful to the word of Lawrence, but it is to his spirit, totally. And I can't think of another way that I would have done it. Eventually it just came together and ended up being broadcast as two parts of ninety-odd minutes and it is one of the things that I'm genuinely proudest to have written. Howard Jacobson, who was another one of Leavis's students, wrote a review in the *Independent* saying, 'It is superb [...] It transfixed me for 90 minutes as nothing I have seen on television ever has'.[3]

In terms of adapting Lawrence's dialogue, there were moments where it felt quite theatrical, too theatrical in fact, even by my standards. So I had to tone it down a little. But there were times, such as when Ursula says the biblical line 'It's you who must return, like a dog to his vomit' (which is some of the most extraordinary dialogue that I've ever read anywhere), when the original sat very nicely within the confines of the piece.[4] And it felt wonderful to be able to help place those lines before a modern audience in a TV drama. What I discovered generally with the language, was that if a purple patch lay ahead, or there was something which was extremely vivid and which I wanted to keep, then a few scenes before that moment I had to start feeding in the odd bit of texture linguistically – to begin turning up the colour, almost, so that when we got to the really rich moment, the viewer was attuned. In that respect, I felt a bit like a gardener, tilling the soil, shading some areas, watering others, encouraging growth so that any sudden burst of colour felt appropriate.

I also found that Lawrence wrote many things in his prose descriptions which when made into dialogue were sensational examples of dramatic writing. These sentences I could put straight into the characters' mouths. For him, I think, the landscape *was* so alive, that it spoke to him almost like a person, and so for me, the job was simply to pull out those moments and choose who to give them to.

Of course, some people didn't like the liberties that I had taken with *Women in Love*. When my film was premiered in Santa Fe (just down the road from Taos) in New Mexico, someone asked me if I'd even read Lawrence's work. But I have always been extremely happy with what I did. What is more, because I was determined to reflect the spirit of Lawrence I wanted the work to have a strong taste, extremely strong, and I knew that would not be to everyone's palate. Anyway, for me, all of the important aspects of Lawrence's *Women in Love* are present in my film; it's simply that a lot of it is rendered in quite an unfamiliar way. And I was extremely proud that Vintage reissued some of their Lawrence books on the back of the film, even though that involved me having some very strange conversations about front-cover artwork with them.

I don't think I would adapt another Lawrence piece for the screen. A year or two ago I was approached to see whether I wanted to do a version of *Lady Chatterley*, but I think that text has been done to death. Perhaps there are some short stories that could be turned into a movie, but I think I've done what I want to with Lawrence, beyond read him again. Nevertheless, he remains, for me, such an extraordinary writer, and I will always retain a fascination for him as well as his work. I visited Taos at one point during my writing of the *Women in Love* screenplay and I went up to his grave, and I was 6,000 or 7,000 feet up the side of this mountain, I could hardly breathe, the sky was piercing blue and I was just imagining the little birthplace back in Eastwood, and how he went from there to end up here, and I couldn't stop thinking: what a journey. What a journey, in every sense.

CHAPTER 8
AN INTERCULTURAL PERSPECTIVE
Soudabeh Ananisarab

Soudabeh Ananisarab was born in Tehran, Iran, in 1989, and studied English literature at the University of Shahid Beheshti. She travelled to the UK in 2010 in order to pursue her postgraduate studies in the School of English, University of Nottingham, and has since worked as an undergraduate tutor at the university, where she teaches the history, theory and practice of drama. She has also been working with the Nottingham Theatre Royal on a series of public activities designed to commemorate, in 2015, the 150th anniversary of the opening of the playhouse. Her current research focuses mainly on the theatre of the English Midlands and she is completing a book-length study about George Bernard Shaw and the Malvern Theatre Festival.

In the years since D.H. Lawrence wrote his 'Eastwood Trilogy' of plays, the areas of Nottinghamshire that he knew and described have shifted and altered in innumerable ways. In Eastwood, the old Congregationalist chapel that he attended in his youth has been demolished and replaced with a branch of the Iceland supermarket. At Brinsley, the headstocks have been re-erected as a strictly ornamental feature of the local picnic area, and the original coalmine has long been abandoned. In Nottingham town centre, the music halls have almost completely vanished, and the Unitarian chapel on High Pavement Street is now a branch of the Pitcher and Piano pub, with many of the church fittings still in place. These architectural shifts also signify changes in the lifestyle depicted in the plays, as old patterns of British manual labour have been replaced by service industry, and as the family template described in Lawrence's drama has also been displaced, in many cases with a more varied network of personal relationships. What, then, is the relevance of a play such as *The Widowing of Mrs Holroyd*? Is it merely a museum piece?

In this chapter, I will make the case that aspects of Lawrence's playwriting still resonate in contemporary British society, which has become, since Lawrence's time, a more varied amalgamation of different cultures as a result of the increase in immigration to the country. I will also show how Lawrence's drama has the potential to find affinities with those living in locations far beyond the shores of the UK. From my own perspective, as an Iranian who is resident in Britain, I find there is much in *The Widowing of Mrs Holroyd* – in terms of its depiction of a change in the traditional roles of husband and wife in a marriage, and the struggles of its female protagonist as a result of her social aspirations – which connects with the recognizable experiences of members of certain Asian diasporic communities living in the country. As a result, I argue that while many of the specific domestic details that Lawrence depicted in this play have mutated or disappeared, Lawrence's work continues to chime with these evolving twenty-first century contexts.

Prior to arriving in Britain, my experience of Lawrence's writing was limited, as he is not a well-known figure outside academic circles in Iran. In my home country today, similar to the original reception of Lawrence's work in Britain, his writing struggles with state-sponsored controls and regulations. The Iranian translator of Paul Strathern's *D.H. Lawrence in 90 Minutes*, Shirin Maghanloo, explained in an interview of 2008: 'The issues concerning the translation of Lawrence for us goes back to censorship regulations and is already out of the question and I don't think any translator would go near them'. However, the interviewer describes Lawrence as 'a progressive figure who was able to advance beyond his own community and later force his progress onto his own society'. Other online articles in Farsi similarly praise Lawrence's courage in breaking taboos and providing alternative narratives, seeing his battles against the censor as having particular resonance in an Iranian society where art and drama are also used for challenging established beliefs and opinions.[1]

Yet, since arriving in Britain, I have read more widely in Lawrence's work, and have often felt suspicious of, and alienated by, some of his political and personal sympathies, particularly as manifested his later career. After all, Lawrence is a writer who wrote from Tahiti in 1922 to tell Compton Mackenzie, 'If you are coming here don't. The people are brown and soft' (*Letters* IV, 268). Lawrence is also a writer whose 'Autobiographical Fragment' of 1927 laments the fact that 'ours is the generation of "free" womanhood' which has created 'pathetic' men.[2]

Nonetheless, despite my suspicions, I have found in Lawrence's writing, and especially in plays such as *The Widowing of Mrs Holroyd*, much that feels well-observed, sensitive and pertinent. In *The Widowing*, his second full-length play, Lawrence set about describing, in minute detail, the lives of the white working-class living in Bestwood, a fictional version of his hometown. To me, what is remarkable about this drama is the attention that Lawrence pays to the woman struggling to reconcile her own aspirations with her society's norms of female behaviour, particularly the expectation that a wife should obey her husband's will. Mrs Holroyd, or Lizzie as her name is later revealed, married out of necessity rather than choice, as she pursued marriage as a means of escape: 'I felt I'd nowhere to go, I belonged to nowhere, and nobody cared about me, and men came after me, and I hated it. So to get out of it, I married the first man that turned up' (92). This 'first man' was Charlie, a miner for whom Lizzie relocated to Bestwood. However, at the point when we join the couple in the play, Lizzie is increasingly dissatisfied with her life. Charlie now spends his nights drinking at the local pub with other women, while she is left with her domestic duties – and is pictured doing her laundry at the start of both the first and second scenes (in a particularly fruitless way – the washing is no sooner dried than she discovers it to be covered with 'smuts' (67)). Through Blackmore, Lizzie imagines a life away from her husband and this life of repetitive duty. She expresses her aspirations for relocating from Bestwood as she finds this place to have little to offer: 'There's less than nothing if you can't be like the rest of them – as common as they're made'. However, as Blackmore indicates, possessing such aspirations for a life beyond Bestwood is problematic, 'particularly for a woman' (68).

Obviously, the work, leisure and religious culture of such white, working-class women in Britain has changed a great deal in the century since Lawrence first wrote this script. Today, Lizzie Holroyd would undoubtedly be using a washing machine. But, as Jeremy Seabrook observes, much of the rhetoric of poverty remains much the same today as it did in the early twentieth century, and many of the new minorities of the UK have come to occupy the economic and geographical positions once inhabited by the particular section of the white working-class whose daily worries and concerns so interested Lawrence. In particular, Seabrook describes the correspondences between the kind of figures who populate Lawrence's dramas and many Asian communities in Britain of our own day, and the way that women may still feel trapped by the same kinds of power structure that Lizzie Holroyd's dilemma reveals. Seabrook observes that today, in Britain's Asian migrant communities, very often:

Women have the same protective role, using up their energies to keep body and soul – and the family – together. The same mothers look anxiously at their sons, wondering at the company they keep [...] Similar doubts clouded the eyes of mothers two or three generations ago, when their young formed friendships with boys or girls who were not chapel, or came from the rough, rather than the respectable, parts of town. The men, too, privileged patriarchs, whose word is no longer law, seek in vain to compel their refractory children to habits of obedience, sometimes using canes or fists [...] How familiar it is. For the old working class lived, like communities of Bengalis and Pakistanis, a life apart. Of course, migrants and their children are minorities; but the working class (always a majority of the population), rarely figured in the iconography of the nation, except as 'masses', workers, or when wars were fought, as soldiers and dead heroes.[3]

It may be that, for Lawrence's reputation as a playwright to flourish in the future, a new generation of migrant or diasporic audiences need to find this kind of renewed sense of relevance in his 'Eastwood Trilogy', and to recover the Lawrence who depicted the lives of those who exist outside the 'iconography of the nation'. Indeed, a reading and discussion of these playscripts in modern urban Britain; a cross-cultural casting of the Eastwood dramas; or even radically rewritten versions which updated the characters and setting, might highlight the ways in which, for example, the day-to-day experience of the Asian-Muslim working-class woman is today often just as circumscribed, and obfuscated in public and political discourse, as the realm of the collier's wife in Lawrence's time.

As an Iranian woman myself, I find that the themes of *The Widowing of Mrs Holroyd* exert a particular fascination. There are aspects of the Holroyd's marriage, with its breakdown of traditional roles of husband and wife and the implications of Lizzie's social aspirations on her marriage to Charlie, which connect with the changing dynamics of society and culture experienced by those from my home country. In recent years, the number of women entering university in Iran has increased as female students currently occupy 60 per cent of university seats. A natural outcome of this rise in education has been the entrance of women into a variety of different fields of employment (with 30 per cent of women listed as wage earners by the International Labour Organization in the late 2000s compared with 12 per cent prior to the revolution).[4] As a result, some women have gained relative financial independence, and the role of the husband as the sole provider is increasingly undermined. This financial independence and education means that many of such women, similar to Lizzie, are now searching for much more than just a provider and protector in a husband, hence the rising age of marriage amongst the university-educated female population.[5] In Iran, the traditional family structure is still in the process of being refigured in order to accommodate for women working outside the home, something which often continues to cause tension for many couples. In addition, for women who can financially support themselves without a husband, imagining a means of escape from a marriage in which they are unhappy becomes logistically easier, hence the current rise of divorce in the country.

To me, then, there feels something very familiar about the way that the main characters of *The Widowing of Mrs Holroyd* seek to redefine their roles and responsibilities. Lizzie's husband Charlie, for example, is frustrated by Lizzie's lack of respect which, he feels, undermines his status as the 'man' of the house, asking: 'Do you think I'm a dog in the house, an' not a man, do you[?]' (79). Charlie is unable to play the traditional role of provider because of a major issue in their marriage: the fact that Lizzie has inherited money from her uncle. Charlie repeatedly refers to the money and claims that this inheritance has instilled a sense of superiority in Lizzie: 'You think you're something, since your uncle left you that money' (79). Charlie then uses his physical strength to reinforce his authority in the house and regain some of the power and the sense of masculinity lost as a result of Lizzie's relative financial independence. Charlie bangs his fist on the table in scene two as he insists: 'We'll see who's master i' this house. I tell you, I'm going to put a stop to it' (79). Thus this loss of the role of sole breadwinner and possessor of money in the relationship and its implications for Charlie's sense of masculinity has influenced his violent and reckless behaviour. Charlie attempts to reinforce his role as the man of the house through his physical strength and also seeks to regain his lost sense of self-respect by pursuing women other than Lizzie.

Blackmore, by contrast, may have the higher social status of electrician ('He's a gentleman, he is' (83)), but he enters a relationship with Lizzie that allows her to take a more active role in the relationship. Blackmore is five years younger than her, admits 'I don't know anything about love' (89), and is willing to allow Lizzie to direct the relationship in order to form a bond in which she also feels happy and comfortable. In scene one, Lawrence presents us with the image of the couple folding the sheets together (67), with Lizzie giving Blackmore orders as she hands him over sheets to fold and Blackmore then using housework as a means to extend his intimacy with Lizzie. When Charlie arrives home injured, it is Blackmore who cleans his face, in a premonition of the washing that Lizzie will do at the end of the play. Blackmore's attitude towards housework is refreshing and pleasing to Lizzie. She concludes that Blackmore is 'different from most men' (69), although with a typical Lawrentian ambiguity we might wonder whether Blackmore's joking confession that 'I had to drink three whiskies' (82) and his personal jealousy of Charlie ('Why should *he* have you – and I've never had anything' (91)) mean that he is really all that different from her husband.

If the men of the play are struggling to reconceive ideas of masculinity, then the idea that female identities might be fixed and unchanging is also brought into question. Lizzie, of course, is actively seeking a new way of living. But even the grandmother in the play, although ostensibly the figure who endorses unchanging and traditional gender boundaries, is revealed to be someone who embraces a certain fluidity of identity. This character, Charlie's mother, insists that a woman must be aware of her responsibility to manage the home and to provide a peaceful environment for her husband, asking: 'what man wouldn't leave a woman that allowed him to live on sufferance in the house with her, when he was bringing the money home?' (99). Consequently, according to the grandmother, a husband's role as a provider for his family obliges the woman to complete submission to his will. Yet this grandmother is herself conscious of the way that modes of female behaviour might be, in Richard Schechner's famous terms, examples of 'restored behaviour'. She enters the stage, inspecting the house in Lizzie's absence, and then '*puts on*' a sorrowful expression as soon as she hears Lizzie approaching, consciously adopting the role of a concerned mother who is worried about her son's well-being (97). She is therefore quick to adopt the pose that society expects from her, yet she evidently appreciates that there are alternatives: indeed, the grandmother's acknowledgement that a husband requires 'a bit of coaxing and managing' (99) perhaps suggests that – despite all her statements to the contrary – the real power in a marriage lies with the woman. She also admits to Lizzie that she too has suffered as a result of Charlie's behaviour: 'Charlie's been a handful of trouble. He made my heart ache once or twice afore you had him, and he's made it ache many, many's the time since' (98).

By the end of the play, Lizzie has therefore discovered an unlikely affinity with this mother-in-law. Earlier in the script Lizzie had complained of her husband Charlie that he was little more than an insensate 'brute' (83), and that, 'You can't *get* anywhere with him. There's just his body and nothing else' (92). But by the close of the drama, when Charlie is found dead, the grandmother admits that she has experience of something very similar, revealing that: 'when I waked his father up and told him, he sat up in bed staring over his whiskers, and said should he come up? But when I'd managed to find the shirt and things, he was still in bed. You don't know what it is to live with a man that has no feeling' (109).

Charlie's brute nature has, ultimately, followed the example of his own father, who prefers to stay in bed (presumably asleep) upon the news of his son's death. Thus, although Lizzie has argued with her mother-in-law in the earlier parts of the play, the drama ends with them washing the body together, in an act of comradeship that arises from their newly discovered appreciation of one another's struggles.

It is at this point in the play that Lizzie is most comfortable to reveal her feelings to Charlie and speak honestly to him. As Lizzie washes Charlie, in a tragic monologue she begins to tell him: 'Oh – I can't bear it, for you. Why couldn't I do anything for you? The children's father – my dear – I wasn't good to you. But you shouldn't have done this to me' (108). This scene is reminiscent to me of Atiq Rahimi's novel, *The Patience Stone* (2010), which is a monologue of an Afghan woman speaking to her husband as she cares for him while he remains in a vegetative state as a result of a shot to his neck. Similar to Lizzie, now that her headstrong husband is without an option but to listen, this unnamed woman begins to speak unguardedly and truthfully with him. She begins with similar feelings of guilt as those demonstrated by Lizzie, before gaining the strength to analyse her situation and the injustice she feels to have been committed against her. In *The Widowing of Mrs Holroyd*, it is left to the audience to wonder about the manner in which Lizzie's feelings may have changed if a longer opportunity presented itself for her to continue speaking to Charlie without interruption. Khaled Hosseini describes *The Patience Stone*'s greatest achievement as 'giving voice', and I would argue that Lawrence accomplishes a similar effect in *The Widowing of Mrs Holroyd*.[6]

After all, *The Widowing of Mrs Holroyd* is not simply a melodramatic portrayal of the victimization of a woman at the hands of a cruel and domineering husband. It is a more intricate and nuanced analysis of a marriage formed as a result of necessity rather than personal compatibility and may, as a result, speak particularly to those members of modern Britain whose cultural or religious traditions facilitate similar arrangements. Indeed, despite the arguments of the married couple, Lizzie and Charlie do demonstrate rare glimpses of caring for one another, albeit each in a language incomprehensible to each other. As a result they are trapped in a cycle of misunderstandings, acts of revenge and emotions left unexpressed. For instance, Lizzie immediately defends her husband when his potential replacement, Blackmore, implies Charlie is 'getting fat': she insists that Charlie is 'big made – he has a big frame' (82). When Charlie confronts a rat she also, with comic protectiveness, urges, 'Don't, he'll fly at you [...] they're poisonous' (72). In return, Charlie demonstrates his affection towards Lizzie in his own small ways, for example, after the incident with the paper-bonnet girls, Charlie is 'ashamed but defiant, withal anxious to apologize' (78).

Lawrence is able to draw such nuances through the realist form that he has chosen for the play, allowing the action to occur in a domestic space that places great emphasis on the dialogue between the characters. For me at least, this recalls current trends in Iranian cinema, which is also heavily reliant on dialogue-based scenarios occurring in a limited number of locations, most often in the domestic space of family homes. Consequently, and similarly to Lawrence's drama, this allows the director to critique and analyse contemporary social issues. A celebrated instance of such an outlook is Asghar Farhadi's Oscar-winning film A Separation, in which intense dialogue between its characters depicts the lives of two couples and analyses their internal family interactions and also their relationship with one another. The film uses these depictions in order to critique and analyse specific Iranian cultural issues such as the class system and also male and female interaction. A Separation begins with a couple requesting a divorce based on irreconcilable differences. Simin has boldly placed an ultimatum for her husband to choose between migrating abroad with her or a divorce. In this way, Simin's refusal to submit to her husband's will and her determination and aspirations for change has left her marriage at breaking point. Thus, if Lawrence's plays gained widespread critical attention in Britain during the 1960s in part because of the way in which they chimed with the social and legislative reordering of that decade, The Widowing of Mrs Holroyd continues to have the potential to speak to other diasporic communities in Britain as new cultural changes and transformations are enacted.

Do such affinities mean that we can expect to see a rash of Lawrence productions in Iran or amongst Iranians in Britain? Well, perhaps not. For one thing, there does often exist a mutual cultural suspicion at present between the Iranian world and the sphere of Anglo-American influence. But the temporal and spatial boundaries of modernity have increasingly been questioned by scholars in recent years, with modernist literature such as that of Lawrence developing quite unexpected echoes across quite different time frames and geographies.[7] Lawrence's own move from working-class Eastwood to become one of the pre-eminent literary figures of the mid-twentieth-century Anglosphere, means that his life and work may still provide a set of powerful exemplars for those communities who may have little economic and political power but whose members are determined to accrue, in Pierre Bourdieu's terms, various forms of cultural capital.

Ultimately, while Lawrence refuses to provide solutions to the conflicts in *The Widowing of Mrs Holroyd* and presents his characters as caught in cycles of repetitive behaviour, the act of depiction itself is significant. His drama shows lives as lived by the marginalized and thus provides an alternative to the dominant historical narrative, which fails to represent such groups adequately, as has been widely discussed in post-colonial theory. For instance, subaltern studies initially aimed to use neglected sources to provide an alternative history of nationalism in India, countering the dominant narrative in which the masses were not considered as active participants or instigators of action. Edward Said, in his introduction to *Selected Subaltern Studies*, connects the work of such scholars to a wider movement for offering voice to subordinate groups beyond categories defined by class and race, and here Said specifically includes women: 'as an alternative discourse then, the work of the subalterns can be seen as an analogue of all those recent attempts in the West and throughout the rest of the world to articulate the hidden or suppressed accounts of numerous groups, – women, minorities, disadvantaged or dispossessed groups, refugees, exiles, etc'.[8] Lawrence may have included terrible racist and misogynist comments in some of his work, yet in his 'Eastwood Trilogy' he attempts to depict life as lived by the miners' wives in his home town, and so does offer a commendable model for emulation by those who wish to draw attention to such overlooked minorities. As with the industrial English midlands at the beginning of the twentieth century, there remain many marginalized groups in our current societies whose untold narratives require a voice. Lawrence's drama might just encourage us to look beyond the theatre, and to examine other lives that are outside the hegemonic modes of representation and discussion.

CONCLUSION

In 1953, the BBC Home Service broadcast a radio version of *The Widowing of Mrs Holroyd*, and the *Sunday Times* declared that although Lawrence had once been a revolutionary, the writer's time had now passed. The newspaper's critic, Maurice Wiggin, commented: 'what would I not give for a time-machine to enable me to hear it for the first time in 1914! The BBC can safely go ahead digging up Lawrence; a rich vein of ore, certified no longer radioactive.'[1]

Frieda Lawrence read those words in the newspaper, and responded with fury, asking:

> Who 'certifies' that he is no longer radioactive? That is wishful thinking.
> Young men, very young men, come to me to tell me how reading him
> has changed them, given their lives a new direction and meaning.
> Lawrence will be read when a great many more of us will be under the
> daisies.[2]

Frieda's viewpoint would be endorsed in the following decade, when the British theatre revived Lawrence's reputation as a playwright and a Butler-Act generation of directors, performers and critics found a new connection with Lawrence's dramas. Peter Gill was responsible for promoting Lawrence's 'Eastwood Trilogy' through skilfully realized productions in the late 1960s, with writers such as Stephen Lowe – and later William Ivory – then ensuring that Lawrence's theatrical influence endured in a range of new dramatic scripts. As Soudabeh Ananisarab argues, Lawrence's plays may have an even longer reach into the twenty-first century, as they potentially challenge the comfortable assumptions and horizons of the bourgeois theatre-goer, and ask still-pertinent questions about the representation of marginalized groups.

It is tempting to imagine how literary history may have been different if Lawrence had achieved, during his own early career, this kind of theatrical acclaim and admiration. What would have happened if Granville Barker had successfully produced Lawrence's drama in 1911, if Iden Payne had done so in 1912, or if the Stage Society had taken a punt in 1913? Would there have been more theatre scripts from Lawrence, and would these have been achieved at the expense of his novel writing? Of course, the answers to such a question remain in the realm of historical counterfactuals.[3] But what we can say, with some certainty, is that Lawrence maintained an interest in drama and acting throughout his life, and that such an interest is consistently manifested in his overall body of work.

Of his plays, only the 'Eastwood Trilogy' has maintained a presence in the theatrical repertoire during recent years, even though Lawrence himself felt desperately keen to see his other scripts on the stage as well. Ultimately, it may be that, in order to thrive in the playhouse, the dramas from outside that trilogy require the kind of careful reshaping by actors and directors who appreciate the requirements of the professional world of theatre, a world that Lawrence himself tried, and failed, to know. After all, Lawrence was always refreshing unfussy about having those scripts edited and rearranged for that purpose, acknowledging that even some of his best playwriting 'wants weeding out a bit' (*Letters* I, 500–501). His advice to potential theatrical collaborators was: 'My idea of a play is that any actor should have the liberty to alter as much as he likes – the author only gives the leading suggestion' (*Letters* III, 509–510).

The plays from outside the 'Eastwood Trilogy', then, may be relatively unknown, but it is nonetheless apparent that, in recent times, Lawrence has become extremely familiar to audiences through drama. Indeed, these days, many people who know Lawrence's work will often have primarily encountered the texts not on the page, but being spoken by actors. Throughout the late twentieth and early twenty-first centuries, as William Ivory attests, Lawrence's novels have proven particularly appealing to screenwriters; and perhaps we should not be surprised by this, as Lawrence's achievements in prose were always informed by an admirably enquiring and experimental dramatic sensibility. When we look at Lawrence's oeuvre, we find that his well-known novels return to performance again and again. As Hans-Wilhelm Schwarze and John Worthen put it, much of the author's broader work 'was always and essentially dramatic'.[4]

In conclusion, then, the young Lawrence showed an impressive ability to craft plays; the mature writer channelled that theatrical sensibility into his novel writing; and throughout his career Lawrence showed an engagement with dramatic experiment. The sex described in his novels may remain the single best-known thing about the writer, but even these descriptions consistently depend upon Lawrence's thoughts about theatre. In the playhouse itself, Lawrence faced great disappointment in staging his work during his own lifetime, but his posthumous dramatic legacy has been far more impressive. Not only did the productions of the 'Eastwood Trilogy' in the 1960s receive much praise, but as the contributors to this volume have shown, Lawrence has continued to provoke theatrical inspiration and emulation in subsequent decades. His own plays still enjoy varying fortunes on the British stage, with some of the scripts remaining almost entirely unperformed. Yet, when Lawrence's dramas do appear, as Michael Billington said of *The Widowing of Mrs Holroyd* in 2014, they may nonetheless catch 'you by the throat and [make] you wish Lawrence's palpable dramatic gifts had been encouraged'.[5]

LAWRENCE'S THEATRE:
A TIMELINE

1885   D.H. Lawrence born in Eastwood on 11 September.

1907   Lawrence publishes his first work, the short story 'A Prelude', about an amateur theatrical performance staged on Christmas Eve in the English midlands.

1909   Lawrence writes his first play, *A Collier's Friday Night*. The play will not be performed until March 1939, when it is presented by the Morely Adult School Players, Yorkshire (an amateur group), and will not be published until 1934 (by Martin Secker in London).

1910   Lawrence drafts the first version of his play *The Widowing of Mrs Holroyd*, which he will rework in 1913.

1910–11 Lawrence writes *The Merry-go-Round*, a play that will be first performed in 1973 at the Royal Court Theatre, and first published in 1941 in the *Virginia Quarterly Review* (Winter 1941, pp.1–44).

1912   Lawrence writes *The Married Man* in the spring, a play that will eventually be premiered onstage in 1997, by students at the Royal Academy of Dramatic Art, and first published in 1940 in the *Virginia Quarterly Review* (Fall 1940, pp.523–547). In autumn 1912 Lawrence also writes *The Fight For Barbara*, a play that will be premiered in 1967 at the Mermaid Theatre, Blackfriars, and first published in 1933 as a shortened version under the name *Keeping Barbara* (in *The Argosy*, December 1933, pp.68–90).

1913   In January, Lawrence's play *The Daughter-in-Law* is written. It will not be premiered onstage until 1967 at the Traverse Theatre in Edinburgh, and will only appear in print in 1965 in *The Complete Plays of D.H. Lawrence* (published by Heinemann in London). In 1913 Lawrence also writes an essay about watching drama in Italy: the essay is entitled 'The Theatre' and appears in the *English Review* in September 1913, and in revised form in the 1916 volume of essays, *Twilight in Italy*.

1914 Lawrence publishes a play for the first time: a revised version of the script he first wrote in 1910, *The Widowing of Mrs Holroyd* (published by Mitchell Kennerley in New York).

1916 First staged production of a Lawrence play, when *The Widowing of Mrs Holroyd* is performed at the Los Angeles Little Theatre.

1918 Lawrence writes his play *Touch and Go*, and revises it the following year. It will be first performed in 1973 by the amateur Questors Theatre, Ealing, and first published in 1920 (by Thomas Seltzer in New York).

1920 An amateur group, the Altrincham Garrick Society, gives the British stage premiere of Lawrence's playwriting, performing *The Widowing of Mrs Holroyd* near Manchester.

1924 Lawrence writes the incomplete play *Altitude* as well as three non-fictional essays about the ritual dramas of the Native Americans of the South-western United States: 'Indians and Entertainment', 'The Dance of the Sprouting Corn', and 'The Hopi Snake Dance' (the first of which first appeared in the *New York Times Magazine*, the other two in *Theatre Arts Monthly*).

1925 Lawrence begins his play *Noah's Flood*, which remains uncompleted, but he does complete his play *David*, which will be first performed in 1927 at the Regent Theatre, London, and first published in 1926 (by Knopf in New York).

1926–27 The Stage Society in London gives the British professional premieres of Lawrence's plays *The Widowing of Mrs Holroyd* and *David*.

1928 Lawrence writes his last complete story, 'The Blue Moccasins', about an amateur theatrical performance staged on Christmas Eve in the English midlands.

1930 Lawrence dies on 2 March in Vence, France, at the age of 44.

1960 Penguin books publishes Lawrence's novel *Lady Chatterley's Lover* and the company is tried, and found not guilty, under the Obscene Publications Act.

1961 An edited version of *The Widowing of Mrs Holroyd* is televised by ITA.

1965 Publication of Lawrence's *Complete Plays* by Heinemann.

1968 Peter Gill stages the celebrated 'Eastwood Trilogy' at the Royal Court (following his successful staging of the individual plays *A Collier's Friday Night* in 1965, and *The Daughter-in-Law* in 1967).

1999 Definitive edition of the plays published by Cambridge University Press.

NOTES

Foreword

1. Lawrence, 'The Old Idea of Sacrifice', in *The Poems*, ed. by Christopher Pollnitz, 2 vols (Cambridge: Cambridge Univeristy Press, 2013), I, 586.
2. Lawrence, *The Letters of D.H. Lawrence*, ed. by James Boulton et al., 8 vols (Cambridge: Cambridge University Press, 1979–2001), I, 509.
3. Lawrence, *The Letters of D.H. Lawrence*, I, 509.
4. Lawrence, *Lady Chatterley's Lover and A Propos of 'Lady Chatterley's Lover'*, ed. by Michael Squires (Cambridge: Cambridge University Press, 2002), p.95.
5. Lawrence, *Lady Chatterley's Lover and A Propos of 'Lady Chatterley's Lover'*, p.5.
6. Shaw quoted by Esmé Percy, 'Bernard Shaw: A Personal Memory', *The Listener*, 26 May 1955, pp.929–931, p.929.
7. Lawrence, *The Plays*, ed. by Hans-Wilhelm Schwarze and John Worthen (Cambridge: Cambridge University Press, 1999), p.312.

Overview

1. Lawrence, *The Letters of D.H. Lawrence*, ed. by James Boulton et al., 8 vols (Cambridge: Cambridge University Press, 1979–2001), I, 477. Further references to this publication will be given parenthetically in the text.
2. Dollimore, *Sexual Dissidence: Augustine to Wilde, Freud to Foucault* (Oxford: Oxford University Press, 1991), p.268.
3. Clarke, 'Dialogue and Dialect in Lawrence's Colliery Plays', *The Journal of the D.H. Lawrence Society* (2001), 39–61 (p.39). Becket, *The Complete Critical Guide to D.H. Lawrence* (London: Routledge, 2004), p.37.
4. Seabrook, *Pauperland: Poverty and the Poor in Britain* (London: Hurst, 2014), p.204.
5. Jones, *Chavs: The Demonization of the Working Class*, rev. 2nd edn (London: Verso, 2012).

Introduction

1. Lawrence, *The Complete Plays of D.H. Lawrence* (London: Heinemann, 1965).
2. 'Mr. D.H. Lawrence: Novelist and Poet', *Manchester Guardian*, 4 March 1930, p.12.

Notes

3. 'Mr. D.H. Lawrence: A Writer of Genius', *The Times*, 4 March 1930, p.11.

4. Lowell, 'A Voice in Our Wilderness: D.H. Lawrence's Unheeded Message "to Blind Reactionaries and Fussy, Discontented Agitators"', *New York Times Book Review*, 22 August 1920, Section 3, p.7, reprinted in Lowell, *Poetry and Poets: Essays* (Boston and New York: Houghton Mifflin, 1930), pp.175–186.

5. Aldington, *D.H. Lawrence: An Appreciation* (Harmondsworth: Penguin, 1950), p.30.

6. In 1922 Aldington translated Goldoni's *Le Donne di Buon' Umore*, and Lawrence was invited, but declined, to write the introduction (*Letters*, IV, 242). Lawrence did later mention 'the Goldoni plays' in *Lady Chatterley's Lover*, but Arthur Symons ended up writing the introduction for Aldington. See Lawrence, *Lady Chatterley's Lover and A Propos of 'Lady Chatterley's Lover'*, p.258; and Carlo Goldoni, *The Good-Humoured Ladies*, trans. by Richard Aldington (London: Beaumont, 1922).

7. Lawrence, *The Complete Plays of D.H. Lawrence* (London: Heinemann, 1965), p.222.

8. 'Original Play by Lawrence Revived', *The Times*, 28 January 1967, p.13.

9. Worthen, 'Towards a New Version of D.H. Lawrence's "The Daughter-in-Law": Scholarly Edition or Play Text?', *The Yearbook of English Studies*, 29 (1999), 231–246 (p.237).

10. O'Casey, 'A Miner's Dream of Home', *New Statesman*, 28 July 1934, p.124.

11. O'Casey, 'A Miner's Dream', p.124.

12. The first quote was remembered by Esmé Percy, 'Bernard Shaw: A Personal Memory', *The Listener*, 26 May 1955, pp.929–931, p.929. The second quote appears in Shaw, 'Mr. Bernard Shaw on D.H. Lawrence and "The Savage Pilgrimage"', *Time and Tide*, 6 August 1932, p.863. Shaw also felt fascinated by the performances of Lawrence's personal life, asking Frieda, 'Is it true that you broke a plate over your husband's head?' Frieda Lawrence, 'Lunch with Mr and Mrs Bernard Shaw', in *Frieda Lawrence: The Memoirs and Correspondence*, ed. by E.W. Tedlock (London: Heinemann, 1961), pp.147–148, p.147.

13. Eliot, 'London Letter', *Dial*, 73 (1922), 329–331 (p.331).

14. See R.P. Draper, ed., *D.H. Lawrence: The Critical Heritage* (London: Routledge, 1997), p.298.

15. For the abandoned Secker plan see Worthen, 'Towards a New Version', p.234.

16. *My Son's My Son* premiered in London's Playhouse Theatre in London in May 1936, and first appeared at Stockholm's Blancheteatren in March 1937. See Marko Modiano, 'An Early Swedish Stage Production of D.H. Lawrence's *The Daughter-in-Law*', *D.H. Lawrence Review*, 17 (1984), 49–59. In Greenwood's version, the matriarch shows pleasure at having an illegitimate grandchild and decides to provide financial support. See University of Salford Library, Greenwood and Lawrence, *My Son's My Son*, Prompt Copy, WGC/1/4/1.

17. D.B., 'Old Woman Dominates D.H. Lawrence Play', *Evening Standard*, 27 May 1936, p.10.

18. See Schwarze and Worthen, 'Introduction', in D.H. Lawrence, *The Plays*, ed. by Hans-Wilhelm Schwarze and John Worthen (Cambridge: Cambridge University Press, 1999), pp.xxiii–cxxiv.

19. F.R. Leavis, *D.H. Lawrence: Novelist* (London: Chatto and Windus, 1962 [1955]), p.107.

20. Richard Storer, *F.R. Leavis* (Abingdon: Routledge, 2009), p.82.

21. Leavis, *D.H. Lawrence: Novelist*, p.159, p.161.

22. Leavis, *Thought, Words and Creativity: Art and Thought in Lawrence* (London: Chatto and Windus, 1976), p.32.

23. Leavis, *Thought*, p.56. The pieces first appeared in *Theatre Arts Monthly*, VIII (July 1924), 447–457 and *Theatre Arts Monthly*, VIII (December 1924), 836–860. They were later published in the volume *Mornings in Mexico* (London: Martin Secker, 1927), which is where Leavis read them.

24. Philip Carter, 'Lady Chatterley's Lover Trial', *Oxford Dictionary of National Biography*. Available online: http://www.oxforddnb.com/templates/theme-print. jsp?articleid=101234 [accessed 15 September 2014].

25. Lawrence, *The Plays*, ed. by Hans-Wilhelm Schwarze and John Worthen (Cambridge: Cambridge University Press, 1999), pp.49–50. Further references to the Cambridge *Plays* will be given parenthetically in the text.

26. Granada (ITA), 23 March 1961, dir. Claude Whatham.

27. Eric Shorter, 'Lawrence's First Play Well Acted', in Nottingham University Manuscripts and Special Collections, La-Z-13/3/223.

28. Wardle, 'Lawrence Play with a Strindberg Touch', *The Times*, 17 March 1967, p.12.

29. Williams, 'Introduction', in Lawrence, *Three Plays* (Harmondsworth: Penguin, 1969) pp.7–14, p.8, p.14.

30. [Andor Gomme], 'Drama', *Times Literary Supplement*, 6 March 1969, p.253.

31. Billington, 'Fine Way with a Lawrence Play', *The Times*, 8 March 1968, p.12. Billington, 'The Merry-go-Round at the Royal Court', *Guardian*, 8 November 1973, p.12.

32. Sklar, *The Plays of D.H. Lawrence: A Biographical and Critical Study* (London: Vision, 1975), p.262.

33. Indeed, Osborne's playwriting was advertised on a full-page of the 1968 Royal Court programme.

34. Peter Lewis, 'D.H. Lawrence's Own Painful Love Story', *Daily Mail*, August 1967, from Nottingham University Manuscripts and Special Collections, La-Z-13/3/283.

35. Toril Moi, *Henrik Ibsen and the Birth of Modernism* (Oxford: Oxford University Press, 2006), p.302.

36. Patricia D. Denison, ed., *John Osborne: A Casebook* (New York: Routledge, 2007), p.xxviii.

Notes

37. 'Fine Way with a Lawrence Play', *The Times*, 8 March 1968, p.12.

38. Of the two, *The Fight for Barbara* is more performed, having appeared at London's Mermaid Theatre in 1967, and at New York's Nat Horne Theater in 1978.

39. Kermode, *Lawrence* (London: Fontana/Collins, 1973), pp.129–130.

40. Lodge, *Lives in Writing: Essays* (London: Harvill Secker, 2014), p.156.

41. Quote about *St Mawr* made in c1930, printed in James Knowlson, *Damned to Fame* (New York: Touchstone, 1997), p.122. Jacqueline Thomas, 'Happy Days: Beckett's Rescript of Lady Chatterley's Lover', *Modern Drama*, 41:4 (1998), 623–634 (pp.631–632).

42. Lawrence, *Lady Chatterley's Lover and A Propos of 'Lady Chatterley's Lover'*, p.246.

43. Beckett, *Trilogy* (London: Calder, 1994), p.56.

44. Fedder, *The Influence of D.H. Lawrence on Tennessee Williams* (London: Mouton, 1966).

45. Quoted in Williams, *The Collected Poems of Tennessee Williams*, ed. by David Roessel and Nicholas Moschovakis, rev. edn (New York: New Directions, 2002), p.224.

46. Williams, *Tennessee Williams: Notebooks*, ed. by Margaret Bradham Thornton (New Haven, Conn.: Yale University Press, 2006), p.162.

47. See Gerri Kimber, 'The Night of the Zeppelin', *Times Literary Supplement*, 5 September 2014, pp.14–15.

48. See Gilbert Debusscher, 'Creative Rewriting: European and American Influences on the Dramas of Tennessee Williams', in *The Cambridge Companion to Tennessee Williams*, ed. by Matthew Roudané (Cambridge: Cambridge University Press, 1997), pp.167–188.

49. Williams, 'Preface', *I Rise in Flame, Cried the Phoenix* (Norfolk, Conn.: New Directions, 1951), p.6.

50. Williams, *I Rise*, p.19.

51. Williams, *I Rise*, pp.27–28.

52. Frieda Lawrence, 'A Note by Frieda Lawrence', in *I Rise in Flame*, p.8.

53. Irving Wardle, 'Pay Day for Young Lawrence', *The Times*, 1 March 1968, p.12.

54. Bennett, *Alan Bennett: Plays One* (London: Faber, 1996), p.276.

55. Bennett, *Plays One*, p.310.

56. Millett, *Sexual Politics* (London: Virago, 1993 [1970]), p.277.

57. Millett, p.292.

58. For the references to actresses, see Lawrence, *Aaron's Rod*, ed. by Maria Kalnins (Cambridge: Cambridge University Press, 1988), p.79; Lawrence, 'Delilah and Mr. Bircumshaw', in *Love Among the Haystacks and Other Stories*, ed. by John Worthen (Cambridge: Cambridge University Press, 1987), pp.143–151, p.146; Lawrence, *Sons and Lovers*, ed. by Helen Baron and Carl Baron (Cambridge:

Cambridge University Press, 1992), p.126. Lawrence, 'Women are So Cocksure', in *Late Essays and Articles*, ed. by James Boulton (Cambridge: Cambridge University Press, 2004), pp.116–118, p.117.

59. Lawrence, *Sea and Sardinia*, ed. by Mara Kalnins (Cambridge: Cambridge University Press, 1997), p.188, p.190.

60. Fernihough, 'Introduction', in D.H. Lawrence, *The Rainbow*, ed. by Mark Kinkead-Weekes (Harmondsworth: Penguin, 1995), pp.xiii–xxxiv, p.xiv. Harrison, 'Meat Lust: An Unpublished Manuscript by D.H. Lawrence', *Times Literary Supplement*, 29 March 2013, p.15.

61. Lawrence, 'The Theatre' [B], in *Twilight in Italy and Other Essays*, ed. by Paul Eggert (Cambridge: Cambridge University Press, 1994), pp.133–153, p.141.

62. Rosenthal, 'Lawrence the Playwright', in *The Widowing of Mrs Holroyd* theatre programme (London: Orange Tree, 2014), pp.8–9, p.9.

63. See Dramatis Personae in *William Shakespeare: The Complete Works*, ed. by Stanley Wells et al. (Oxford: Clarendon Press, 1988), p.654. Shaw, *Saint Joan*, ed. by Dan H. Laurence (Harmondsworth: Penguin, 1957), p.160.

64. Wallis and Shepherd, *Studying Plays*, 3rd edn (London: Bloomsbury, 2010), pp.112–113.

65. Christopher Innes, *Modern British Drama: The Twentieth Century* (Cambridge: Cambridge University Press, 2002), p.71.

66. Hoggart, *The Uses of Literacy* (Harmondsworth: Penguin, 1969 [1957]), p.49.

67. See, for example, Terry Eagleton, *The English Novel: An Introduction* (Oxford: Blackwell, 2005), pp.270–271.

68. Philip French, 'A Major Miner Dramatist', *New Statesman*, 22 March 1968, p.390.

69. Indeed, the theatre programme for *The Daughter-in-Law* included a glossary when staged by the Royal Court in 1967, by the Canadian Centaur company in 1975 and by the Nottingham Playhouse in 1980. See 'Material Related to Stage Productions of Works by D.H. Lawrence', Nottingham University Manuscripts and Special Collections, For-3/1.

70. Lawrence, 'Introduction to *Mastro-Don Gesualdo*, by Giovanni Verga', in *Introductions and Reviews*, ed. by N.H. Reeve and John Worthen (Cambridge: Cambridge University Press, 2005), pp.145–156, p.148.

71. Jones, *Chavs*, p.6.

72. 'Items Related to the Royal Academy of Dramatic Art Production of *The Daughter-in-Law*', Nottingham University Manuscripts and Special Collections, For-L-3/1/3/5/1.

73. '*Collier's Friday Night*: 1965–1992', Nottingham University Manuscripts and Special Collections, For-L-3/1/2/5/2.

74. Stuart Jeffries, 'The Hole Truth: Television', *Guardian*, 16 October 1995, p.A9.

75. Warren Roberts and Paul Poplawski, *A Bibliography of D.H. Lawrence*, 3rd edn (Cambridge: Cambridge University Press, 2001), p.24.

Notes

76. '20 Questions With…Anne-Marie Duff', The *Stage*, 9 September 2002. Available online: http://www.whatsonstage.com/west-end-theatre/news/09-2002/20-questions-withanne-marie-duff_27302.html [accessed 15 September 2014].

77. Katie Galbraith, 'The Daughter-in-Law', *Stage*, 14 March 2013. Available online: http://www.thestage.co.uk/reviews/review.php/38321/the-daughter-in-law [accessed 15 September 2014].

78. Hickling, 'The Daughter-in-Law – Review', *Guardian*, 5 March 2013. Available online: http://www.theguardian.com/stage/2013/mar/05/the-daughter-in-law-review [accessed 15 September 2014].

79. Clapp, 'The Widowing of Mrs Holroyd Review', 14 September 2014. Available online: http://www.theguardian.com/stage/2014/sep/14/widowing-of-mrs-holroyd-review-orange-tree-richmond-dh-lawrence [accessed 21 October 2014]. Cavendish, 'Bring the Classics Back to the Theatre', *Daily Telegraph*, 16 September 2014. Available online: http://www.telegraph.co.uk/culture/theatre/11099518/Bring-the-classics-back-to-the-theatre.html [accessed 21 October 2014].

80. Spenser, 'A Long, Bad Friday with D.H. Lawrence', *Daily Telegraph*, 7 July 1994, p.16.

81. Spenser, 'Proof that D.H. Lawrence was a Better Playwright than a Novelist', *Daily Telegraph*, 8 September 2006. Available online: http://www.telegraph.co.uk/culture/theatre/drama/3655141/Proof-that-DH-Lawrence-was-a-better-playwright-than-a-novelist.html [accessed 15 September 2014].

82. Nightingale, *Great Moments in the Theatre* (London: Oberon, 2012), p.140.

83. See Wallis and Shepherd, *Studying Plays*, 1st edn (London: Arnold, 1998), pp.100–101, p.132; 2nd edn (London: Arnold, 2002), pp.105, p.110, p.113, p.115, p.157; 3rd edn (London: Bloomsbury, 2010), p.108, p.112, p.159.

84. Sagar, *D.H. Lawrence: Life into Art* (Harmondsworth: Penguin, 1985), p.61.

85. Lawrence, 'Just Back from the Snake Dance', in *Mornings in Mexico and Other Essays*, ed. by Virginia Crosswhite Hyde (Cambridge: Cambridge University Press, 2009), pp.183–187, p.187. He later rewrote the piece as 'The Hopi Snake Dance', a less satirical piece, after his white American host felt offended by what he had written.

86. Lawrence, 'Studies in Classic American Literature: First Version (1918–19)', in *Studies in Classic American Literature*, ed. by Ezra Greenspan, Lindeth Vasey and John Worthen (Cambridge: Cambridge University Press, 2003), pp.163–304, p.176.

Chapter 1

1. Ada Lawrence and G. Stuart Gelder, *Young Lorenzo: Early Life of D.H. Lawrence* (New York: Russell & Russell, 1966), p.13.

2. Worthen, *D.H. Lawrence: The Early Years 1885–1912* (Cambridge: Cambridge University Press, 1991), p.14.

3. Worthen, *Early Years*, pp.5–6.

4. Rev. A. Hervey, *Nottingham Theatre: The Warning!*, quoted by Robinson, 'The Performance of Anti-Theatrical Prejudice in a Provincial Victorian Town: Nottingham and its New Theatre Royal, 1865', *Nineteenth Century Theatre and Film*, 35:2 (2008), 10–28 (p.14). Clement Clemance, *The Theatre, Considered Chiefly in its Moral Aspects* (Nottingham: Burton, 1865), p.12.

5. 'Local and District News', *Eastwood and Kimberley Advertiser*, 6 February 1903, p.2.

6. Worthen, *Early Years*, p.23.

7. Leavis, 'Mr. Eliot and Lawrence', *Scrutiny*, 18:1 (1951), 66–73 (p.73). Leavis later recycled this phrase as the ringing conclusion to the introduction of *D.H. Lawrence: Novelist* (p.15).

8. Hopkin Hilton, *More Than One Life: A Nottinghamshire Childhood with D.H. Lawrence* (Phoenix Mill: Alan Sutton, 1993), p.23.

9. Hopkin Hilton, p.23.

10. Edward Nehls, *D.H. Lawrence: A Composite Biography*, 3 vols (Madison: University of Wisconsin Press, 1958), III, 746 n.90. Keith Sagar, *Life into Art*, p.34.

11. See Nottingham Central Library card-catalogue entry for 'Rayner, Sammy', and the description given by William Holbrooke in Nehls, III, 746.

12. Nehls, III, 746.

13. University of Kent at Canterbury, Frank Pettingell collection, *The Chilwell Ghost*, Harvester Code No. Cm21.

14. 'Shot, Hanged, and Stabbed: Adventures of a Notts. Actor', *Nottingham Evening Post*, 29 December 1934, p.7.

15. 'Shot, Hanged, and Stabbed: Adventures of a Notts. Actor', *Nottingham Evening Post*, 29 December 1934, p.7.

16. William Holbrooke, quoted in Nehls, III, 746.

17. Less than six miles up the road, Ripley's October horse-fair also featured regular 'dramar' of ghostly apparitions and 'blood-spilling'. 'Ripley October Fair', *Eastwood and Kimberley Advertiser*, 25 October 1895, p.4.

18. Lawrence, *The White Peacock*, ed. by Andrew Robertson (Cambridge: Cambridge University Press, 1983), pp.63–64.

19. Lawrence, *Kangaroo*, ed. by Bruce Steele (Cambridge: Cambridge University Press, 1994), p.230.

20. *Eastwood and Kimberley Advertiser*, 20 September 1895, p.5.

21. Hoggart, pp.27–28.

22. Hoggart, p.340.

23. Hoggart, p.340.

24. Lawrence, 'The Theatre' [A], in *Twilight in Italy*, pp.69–80, p.77.

Notes

25. Quoted by Worthen, *Early Years*, p.79.

26. Worthen, *Early Years*, p.111.

27. Jessie Chambers, *D.H. Lawrence: A Personal Record by E.T.* (London: Frank Cass, 1935), p.92.

28. *The Merry-go-Round* puts Job Arthur into a version of Portia's trial scene (183); *David* pictures the doomed King Saul torn between heaven and hell like Doctor Faustus (503–504); and *The Widowing of Mrs Holroyd* includes the Shakespearean consolation 'Prithee, prithee, Lizzie' (110).

29. Chambers, p.94.

30. Chambers, p.42, p.108.

31. Hopkin Hilton, p.23.

32. 'Amusements', *Nottingham Evening Post*, 26 February 1903, p.2. Chambers, p.109.

33. Chambers, p.109.

34. Chambers, pp.61–62.

35. 'Amusements in Nottingham', *Nottingham Evening Post*, 29 August 1905, p.3.

36. Chambers, p.108. Jessie also intriguingly refers to how she and Lawrence admired *Lorna Doone*, 'which we all re-enacted in fancy on our own Annesley Hills' (p.96).

37. 'Printed Programme for the University College Students' Association', Nottingham University Manuscripts and Special Collections, La-B225. The letter is printed by James Boulton, *Lawrence in Love* (Nottingham: Nottingham University, 1968), pp.173–174.

38. 'University College, Nottingham notebook of D.H. Lawrence', Nottingham University Manuscripts and Special Collections, La-L-1 (Essays), ff.23v–24.

39. 'University College, Nottingham notebook of D.H. Lawrence', Nottingham University Manuscripts and Special Collections, La-L-1 (Essays), ff.23v–24.

40. 'University College, Nottingham notebook of D.H. Lawrence', Nottingham University Manuscripts and Special Collections, La-L-1 (Essays), ff.16–17.

41. Boulton, *Lawrence in Love*, pp.173–174.

42. 'Autograph Poem by D.H. Lawrence, entitled "From a College Window", in University College Notebook', Nottingham University Manuscripts and Special Collections, La-L-2/7, f.75r.

43. 'Local and District News', *Eastwood and Kimberley Advertiser*, 24 April 1896, p.5. 'Local and District News', *Kimberley and Eastwood Advertiser*, 7 February 1902, p.2.

44. Lawrence, *The Poems*, I, 428.

45. See Worthen, 'Lawrence as Dramatist', in *The Cambridge Companion to D.H. Lawrence* (Cambridge: Cambridge University Press, 2001), pp.137–153, p.137.

46. See for example, Gāmini Salgādo, *D.H. Lawrence: 'Sons and Lovers': A Casebook* (London: Macmillan, 1969), p.12; or Brenda Maddox, *D.H. Lawrence: The Story of a Marriage* (New York: Simon and Schuster, 1994), p.33.

47. Chambers, p.30.

48. Ada Lawrence and Gelder, p.23.

49. Lawrence, *Sons and Lovers* (1992), p.31.

50. 'Local and District News', *Eastwood and Kimberley Advertiser*, 19 May 1899, p.2.

51. 'Local and District News', *Eastwood and Kimberley Advertiser*, 16 February 1900, p.2.

52. Ralph Louis Woods, ed., *A Second Treasury of the Familiar* (New York: Macmillan, 1950), p.144.

53. Gemini, 'Eastwood: II, Its Institutions', *Eastwood and Kimberley Advertiser*, 10 April 1903, p.3.

54. Quoted by Worthen, *Early Years*, p.110.

55. The Eastwood Amateur Dramatic Society performed sporadically between 1900 and 1902, giving versions of *Aunt Maxwell's Return*, and *The Lady of Lyons*, as well as their charity double-bill of *Honour Before Wealth* and *Popping the Question*, 21 February 1902, *Eastwood and Kimberley Advertiser*, p.2. 'Local and District News', *Eastwood and Kimberley Advertiser*, 14 February 1902, p.2. For the society's predecessor see 'Amateur Theatricals at Eastwood', *Eastwood and Kimberley Advertiser*, 20 December 1895, p.4.

56. 'Local and District News', *Eastwood and Kimberley Advertiser*, 14 February 1902, p.2.

57. The local newspaper reported, for example, that 'in Mr. Fred. Hanson, who is always of a humorous nature, this character [a page boy] found an excellent representative'. 'Amateur Theatricals at Eastwood', *Eastwood and Kimberley Advertiser*, 20 December 1895, p.4.

58. The musician had the Lawrentian name of J. Birkin. See 'Fancy Dress Ball', *Eastwood and Kimberley Advertiser*, 29 December 1899, p.2.

59. 'Fancy Dress Ball at Eastwood', *Eastwood and Kimberley Advertiser*, 28 February 1896, p.4.

60. Lawrence, *Sons and Lovers* (1992), p.75.

61. Lawrence, *Sons and Lovers* (1992), pp.75–77.

62. Ada Lawrence and Gelder, p.23, pp.43–44.

63. Chambers, p.42.

64. Elaine Aston, *Sarah Bernhardt, A French Actress on the English Stage* (Oxford: Berg, 1989), p.47. 'Mme. Sarah Bernhardt in Nottingham', *Nottingham Daily Express*, 16 June 1908, p.5. 'Fancy Dress Ball at Eastwood', *Eastwood and Kimberley Advertiser*, 28 February 1896, p.4.

65. The Lawrences owned volume 18 of Richard Garnett, *The International Library of Famous Literature*, 20 vols (London: E. Lloyd, [1900]), which includes Bernhardt's image and an extract from Matilda Heron's (1856) English translation of the play. James Boulton, 'Introduction', in Lawrence, *Letters* I, 1–20, p.5.

66. 'Madame Sarah Bernhardt in Nottingham', *Nottingham Evening Post*, 16 June 1908, p.3.

67. Chambers, p.109.

68. Lawrence, *White Peacock*, p.30. *Sons and Lovers*, pp.382–384.

69. Chambers, p.166.

70. 'Mme. Sarah Bernhardt in Nottingham', *Nottingham Daily Express*, 16 June 1908, p.5.

71. See Worthen, *Early Years*, pp.45–47.

72. Sklar, p.52.

73. Compare Lawrence, *Sons and Lovers* (1992), p.253, with Lawrence, *The Plays*, p.49.

74. Lawrence, *Sons and Lovers* (1992), p.254; the preceding passage follows Lawrence, *The Plays*, pp.33–34.

75. Shaw, *The Quintessence of Ibsenism* (London: W. Scott, 1891).

76. Worthen, *Early Years*, p.244.

77. Chambers, p.109. See also Lawrence, *Letters* III, 83 and *Letters* II, 213.

78. Worthen, 'Lawrence as Dramatist', p.137.

79. Catherine Carswell, *The Savage Pilgrimage: A Narrative of D.H. Lawrence* (London: Chatto and Windus, 1932), pp.135–136.

80. Jessie Chambers, p.121.

81. Michael Marland, 'Introduction', in D.H. Lawrence, *The Widowing of Mrs Holroyd and The Daughter-in-Law* (London: Heinemann, 1968), xi–xxxvi, p.xvii. Lawrence, *Letters* I, 385.

82. Lawrence, *White Peacock*, p.282.

83. Jessie Chambers remembers the visit to the theatre with Lawrence to watch this show, and she is probably correct as she dates the time and venue of the show accurately, and Lawrence's later work is certainly influenced by Galsworthy's play. Chambers, p.172.

84. Chambers, p.123.

85. 'The Death of Mr. J.M. Synge', *Manchester Guardian*, 25 March 1909, p.6.

86. 'Dramatis Personae', *Observer*, 24 October 1909, p.7. 'The New Irish Plays', *Manchester Guardian*, 25 October 1909, p.5. 'The New Irish Drama: Its Sources in Legend and Peasant Life', *Manchester Guardian*, 28 October 1909, p.8. 'Gaiety Theatre: The Irish Plays', *Manchester Guardian*, 24 November 1909, p.10. 'Gaiety Theatre: "The Playboy of the Western World"', *Manchester Guardian*, 23 November 1909, p.9.

87. Chambers, p.122.

88. Lawrence quoted by Worthen, *Early Years*, pp.537–538.

89. By autumn 1911, Lawrence had also attempted to turn this story into a poem, 'The Collier's Wife'. See Lawrence, *The Poems*, pp.15–16.

90. See Worthen, *Early Years*, pp.42–43.

91. Synge, *The Playboy of the Western World and Other Plays*, ed. by Ann Saddlemyer (Oxford: Oxford University Press, 1995), p.9.

92. 'Mr Synge's New Play', *Irish Times*, 26 February 1904, p.6.

93. ' "The Widowing of Mrs Holroyd": A Play. By D.H. Lawrence', *Sunday Times*, 19 December 1926, p.4.

94. A Correspondent [Catherine Carswell], ' "The Widowing of Mrs Holroyd", an Amateur Performance', *The Times*, 12 March 1920, p.14. Carswell, *The Savage Pilgrimage*, p.135.

95. Desmond MacCarthy, 'A Poet's Realism', *New Statesman*, 18 December 1926, p.310. *Outlook*, 24 December 1926, p.629.

96. Esmé Percy's Prompt Copy of 'The Widowing of Mrs Holroyd', Nottingham University Manuscripts and Special Collections, La-Z-1/5, p.93.

97. Irving Wardle, 'Not an Ordinary Relationship', *The Times*, 15 March 1968, p.13.

98. Julius Novick, 'D.H. Lawrence Wrote Plays, Too', *New York Times*, 25 November 1973, p.3.

99. Quoting from Nehls, I, 86.

100. Lawrence, *Rainbow*, p.310.

101. Lawrence, 'The Theatre' [A], in *Twilight in Italy*, p.75.

102. Worthen, *D.H. Lawrence: The Life of an Outsider* (London: Allen Lane, 2005), p.100.

103. 'School Concert', *Eastwood and Kimberley Advertiser*, 1 December 1911, p.2.

104. Nehls, I, 87.

105. Carlson, *Women of Grace: James's Plays and the Comedy of Manners* (Ann Arbor: UMI Research Press, 1985), p.131.

106. Billington, 'The Merry-go-Round at the Royal Court', *Guardian*, 8 November 1973, p.12.

107. Waterman, 'The Plays of D.H. Lawrence', *Modern Drama*, 2:4 (1959), 349–357 (p.351).

108. Spurling, 'Old Folk at Home', *Spectator*, 22 March 1968, pp.378–379, p.379.

109. Spenser, 'A Long, Bad Friday with D.H. Lawrence', *Daily Telegraph*, 7 July 1994, p.16.

110. 'Items relating to the English Stage Company production of "The Merry-Go-Round" ', Nottingham University Manuscripts and Special Collections, For-L-3/1/7/3/19.

Notes

111. See Worthen, *Early Years*, pp.220–221.

112. David Garnett, *The Golden Echo* (London: Chatto and Windus, 1953), p.245.

113. Yeats, *The Collected Works of W.B. Yeats: Volume II, The Plays*, ed. by David R. Clark and Rosalind E. Clark (New York: Scribner, 2001), p.109.

114. Yeats, *Plays*, p.686. In fact, Lawrence even forgot the name of the Yeats–Gregory play at one point (*Letters*, II, 557).

115. Worthen, *Early Years*, p.377. See also S.J. Hills, 'Frieda Lawrence', *The Times Literary Supplement*, 6 September 1985, p.975.

116. Adrian Frazier, *Behind the Scenes: Yeats, Horniman, and the Struggle for the Abbey Theatre* (Berkeley: University of California Press, 1990), p.197. Keith Sagar, 'D.H. Lawrence: Dramatist', *D.H. Lawrence Review*, 4:2 (1971), 154–182 (p.160).

Chapter 2

1. See also Violet Hunt, *The Flurried Years* (London: Hurst & Blackett, [1926]), p.151.

2. Quoted by Jan McDonald, *The 'New Drama' 1900–1914* (Houndmills: Macmillan, 1986), p.11.

3. MacCarthy, *The Court Theatre* (London: A.H. Bullen, 1907), p.15.

4. 'Amusements in Nottingham', *Nottingham Guardian*, 7 September 1909, p.10.

5. Dennis Kennedy, *Granville Barker and the Dream of Theatre* (Cambridge: Cambridge University Press, 1985), p.100, p.103. *Stage*, 3 March 1910, p.20, quoted by Kennedy, *Granville Barker*, p.101.

6. C.B. Purdom, *Harley Granville Barker* (London: Rockliff, 1955), p.127.

7. Worthen, *Early Years*, pp.320–321.

8. Frederick Harrison quoted by Carolyn G. Heilbrun, *The Garnett Family* (London: George Allen & Unwin, 1961), p.84.

9. 'A Talk with "the Most Abused Man in England"', *New York Times*, 1 December 1907, p.SM6.

10. Shaw quoted by George Jefferson, *Edward Garnett: A Life in Literature* (London: Cape, 1982), p.121.

11. David Garnett, p.133.

12. Although this scene may not, in fact, have been the original beginning, as the only surviving manuscript begins on the page numbered '6'. See Schwarze and Worthen, p.cxiv.

13. See Neville, *A Memoir of D.H. Lawrence (The Betrayal)*, ed. by Carl Baron (Cambridge: Cambridge University Press, 1981), p.26.

14. Worthen, *Early Years*, p.55.

15. Edward Garnett, *A Censured Play: The Breaking Point* (London: Duckworth, 1907), p.114.

16. Edward Garnett, *The Trial of Jeanne d'Arc and Other Plays* (London: Cape, 1931), p.118.

17. G.H.M., 'Gaiety Theatre: The Feud', *Manchester Guardian*, 12 April 1909, p.10.

18. See James Moran, 'Pound, Yeats, and the Regional Repertory Theatres', in *Regional Modernisms*, ed. by Neal Alexander and James Moran (Edinburgh: Edinburgh University Press, 2013), pp.83–103.

19. Ros Merkin, *Liverpool Playhouse: A Theatre and its City* (Liverpool: Liverpool University Press, 2011), p.26.

20. Viv Gardner, 'No Flirting with Philistinism: Shakespearean Production at Miss Horniman's Gaiety Theatre', *New Theatre Quarterly*, 14 (1998), 220–233 (p.232).

21. Jefferson, pp.124–125. David Garnett, p.134.

22. Worthen, *Early Years*, p.458.

23. Lawrence, 'The Theatre' [A], in *Twilight in Italy*, p.70.

24. Schwarze and Worthen, p.xxxv.

25. The two versions are published in *Twilight in Italy*, ed. by Paul Eggert (Cambridge: Cambridge University Press, 1994), pp.69–80 and pp.133–153.

26. In turn, Lawrence wrote another short skit about Frieda in a letter of 1924 (*Letters* II, 244). See Worthen, *Early Years*, p.452.

27. Clarke, 'The Fight for Barbara: Lawrence's Society Drama', in *D.H. Lawrence in the Modern World*, ed. by Peter Preston and Peter Hoare (Houndmills: Macmillan, 1989), pp.47–68, p.49.

28. Frieda Lawrence, Letter to Nancy Pearn of c.1933, Nottingham University Manuscripts and Special Collections, La-Z-4/5/14/1.

29. Worthen, *Early Years*, p.398.

30. Edward Garnett, *Censured Play*, p.102.

31. Frieda Lawrence, Letter to Nancy Pearn of c.1933, Nottingham University Manuscripts and Special Collections, La-Z-4/5/14/1.

32. Kinkead-Weekes, *D.H. Lawrence: Triumph to Exile* (Cambridge: Cambridge University Press, 1996), p.60.

33. Lawrence, *The Poems*, I, 43.

34. Edward Garnett, *Censured Play*, p.51.

35. Bruce Steele, 'Introduction', in *England, My England* (Cambridge: Cambridge University Press, 1990), pp.xix–li, p.xlv.

36. Dennis Kennedy, ed., *The Oxford Encyclopedia of Theatre & Performance: Volume 2: M–Z* (Oxford: Oxford University Press, 2003), p.1278. Jonathan Law et al., eds, *Brewster's Theatre* (London: Cassell, 1994), p.441.

Notes

37. Houghton, *Hindle Wakes* (London: Sidgwick and Jackson, 1919), p.23.

38. 'The Stage Society', *The Times*, 18 June 1912, p.10.

39. Schwarze and Worthen, p.xliii.

40. Kinkead-Weekes, pp.92–93.

41. Schwarze and Worthen, p.xl.

42. Printed in 'The Widowing of Mrs Holroyd', *Sunday Times*, 19 December 1926, p.4: the newspaper reviewer said of this verdict, 'I do not even begin to agree'.

43. 'A Fine Play', *The Times*, 24 April 1914, p.4.

44. The others were Harold V. Neilson and Lena Ashwell (*Letters* II, 187, 201).

45. 'Amusements in Nottingham', *Nottingham Guardian*, 19 March 1912, p.12.

46. Eric Salmon, *Granville Barker: A Secret Life* (London: Heinemann, 1983), p.111. Iden Payne, *A Life in a Wooden O: Memoirs of the Theatre* (New Haven: Yale University Press, 1977), p.128.

47. 'Modern Drama', *New York Times*, 4 October 1914, p.52.

48. 'At the Theaters: Little Theater', *Los Angeles Times*, 29 December 1916, p.II3. Norman M. Karasick and Dorothy K. Karasick, *The Oilman's Daughter: A Biography of Alice Barnsdall* (Encino: Carleston, 1993), pp.49–53.

49. Kingsley, 'Nth Power Realism: Widowing of Mrs. Holroyd at Little Theater', *Los Angeles Times*, 28 December 1916, p.II3.

50. Marie Coleman, *The Irish Revolution, 1916–1923* (Oxford: Routledge, 2014), p.23.

51. Lawrence, *Women in Love*, ed. by David Farmer (Cambridge: Cambridge University Press, 1987), p.419.

52. Elvery had earlier worked with Pearse on a book project, and had considerable sympathy for Irish nationalism. Beatrice Elvery, *Today We Will Gossip* (London: Constable, 1964), p.91.

53. Elvery, p.89.

54. Elvery, p.91

55. The play eschews political discussion in favour of a focus on (homoerotic) personal relationships. Farjeon, *Friends* (London: Samuel French, 1923).

56. An Englishman [Goldring], *A Stranger in Ireland* (Dublin: Talbot Press, 1918), p.129.

57. Goldring, *The Nineteen Twenties: A General Survey and Some Personal Memories* (London: Nicholson & Watson, 1945), p.115, p.121.

58. Goldring, *Odd Man Out: The Autobiography of a 'Propaganda Novelist'* (London: Chapman and Hall, 1936), p.184, p.207.

59. [Goldring], *A Stranger*, p.23.

60. Goldring, *Odd Man*, p.251.

61. Goldring, *Odd Man*, p.256.

62. John Worthen and Lindeth Vasey, 'Introduction', in Lawrence, *The First 'Women in Love'*, ed. by John Worthen and Lindeth Vasey (Cambridge: Cambridge University Press, 1998), pp.xvii–lv, p.xxxviii.

63. Compare Lawrence, *The First 'Women in Love'*, p.212 with Lawrence, *The Plays*, pp.394–395.

64. Goldring, *Odd Man*, p.253.

65. 'Theatre Royal', *Nottingham Daily Express*, 7 September 1909, p.6.

66. Nehls, I, 447.

67. 'From each according to his abilities, to each according to his needs': Louis Blanc's slogan popularized by Marx. See 'Critique of the Gotha Programme' in Marx, *The First International and After: Political Writings Volume 3*, ed. by David Fernbach (London: Verso, 2010), pp.339–359, p.347.

68. *Touch and Go* Autograph Manuscript, Nottingham University Manuscripts and Special Collections, La-L-13/3/2, f.71.

69. 'Amusements in Nottingham', *Nottingham Guardian*, 7 September 1909, p.10.

70. He contacted Cythia Asquith, knowing that she was secretary to the playwright James Barrie, and suggested that she might get the play read by one of her actor acquaintances: 'if you like, show it to Mrs Patrick Campbell' (*Letters* III, 315). The manuscript of *Touch and Go* begins with a list of *dramatis personae* divided into male and female roles, something that, as Worthen and Schwarze have emphasized, is unique in his play manuscripts, and reveals how much Lawrence hoped to see a production. *Touch and Go* Autograph Manuscript, Nottingham University Manuscripts and Special Collections, La-L-13/3/2, cover page verso. Schwarze and Worthen, p.xlvii.

71. Douglas Goldring, 'Introduction', in Goldring, *The Fight for Freedom: A Play in Four Acts* (New York: Thomas Seltzer, 1920), pp.5–11, pp.10–11.

72. Goldring, *Odd Man*, p.257.

73. Compton Mackenzie, *My Life and Times: Octave 5, 1915–1923* (London: Chatto and Windus, 1966), p.182.

74. 'Mrs. Compton's Debut', *Nottingham Evening News*, 21 September 1920, p.3.

75. Account by Albert James Marshall, Nottingham Library, Local Studies Section, Swann scrapbook, f.383.

76. Mackenzie, p.198, p.257.

77. 'Reminiscences of An Old Playgoer', Nottingham Library, Local Studies Section, Swann scrapbook, f.389.

78. 'Where Shall We Go Tonight?', *Nottingham Evening News*, 17 July 1923, p.8.

79. Account by Albert James Marshall, Nottingham Central Library, Local Studies Section, Swann scrapbook, f.383.

80. 'The Rep's Future', *Nottingham Journal*, 24 July 1923, p.5.

Notes

81. 'Repertory Reopening', *Nottingham Evening Post*, 26 July 1923, and card index notes for Grand Theatre, Radford Road, in Nottingham Central Library.

82. Brigit Patmore quoted by Derek Patmore, 'A Child's Memories of D.H. Lawrence' in *A D.H. Lawrence Miscellany*, ed. by Harry T. Moore (Carbondale: Southern Illinois University Press, 1959), pp.134–136, p.135.

83. John Middleton Murry, *Between Two Worlds* (London: Cape, 1935), pp.321–322.

84. The account of Lawrence's directing in 1917 is given by Kinkead-Weekes, p.425.

85. See, for example, Carswell, p.68.

86. Kyle S. Crichton, quoted in Nehls, II, 418. Mabel Dodge Luhan, *Lorenzo in Taos* (Santa Fe: Sunstone, 2007), p.68.

87. Luhan, p.190.

88. Quoted by Luhan, p.53.

89. Ellis, *D.H. Lawrence: Dying Game 1922–1930* (Cambridge: Cambridge University Press, 1998), pp.181, 647. Brett, *Lawrence and Brett: A Friendship* (London: Martin Secker, 1933), p.49.

90. Brett, p.52.

91. Brett, p.60.

92. Quoted by Schwarze and Worthen, p.lxviii.

93. Pound cited in James Longenbach, *Stone Cottage: Pound, Yeats, and Modernism* (Oxford: Oxford University Press, 1991), p.207.

94. Lawrence, *Sea and Sardinia*, pp.191–192.

95. Quoted by Brett, pp.219–220.

96. 'Notebook Containing the Autograph Manuscript of "David"', Nottingham University Manuscripts and Special Collections, La-Z-1/32, f.104, f.164.

97. Brecht, 'A Short Organum for the Theatre', in *Brecht on Theatre*, ed. by Marc Silberman, Steve Giles and Tom Kuhn, 3rd edn (London: Bloomsbury, 2015), pp.229–255, p.247.

98. Ruderman, *Race and Identity in D.H. Lawrence* (Houndmills: Palgrave, 2014).

99. 'Notebook Containing the Autograph Manuscript of "David"', Nottingham University Manuscripts and Special Collections, La-Z-1/32, f.8, f.14, f.34, f.35.

100. 'Notebook Containing the Autograph Manuscript of "David"', Nottingham University Manuscripts and Special Collections, La-Z-1/32, f.27.

101. Worthen and Schwarze, p.lxxi.

102. Shaw, *The Complete Plays of Bernard Shaw* (London: Hamlyn, 1965), p.942.

103. See also Ellis, pp.364–365.

104. James Agate, 'The Dramatic World', *The Sunday Times*, 29 May 1927, p.6. St John Ervine, 'The Week's Theatres', *Observer*, 29 May 1927, p.15.

105. I.B., 'Mr. D.H. Lawrence's "David"', *Manchester Guardian*, 24 May 1927, p.12.

106. *Festival Theatre Programme, Number 2, David* (Cambridge: Festival Theatre, 1933). I am grateful to John Worthen for supplying this.

107. French, p.390.

Peter Hall Letter of 16 March 1984, Nottingham University Manuscripts and Special Collections, La-R5-19/2.

Chapter 3

1. See James Moran, *The Theatre of Seán O'Casey* (London: Bloomsbury, 2013), p.68.

2. Worthen, 'Lawrence as Dramatist', p.152.

3. Lewis, *The Cambridge Introduction to Modernism* (Cambridge: Cambridge University Press, 2007), p.77.

4. Bailey and Nottingham, *Heartlands: A Guide to D.H. Lawrence's Midlands Roots* (Kibworth: Matador, 2013), p.4.

5. Lawrence did, however, tell Compton Mackenzie, 'I can't act one little bit' (*Letters* III, 510).

6. Chambers, p.42.

7. May Chambers Holbrook, quoted in Nehls, III, 602–603.

8. Ada Lawrence and Gelder, p.43.

9. Ada Lawrence and Gelder, pp.45–46.

10. Hopkin Hilton, pp.23–24.

11. Lawrence, 'A Prelude', in *Love Among the Haystacks*, pp.5–15, p.9.

12. Lawrence, *Love Among the Haystacks*, p.10. For more on these Christmas plays see Alan Brody, *The English Mummers and their Plays* (London: Routledge, 1971), p.60; Lawrence, *The Rainbow*, ed. by Mark Kinkead-Weekes (Cambridge: Cambridge University Press, 1989), p.507.

13. Lawrence, *Rainbow*, p.130.

14. Tom laughingly remembering how, when he played Beelzebub as a child, he received a smack on the head that 'knocked all th' sense out of me as you'd crack an egg'. This memory foreshadows his later death, when he tells his family that he is going to Nottingham to see 'a special show', but gets drunk, caught in a flood, and then, 'Something struck his head, a great wonder of anguish went over him, then the blackness covered him entirely'. Lawrence, *Rainbow*, p.130, p.226, p.229.

15. For example, in Lawrence's *The White Peacock* (published 1911) he includes a Boxing Day party of charades that features a woman who is about to enter into an unhappy marriage, and who turns the acting into a 'small tragedy'. In his early short story, 'Delilah and Mr Bircumshaw' (written 1910, revised 1912), where a man who acts in a Christmas pageant is teased about participating by his wife.

Notes

16. 'Theatre Royal – "Carmen"', *Nottingham Evening Post*, 30 March 1886, p.2.

17. In 1909 he watched the Carl Rosa performance of *Tristan and Isolde*, and in the same month the company performed *Carmen* (*Letters* I, 140): Lawrence was working on *The White Peacock* at this time. 'Music: The Carl Rosa Company at Covent Garden', *Observer*, 24 October 1909, p.6.

18. Lawrence, *White Peacock*, p.248.

19. Lawrence, *White Peacock*, p.248.

20. See Lawrence, *Letters* I, 99, and 'The Carl Rosa Week', *Nottingham Evening Post*, 5 March 1895, p.2; 'Amusements', *Nottingham Evening Post*, 12 December 1903, p.2; 'Amusements', *Nottingham Evening Post*, 8 December 1904, p.2.

21. 'Carl Rosa Company at the Theatre Royal', *Nottingham Evening Post*, 9 December 1902, p.6. Helen Corke, 'The Writing of *The Trespasser*', *D.H. Lawrence Review*, 7:3 (1974), 227–239 (pp.231–232).

22. Indeed, when finishing *The White Peacock*, Lawrence mistakenly wrote 'Siegmund' on three occasions, showing how the name had started to obsess him. Worthen, *Outsider*, p.78.

23. Elizabeth Mansfield, 'Introduction', in Lawrence, *The Trespasser*, ed. by Elizabeth Mansfield (Cambridge: Cambridge University Press, 1981), pp.1–40, p.5.

24. These slips are detailed by Elizabeth Mansfield, 'Explanatory Notes', in Lawrence, *Trespasser*, pp.233–243, p.235, p.242.

25. Sale, *Modern Heroism: Essays on D.H. Lawrence, William Empson, & J.R.R. Tolkien* (Berkeley: University of California Press, 1973), p.104. Stevens, 'From Genesis to the *Ring*: Richard Wagner and D.H. Lawrence's *Rainbow*', *Textual Practice*, 2013, 1–20.

26. Mansfield, 'Introduction', p.6.

27. Malcolm Muggeridge and Helen Corke, 'The Dreaming Woman', *The Listener*, 25 July 1968, 104–107 (p.105).

28. Corke, p.231.

29. Lawrence, *Trespasser*, p.53.

30. Lawrence, *Trespasser*, p.48.

31. '*Psychoanalysis and the Unconscious*' and '*Fantasia of the Unconscious*', ed. by Bruce Steele (Cambridge: Cambridge University Press, 2004), p.141. See also Lawrence, *Letters* I, 53, 80, 101, 509, and Lawrence, 'Introduction to These Paintings', in *Late Essays and Articles*, pp.182–217, p.190.

32. Lawrence, *Lady Chatterley's Lover and A Propos of 'Lady Chatterley's Lover'*, p.319.

33. See Leavis, 'Shaw against Lawrence', *Spectator*, 1 April 1955, pp.397–399.

34. Shaw, 'Mr. Bernard Shaw on D.H. Lawrence', p.863. D.H. Lawrence's response quoted by Frieda Lawrence, *Frieda Lawrence: The Memoirs and Correspondence*, ed. by E.W. Tedlock (London: Heinemann, 1961), pp.147–148, p.147.

35. Frieda Lawrence, *Memoirs*, p.147. Shaw himself commented that '*Lady Chatterley* should be on the shelves of every college for budding girls. They should be forced to read it on pain of being refused a marriage licence'. Quoted by Frank Harris, *Bernard Shaw* (London: Victor Gollancz, 1931), pp.232–233.

36. Frieda Lawrence, '*Not I, But the Wind*' (London: Heinemann, 1935), p.4. Worthen, *Early Years*, p.382.

37. Frieda Lawrence, *Memoirs*, 22–23; Nehls, I, 162–163; Worthen, *Early Years*, p.381. Lawrence may have been following family precedent in organizing this: in August 1910 his younger sister Ada had made a similar playhouse visit in the company of a man who would become her fiancé, with Lawrence observing that Ada 'who is tall and slender and twenty three years old, has cycled to the theatre in Nottingham with her sweetheart' (*Letters* I, 174).

38. Shaw, *Plays*, p.341.

39. Shaw, *Plays*, p.396.

40. Chambers and George Zytaruk, *D.H. Lawrence Review: The Collected Letters of Jessie Chambers: Volume 12 Numbers 1 and 2, Spring and Summer 1979* (Fayetteville: University of Arkansas, 1979), p.67.

41. Lawrence, *Sons and Lovers* (1992), pp.375–376.

42. Lawrence, *Sons and Lovers* (1992), p.381.

43. Until the 1992 Cambridge edition was published, this section read simply, 'He sat up and looked at the room in the darkness, his feet doubled under him, perfectly motionless, listening'. See *Sons and Lovers* (London: Duckworth, 1913), p.338.

44. Lawrence, *White Peacock*, p.248.

45. Lawrence, *Sons and Lovers* (1992), p.375.

46. Lawrence, *Trespasser*, p.48.

47. Lawrence, *Rainbow*, p.211.

48. Lawrence, *Rainbow*, p.211.

49. Lawrence, *Rainbow*, p.213.

50. The entertainment district included the Theatre Royal, the Gaiety Palace of Variety (from 1898), the Empire (from 1898), and the Hippodrome music hall (from 1908). See John Beckett, *Nottingham: An Illustrated History* (Manchester: Manchester University Press, 1997), p.70.

51. See Jack Read, *Empires, Hippodromes & Palaces* (London: Alderman, 1985), p.93.

52. Lawrence, *Rainbow*, p.211.

53. Lawrence had earlier alluded to the lure of the music hall in his 1909 short story 'Lessford's Rabbits', where two schoolboys raise money to 'Go to the Empire'. Lawrence, 'Lessford's Rabbits', in *Love Among the Haystacks*, pp.21–27, p.26.

Notes

54. Lawrence, *Women in Love*, pp.117–120.

55. Lawrence, 'Tickets Please', in *England, My England*, pp.34–45, p.40.

56. Lawrence, *England, My England*, p.38.

57. Lawrence, *England, My England*, p.39.

58. Lawrence, *England, My England*, p.38.

59. Lawrence, 'Monkey Nuts', in *England, My England*, pp.64–76, p.65.

60. Lawrence, *England, My England*, pp.64, 67, 65.

61. Lawrence, *England, My England*, p.69.

62. Lawrence, *England, My England*, p.71.

63. Quoted in Jeffrey Meyers, *D.H. Lawrence: A Biography* (New York: Cooper Square, 2002), p.202.

64. Meyers, p.201.

65. To avoid libeling Duse, Lawrence changed this reference in the English edition eventually published in 1921. Lawrence, *The First 'Women in Love'*, ed. by John Worthen and Lindeth Vasey (Cambridge: Cambridge University Press, 1998), p.414.

66. Carswell, *Savage Pilgrimage*, pp.86–87.

67. Luhan, p.51.

68. Kinkead-Weekes, p.825.

69. Lawrence, *The Lost Girl*, ed. by John Worthen (Cambridge: Cambridge University Press, 1981), p.35.

70. Lawrence, *Lost Girl*, p.117, p.119, p.120.

71. Lawrence, *Lost Girl*, p.140.

72. Lawrence, *Lost Girl*, p.288.

73. Lawrence, *Lost Girl*, p.147.

74. Lawrence, *Lost Girl*, pp.108–109.

75. Lawrence, *Lost Girl*, p.149.

76. Some of the best-known critics of *The Lost Girl* have been irked by its depictions of live drama. F.R. Leavis described 'the Natcha Kee Tawara business' as 'irritating', while Richard Aldington described the 'balderdash about people playing at Red Indians, puerile stuff'. Leavis, *D.H. Lawrence: Novelist*, p.31. Richard Aldington, *D.H. Lawrence* (London: Chatto and Windus, 1930), p.33.

77. 'Local and District News', *Eastwood and Kimberley Advertiser*, 24 July 1903, p.2. 'Local and District News: Belmore's Pavilion Theatre', *Eastwood and Kimberley Advertiser*, 3 July 1903, p.2.

78. 'Local and District News: Belmore's Pavilion Theatre', *Eastwood and Kimberley Advertiser*, 3 July 1903, p.2. 'Local and District News', *Eastwood and Kimberley Advertiser*, 24 July 1903, p.2. 'Local and District News', *Eastwood*

and Kimberley Advertiser, 7 August 1903, p.2. 'Local and District News: Belmore's Theatre', *Eastwood and Kimberley Advertiser*, 9 October 1903, p.2.

79. The venue gave twice-nightly presentations of silent films such as 'The Ship of Lions', or 'The Victim of the Mormons', and winning praise for projecting films 'not yet shown in the City of Nottingham'. 'Local and District News', *Eastwood and Kimberley Advertiser*, 1 November 1912, p.2. 'Visit Parker's Picture Pavilion', *Eastwood and Kimberley Advertiser*, 22 November 1912, p.3.

80. In December 1913 Parker's Picture Pavilion was taken over by Reliance Pictures, which continued to show silent films there for another six years.

81. Lawrence, *Lost Girl*, p.3.

82. Belmont's venture failed because of its owner's failure to find a popular form of drama to appeal to Eastwood, and when the real-life Empire defeated Parker's Picture Pavilion in 1913, the Empire showed a range of live variety acts, including acrobats, comedians and singers. It was in fact the Picture Pavilion which, as its name suggests, operated primarily as a cinema.

83. Auslander, *Liveness: Performance in a Mediatized Culture*, 2nd edn (London: Routledge, 2008), p.11, p.12.

84. *Eastwood and Kimberley Advertiser*, 22 June 1917, p.2. The venue continued to show movies into the 1950s, when it was eventually converted into its present incarnation as a low-budget shop.

85. Lawrence, *Lost Girl*, p.115.

86. Lawrence, *Lost Girl*, p.119.

87. Such melancholy is also indicated in *Lady Chatterley's Lover*, when Connie drives past a fictional version of the Eastwood Empire, and is described as going past the 'plaster-and-gilt horror of the cinema'. Lawrence, *Lady Chatterley's Lover and A Propos of 'Lady Chatterley's Lover'*, p.152. Louis K. Greiff describes this aspect of *Lady Chatterley* in *D.H. Lawrence: Fifty Years on Film* (Carbondale: Southern Illinois University Press, 2001), p.2.

88. Lawrence, 'Indians and Entertainment', in *Mornings in Mexico and Other Essays*, pp.57–68, p.62, p.60.

89. Lawrence, *Lost Girl*, p.116.

90. Lawrence, 'The Theatre' [A], in *Twilight in Italy*, p.78.

91. Lawrence, *Sea and Sardinia*, p.191.

92. Lawrence, *Lost Girl*, p.116.

93. Lawrence's mockery of the movie star was remembered by Brewster Ghiselin, in Nehls, III, 289. I am grateful to Andrew Harrison for his insights about Götzsche.

94. Lawrence, *Aaron's Rod*, p.254, p.108, p.136.

95. The very names of the characters of the novel are often taken from drama: we find Aaron (*Titus Andronicus*), Algy (*The Importance of being Earnest*), Nan (*The Tragedy of Nan*) and even Job Arthur (from Lawrence's own *Touch and Go* and *The Merry-go-Round*).

Notes

96. Asquith, *Diaries: 1915-1918* (London: Hutchinson, 1986), p.365.

97. Asquith, p.365. 'Court and Society', *Observer*, 18 November 1917, p.3.

98. Lawrence, *Aaron's Rod*, p.56.

99. Lawrence, *Aaron's Rod*, p.51.

100. Lawrence has 'there were no taxis – absolutely no taxis. And it was raining' (*Aaron's Rod*, p.56), whereas Shaw's play famously begins with the soaked character of Freddie failing to find a cab and complaining, 'I tell you theyre [*sic*] all engaged. The rain was so sudden' (Shaw, *Collected Plays*, p.716).

101. Lawrence, *Aaron's Rod*, p.47.

102. Le Bon, *The Crowd* (New Brunswick: Transaction Publishers, 1995), pp.89–90.

103. The first quote is from Mussolini's letter of 22 June 1927 to Gastone Monaldi, quoted by Doug Thompson, 'The Organisation, Fascistisation and Management of Theatre in Italy, 1925-1943', in *Fascism and Theatre*, ed. by Günter Berghaus (Providence: Berghahn, 1997), pp.94–112, pp.97–98. The second Mussolini quote is printed by Pietro Cavallo, 'Theatre Politics of the Mussolini Régime and their Influence on Fascist Drama', in *Fascism and Theatre*, ed. by Günter Berghaus (Providence: Berghahn, 1997), pp.113–132, pp.113–114.

104. Lawrence, *Aaron's Rod*, p.47.

105. Lawrence, *Aaron's Rod*, p.48.

106. Lawrence, *Aaron's Rod*, p.299.

107. Hans-Ulrich Thamer, 'The Orchestration of the National Community: The Nuremberg Party Rallies of the NSDAP', in *Fascism and Theatre*, ed. by Günter Berghaus (Providence and Oxford: Berghahn, 1997), pp.172–190, p.175.

108. Quoted by Witter Bynner, *Journey with Genius: Recollections and Reflections Concerning the D.H. Lawrences* (New York: John Day, 1951), p.51.

109. Bynner, p.56.

110. L.D. Clark, 'Introduction', in Lawrence, *The Plumed Serpent*, ed. by L.D. Clark (Cambridge: Cambridge University Press, 1987), pp.xvii–xlvii, p.xlii.

111. Lawrence, *The Plumed Serpent*, ed. by L.D. Clark (Cambridge: Cambridge University Press, 1987), p.8.

112. Lawrence, *Plumed Serpent*, p.16.

113. Lawrence, *Plumed Serpent*, p.18.

114. Lawrence, *Plumed Serpent*, p.20, p.27.

115. Lawrence, 'None of That!', in *The Woman who Rode Away*, pp.211–229, p.215, pp.221–222.

116. Gano had recently retired after having made a fortune, and was involved in public scandal when a woman died at one of his orgies. See Dieter Mehl and Christa Jansohn, 'Explanatory Notes', in Lawrence, *The Women who Rode Away and Other Stories*, ed. by Dieter Mehl and Christa Jansohn (Cambridge:

Cambridge University Press, 1995), pp.383–426, p.413. Lawrence, *The Woman who Rode*, p.214.

117. Lawrence, *The Woman who Rode*, p.227.

118. Lawrence, *The Woman who Rode*, p.229.

119. Millett, p.292.

120. Artaud, 'Theatre and the Plague', in *Artaud on Theatre*, ed. by Claude Schumacher and Brian Singleton (London: Bloomsbury, 2001), pp.127–131, p.130.

121. Artaud, *The Theatre and its Double*, trans. by Mary Caroline Richards (New York: Grove, 1958), p.132. Artaud, *Antonin Artaud: Selected Writings*, ed. by Susan Sontag (Berkeley: University of California Press, 1988), p.389. Gerald Doherty argues that Lawrence's Artaudian understanding of theatre affected *St Mawr*: see *Oriental Lawrence* (New York: Peter Lang, 2001), pp.65–82.

122. Artaud, 'Theatre and Cruelty', in *Artaud on Theatre*, ed. by Claude Schumacher and Brian Singleton (London: Bloomsbury, 2001), pp.120–123, p.120.

123. Ahrends, 'The Nature and Fuction of Cruelty in the Theatre of Artaud and Foreman', in *Chapters from the History of Stage Cruelty*, ed. by Günter Ahrends and Hans-Jürgen Diller (Tübingen: Gunter Narr Verlag Tübingen, 1994), pp.117–128, p.119.

124. Artaud, 'Theatre and Cruelty', p.121.

125. Lawrence, *Mornings in Mexico*, p.66.

126. Bruce Weber, 'Theatre Review: D.H. Lawrence's Young Wisdom', *New York Times*, 16 June 2003, available at: http://www.nytimes.com/2003/06/16/theater/theater-review-d-h-lawrence-s-young-wisdom.html [accessed 15 September 2014].

127. Lawrence, 'The Blue Moccasins', in *The Virgin and the Gypsy and Other Stories*, ed. by Michael Herbert, Bethan Jones, and Lindeth Vasey (Cambridge: Cambridge University Press, 2005), pp.165–179, p.174.

128. Lawrence, *The Virgin*, p.179.

129. The play in Lawrence's story owes something to George Meredith's (1855) prose fiction *The Shaving of Shagpat: An Arabian Entertainment*. Lawrence, *The Virgin*, p.177, p.172.

130. Lawrence, *The Virgin*, p.170.

131. Lawrence, *The Virgin*, p.173.

132. Lawrence, *The Virgin*, p.174.

Chapter 4

1. Nin, 'Novelist on Stage', *New York Times*, 10 April 1966, p.4 and p.33, p.4.

2. Billington, 'Fine Way with a Lawrence Play', *The Times*, 8 March 1968, p.12.

Notes

3. Peel quoted by Nightingale, p.140.
4. Moi, p.25.
5. Thacker, ' "that trouble": Regional Modernism and "little magazines" ', in *Regional Modernisms*, ed. by Neal Alexander and James Moran (Edinburgh: Edinburgh University Press, 2013), pp.22–43, p.33.
6. Malani, *D.H. Lawrence: A Study of His Plays* (New Delhi: Arnold-Heinemann, 1982), p.32.
7. MacCarthy, 'A Poet's Realism', p.310.
8. Carswell, p.135.
9. Darlington, 'Naïvety of Lawrence the Playwright', *Daily Telegraph*, December 1965, in Nottingham University Manuscripts and Special Collections, La-Z-13/3/224/1-2.
10. Sklar, p.121.
11. Kane, *Complete Plays* (London: Methuen, 2001), p.136.
12. Norris, *To Bodies Gone: The Theatre of Peter Gill* (Bridgend: Seren, 2014), pp.68–69.
13. Chaudhuri, *Staging Place: The Geography of Modern Drama* (Ann Arbor: University of Michigan Press, 1997), pp.8–9.
14. Ubersfeld, *L'école de spectateur* (Paris: Edition Sociale, 1981), p.67, cited by Chris Morash and Shaun Richards, *Mapping Irish Theatre* (Cambridge: Cambridge University Press, 2013), p.40.
15. Sklar, p.137.
16. Carlson, 'A Stormy Apprenticeship: Lawrence's Three Comedies', *DHL Review*, 14 (1981), pp.191–211.
17. Sklar, p.189.
18. David Krasner, *A History of Modern Drama: Volume I* (Oxford: Wiley Blackwell, 2012), p.147.
19. Lawrence, *White Peacock*, p.28.
20. Here Lawrence is ostensibly discussing Flaubertian realism in the novel, but he includes an allusion to *Hamlet* that indicates that his thinking had a broader application. 'Introduction to *Mastro-Don Gesualdo*', in *Introductions and Reviews*, pp.145–156, p.149.
21. Ibsen, *Three Major Plays*, trans. by David Rudkin (London: Oberon, 2006), pp.254–255.
22. Chambers, p.108.
23. 'Items relating to the Nottingham Playhouse Company production of "A Collier's Friday Night"', Nottingham University Manuscripts and Special Collections, For-L-3/1/2/2/3.
24. Quoted by Chambers, p.108.

25. Hans-Göran Ekman, 'Strindberg and Comedy', *The Cambridge Companion to August Strindberg*, ed. by Michael Robinson (Cambridge: Cambridge University Press, 2009), pp.70–78, p.75.

26. Strindberg, *Miss Julie and Other Plays*, trans. by Michael Robinson (Oxford, Oxford University Press, 1998), p.308.

27. In October 1912 Lawrence described Strindberg as 'a bit wooden, like Ibsen, a bit skin-erupty' (*Letters* I, 465) and by September 1913 had described the 'certain intolerable nastiness about the real Ibsen: the same thing is in Strindberg'. Lawrence, 'The Theatre' [B], in *Twilight in Italy*, pp.137–138.

28. Lawrence, *Trespasser*, p.224.

29. Hauptmann, *The Dramatic Works of Gerhart Hauptmann: Volume Three*, ed. by Ludwig Lewisohn (New York: Huebsch, 1914), p.128. Leroy R. Shaw, *The Playwright & Historical Change* (Madison: University of Wisconsin Press, 1970), pp.27–28.

30. Like Hauptmann's *Hannele*, Lawrence's 'The Prussian Office' ends by returning from the visionary scenes to a realistic hospital room, where we learn that the main character is now dead.

31. Lawrence, 'The Captain's Doll', in *The Fox, The Captain's Doll, The Ladybird*, ed. by Dieter Mehl (Cambridge: Cambridge University Press, 1992), pp.73–154, p.96.

32. Peter Szondi, *Theory of the Modern Drama*, ed. and trans. by Michael Hays (Cambridge: Polity, 1987 [1956]), p.32.

33. Richard Garnett, *International Library*, XVIII, 8559–8581. Chambers, p.122.

34. Lawrence, *White Peacock*, p.101, p.259; Lawrence, *Trespasser* p.52.

35. Bruce Steele, 'Introduction', p.xxxv.

36. Szondi, *Theory of the Modern Drama*, p.35.

37. McGuinness, *Maurice Maeterlinck and the Making of Modern Theatre* (Oxford: Oxford University Press, 2000), p.214.

38. Lawrence, 'The Blind Man', in *England, My England*, pp.46–63, pp.46–47.

39. Lawrence, *Sea and Sardinia*, p.190.

40. Edward Gordon Craig, 'The Actor and the Übermarionette', *The Mask*, 1:2 (April 1908), 3–15 (p.13).

41. Lawrence, *Trespasser*, p.98. Lawrence, 'The Mortal Coil', in *England, My England*, pp.169–189, p.170. Lawrence, *Women in Love*, p.10.

42. Craig, *Index to the Story of My Days* (London: Hulton, 1957), p.275. See also Craig, *Die Kunst des Theaters*, trans. by Maurice Magnus (Berlin: Seeman Nachfolger, 1905), where Craig does distinguish between theatre and marionette-theatre.

43. Lawrence, *Sea and Sardinia*, p.189.

44. John Balance [Gordon Craig], 'A Note on Masks', *The Mask: The Journal of the Art of the Theatre*, 1:1 (1908), 9–12 (p.10).

Notes

45. Lawrence, *Aaron's Rod*, p.46.

46. In 1914 Lawrence read Marinetti's *I Poeti Futuristi* (Milan: Edizione Futuristi di 'Poesia', 1912). Afterwards Lawrence praised Marinetti's 'revolt against beastly sentiment and slavish adherence to tradition' (*Letters* II, 181).

47. Lawrence, *Sea and Sardinia*, p.189.

48. Two of these essays appeared in *Theatre Arts Monthly*, and the third – 'Indians and Entertainment', Lawrence mistakenly remembered as being published in the same journal, but first appeared in the *New York Times Magazine* (*Letters* V, 595, 636).

49. Isaacs, 'Introduction', in Edith J.R. Isaacs, *Theatre: Essays on the Arts of the Theatre* (New York: Books for Libraries Press, 1927), pp.vii–xviii, p.xviii.

50. Virginia Crosswhite Hyde, 'Introduction', in Lawrence, *Mornings in Mexico and Other Essays*, pp.xxv–lxxxi, p.xliv.

51. Lawrence, 'O! Americans', in *D.H. Lawrence: Complete Poems*, ed. by Vivian de Sola Pinto and F. Warren Roberts (Harmondsworth: Penguin, 1993 [1964]), p.779.

52. Lawrence, *Complete Poems*, p.780.

53. In 1912 Lawrence watched Edward Garnett's son David dancing like Diaghilev's leading dancer (*Letters* I, 429); in November 1918 Lawrence met with Diaghilev in London; and Lawrence's friends including Richard Aldington and Katherine Mansfield remained patrons of Diaghilev's London ballet in 1911–29. Jones, *Literature, Modernism and Dance* (Oxford: Oxford University Press, 2013), p.93. See also Osbert Sitwell, *Laughter in the Next Room* (Boston: Little, Brown and Co, 1948), pp.19–29.

54. Stevens, p.11.

55. Lawrence, *Women in Love*, p.80. Lawrence, *Lost Girl*, p.125.

56. Lawrence, 'The Hopi Snake Dance', in *Mornings in Mexico and Other Essays*, pp.77–94, p.80.

57. Jones, p.113.

58. Jann Pasler, 'Music and Spectacle in *Petrushka* and *The Rite of Spring*', in *Confronting Stravinsky*, ed. by Jann Pasler (Berkeley: University of California Press, 1986), p.74.

59. Jones, p.113.

60. 'Theatres, & c.', *The Times*, 19 October 1911, p.8.

61. Ernst Stern, *My Life, My Stage*, trans. by Edward Fitzgerald (London: Gollancz, 1951), p.87. '*Sumurûn*', *Observer*, 5 February 1911, p.7.

62. J.L. Styan, *Max Reinhardt* (Cambridge: Cambridge University Press, 1982), p.26.

63. Nehls, I, 91–92.

64. Lawrence, *The Woman who Rode*, p.220. Lawrence, *Mornings in Mexico*, p.59.

65. Luhan, pp.209–210.

66. '"Sumurûn"', *The Times*, 20 February 1911, p.10.

67. Brecht, '*Verfremdung* Effects in Chinese Acting', in *Brecht on Theatre*, pp.151–159, p.151 (emphasis in original).

68. Lawrence, *Mornings in Mexico*, p.67.

69. Lawrence, *Mornings in Mexico*, p.61.

70. Lawrence, *Mornings in Mexico*, p.59.

71. Lawrence, *Mornings in Mexico*, p.63, p.67.

72. Chaudhuri, *D.H. Lawrence and 'Difference'* (Oxford: Clarendon Press, 2003), p.156.

73. See Lawrence, 'Autobiographical Fragment', in *Late Essays and Articles*, pp.50–68, p.62 and p.65.

74. ' "From a College Window", f 75r in University College notebook', Nottingham University Manuscripts and Special Collections, La-L-2/7.

75. Jane Ellen Harrison, *Ancient Art and Ritual* (London: Thornton Butterworth, 1913), p.13, p.237. Lawrence, *Letters* II, 90.

76. Lawrence, *Mornings in Mexico*, p.86.

77. Lawrence, *Mornings in Mexico*, p.82.

78. 1913 programme notes to the *Rite* quoted by André Boucourechliev, *Stravinsky*, trans. by Martin Cooper (London: Victor Gollancz, 1987), p.60.

79. Knud Merrild, *A Poet and Two Painters: A Memoir of D.H. Lawrence* (London: Routledge, 1938), pp.321–322.

80. Lawrence, *Lady Chatterley's Lover and A Propos of 'Lady Chatterley's Lover'*, p.5.

81. Lawrence, *The First and Second Lady Chatterley Novels*, ed. by Dieter Mehl and Christa Jansohn (Cambridge: Cambridge University Press, 1999), pp.7–8.

82. McGuinness, p.216.

83. Lawrence, *Lady Chatterley's Lover and A Propos of 'Lady Chatterley's Lover'*, p.5.

84. Lawrence, *Lady Chatterley's Lover and A Propos of 'Lady Chatterley's Lover'*, p.16.

85. Lawrence, *Lady Chatterley's Lover and A Propos of 'Lady Chatterley's Lover'*, p.18.

86. Thomas, p.623.

87. Lawrence, *Lady Chatterley's Lover and A Propos of 'Lady Chatterley's Lover'*, p.51.

88. Opening-night tickets for Arlen's *The Green Hat* cost more than $100; the production lasted on Broadway for twenty-six weeks before touring to other cities; and there were plans afoot for a 1928 film version that would star Greta Garbo. See Julian M. Kaufman, 'A.H. Woods, Producer: A Thrill a Minute, A Laugh a Second!', in Arthur Gewirtz and James J. Kolb, eds, *Art, Glitter, and Glitz: Mainstream Playwrights and Popular Theatre in 1920s America* (Westport: Praeger, 2004), pp.209–216, p.211.

Notes

89. Lawrence, *Lady Chatterley's Lover and A Propos of 'Lady Chatterley's Lover'*, p.54.

90. Lawrence, *Lady Chatterley's Lover and A Propos of 'Lady Chatterley's Lover'*, p.221.

91. Jones, p.71.

92. Davis, *Ballets Russes Style: Diaghilev's Dancers and Paris Fashion* (London: Reaktion, 2010), p.208.

93. Lawrence, *Mornings in Mexico*, p.67.

94. Lawrence, *Lady Chatterley's Lover and A Propos of 'Lady Chatterley's Lover'*, pp.171–172.

95. Lawrence, *Lady Chatterley's Lover and A Propos of 'Lady Chatterley's Lover'*, p.174.

96. Lawrence, *Mornings in Mexico*, p.63.

97. Hyde, 'Introduction', *Mornings in Mexico and Other Essays*, pp.xxv–lxxxi, p.xlv.

98. Lawrence, *Lady Chatterley's Lover and A Propos of 'Lady Chatterley's Lover'*, p.269.

99. Arsène Houssaye, *Man About Paris*, trans. by Henry W. Knepler (London: Gollancz, 1972), p.330.

100. Bernat, *My Autobiography* (New York: Putnam, 1913), p.247.

101. In the British theatre, versions of *Lady Chatterley* have been created by John Hart (London's Arts Theatre Club in 1961); Keith Miles (Coventry Belgrade in 1983); Black Door Theatre Company (London's The Man in the Moon Theatre in 1985); and Marshall Gould (London's Cockpit Theatre in 1996). '*Lady Chatterley's Lover*; 1961–1996', Nottingham University Manuscripts and Special Collections, For-L-3/1/6.

102. Joyce, *Letters of James Joyce: Volume II*, ed. by Richard Ellmann (London: Faber, 1966), p.350.

103. Quoted by Richard Ellmann, *James Joyce*, rev. edn (Oxford: Oxford University Press, 1983), p.462.

Chapter 5

1. Eyre, *Talking Theatre: Interviews with Theatre People* (London: Nick Hern, 2009), p.218.

2. Billington, 'The Merry-go-Round at the Royal Court', *Guardian*, 8 November 1973, p.12.

3. Lawrence, *White Peacock*, p.58.

Chapter 6

1. Lawrence, 'Nottingham's New University', in *The Poems*, p.423.

2. Lawrence, 'Snake', in *The Poems*, p.303.

Chapter 7

1. Lawrence, *Sons and Lovers*, p.88.
2. Lawrence, *Women in Love*, p.7.
3. Jacobson, 'D.H. Lawrence, Forever Misunderstood', *Independent*, 2 April 2011. Available online: http://www.independent.co.uk/voices/commentators/howard-jacobson/howard-jacobson-dh-lawrence-forever-misunderstood-2260014.html [accessed 15 September 2014].
4. Lawrence, *Women in Love*, p.306.

Chapter 8

1. Seyed Mostafa Razili, 'A Discussion with Shirin Maghanloo: D. H. Lawrence in Ninety Minutes'. Available online: http://soodaroo.blogfa.com/post/42 [accessed 25 August 2014].
2. Lawrence, *Late Essays and Articles*, p.52.
3. Seabrook, *Pauperland*, pp.145–146.
4. Alex Shams, *Ajam Reads: Understanding Gender Politics in Iran*. Available online: http://ajammc.com/2013/10/29/ajam-reads-understanding-gender-politics-in-modern-iran/ [accessed 16 September 2014].
5. For instance Mehr News Agency reported in 2010 that the number of unmarried educated women in Iran had tripled in the space of ten years between 1996 and 2006. See: http://www.donya-e-eqtesad.com/news/606017/ [accessed 16 September 2014].
6. Rahimi, *The Patience Stone*, trans by Polly McLean (London: Vintage, 2011), p.iv.
7. See, for example, Douglas Mao and Rebecca L. Walkowitz, 'The New Modernist Studies', *PMLA*, 123:3 (2008), 737–748.
8. Said, 'Foreword', in Ranajit Guha and Gayatri Chakravorty Spivak, eds, *Selected Subaltern Studies* (Oxford: Oxford University Press, 1988), pp.vi–vii.

Conclusion

1. Maurice Wiggin, 'Revolutionaries', *Sunday Times*, 20 September 1953, p.9.
2. Nottingham University Manuscripts and Special Collections, Letter of December 1953 from Frieda Lawrence to *The Times*, La-B-242.
3. For speculation on this issue, see Malcolm Pittock, 'D.H. Lawrence: Dramatist?', *The Cambridge Quarterly*, 43:3 (2014), 256–272.
4. Schwarze and Worthen, p.cxi.

Notes

5. Billington, 'The Widowing of Mrs Holroyd Review: A Cracking Lawrence Revival', *The Guardian*, 11 September 2014. Available online: http://www.theguardian.com/stage/2014/sep/11/widowing-of-mrs-holroyd-review-dh-lawrence-orange-tree-richmond [accessed 16 September 2014].

BIBLIOGRAPHY

Ahrends, Günter, 'The Nature and Function of Cruelty in the Theatre of Artaud and Foreman', in *Chapters from the History of Stage Cruelty*, ed. by Günter Ahrends and Hans-Jürgen Diller (Tübingen: Gunter Narr Verlag Tübingen, 1994), pp.117–128.

Aldington, Richard, *D.H. Lawrence* (London: Chatto and Windus, 1930).

Aldington, Richard, *D.H. Lawrence: An Appreciation* (Harmondsworth: Penguin, 1950).

Artaud, Antonin, *The Theatre and its Double*, trans. by Mary Caroline Richards (New York: Grove, 1958).

Artaud, Antonin, *Antonin Artaud: Selected Writings*, ed. by Susan Sontag (Berkeley: University of California Press, 1988).

Artaud, Antonin, *Artaud on Theatre*, ed. by Claude Schumacher and Brian Singleton (London: Bloomsbury, 2001).

Asquith, Lady Cynthia, *Diaries: 1915–1918* (London: Hutchinson, 1968).

Aston, Elaine, *Sarah Bernhardt, A French Actress on the English Stage* (Oxford: Berg, 1989).

Auslander, Philip, *Liveness: Performance in a Mediatized Culture*, 2nd edn (London: Routledge, 2008).

Bailey, Stephen and Chris Nottingham, *Heartlands: A Guide to D.H. Lawrence's Midlands Roots* (Kibworth: Matador, 2013).

Becket, Fiona, *The Complete Critical Guide to D.H. Lawrence* (London: Routledge, 2004).

Beckett, John, *Nottingham: An Illustrated History* (Manchester: Manchester University Press, 1997).

Beckett, Samuel, *Trilogy* (London: Calder, 1994).

Bennett, Alan, *Alan Bennett: Plays One* (London: Faber, 1996).

Bernat, Julie ['Madame Judith'], *My Autobiography* (New York: Putnam, 1913).

Boucourechliev, André, *Stravinsky*, trans. by Martin Cooper (London: Victor Gollancz, 1987).

Boulton, James, *Lawrence in Love* (Nottingham: Nottingham University, 1968).

Boulton, James, 'Introduction', in Lawrence, *The Letters of D.H. Lawrence*, ed. by James Boulton et al., 8 vols (Cambridge: Cambridge University Press, 1979–2001), I, 1–20.

Brecht, Bertolt, *Brecht on Theatre*, ed. by Marc Silberman, Steve Giles and Tom Kuhn, 3rd edn (London: Bloomsbury, 2015).

Brett, Dorothy, *Lawrence and Brett: A Friendship* (London: Martin Secker, 1933).

Brody, Alan, *The English Mummers and the Plays* (London: Routledge, 1971).

Bibliography

Bynner, Witter, *Journey with Genius: Recollections and Reflections Concerning the D.H. Lawrences* (New York: John Day, 1951).

Carlson, Susan, 'A Stormy Apprenticeship: Lawrence's Three Comedies', *DHL Review*, 14 (1981), 191–211.

Carlson, Susan, *Women of Grace: James's Plays and the Comedy of Manners* (Ann Arbor: UMI Research Press, 1985).

Carswell, Catherine, *The Savage Pilgrimage: A Narrative of D.H. Lawrence* (London: Chatto and Windus, 1932).

Carter, Philip, 'Lady Chatterley's Lover Trial', *Oxford Dictionary of National Biography*. Available online: http://www.oxforddnb.com/templates/theme-print.jsp?articleid=101234 [accessed 15 September 2014].

Cavallo, Pietro, 'Theatre Politics of the Mussolini Régime and their Influence on Fascist Drama', in *Fascism and Theatre*, ed. by Günter Berghaus (Providence: Berghahn, 1997), pp.113–132.

Chambers, Jessie, *D.H. Lawrence: A Personal Record by E.T.* (London: Frank Cass, 1935).

Chambers, Jessie and George Zytaruk, *D.H. Lawrence Review: The Collected Letters of Jessie Chambers: Volume 12 Numbers 1 and 2, Spring and Summer 1979* (Fayetteville: University of Arkansas, 1979).

Chaudhuri, Amit, *D.H. Lawrence and 'Difference'* (Oxford: Clarendon Press, 2003).

Chaudhuri, Una, *Staging Place: The Geography of Modern Drama* (Ann Arbor: University of Michigan Press, 1997).

Clark, L.D., 'Introduction', in Lawrence, *The Plumed Serpent*, ed. by L.D. Clark (Cambridge: Cambridge University Press, 1987), pp.xvii–xlvii.

Clarke, Ian, 'The Fight for Barbara: Lawrence's Society Drama', in *D.H. Lawrence in the Modern World*, ed. by Peter Preston and Peter Hoare (Houndmills: Macmillan, 1989), pp.47–68.

Clarke, Ian, 'Dialogue and Dialect in Lawrence's Colliery Plays', *The Journal of the D.H. Lawrence Society* (2001), 39–61.

Clemance, Clement, *The Theatre, Considered Chiefly in its Moral Aspects* (Nottingham: Burton, 1865).

Coleman, Marie, *The Irish Revolution, 1916–1923* (Oxford: Routledge, 2014).

Corke, Helen, 'The Writing of *The Trespasser*', *D.H. Lawrence Review*, 7:3 (1974), 227–239.

Craig, Edward Gordon, *Die Kunst des Theaters*, trans. by Maurice Magnus (Berlin: Seeman Nachfolger, 1905).

Craig, Edward Gordon [as 'John Balance'], 'A Note on Masks', *The Mask: The Journal of the Art of the Theatre*, 1:1 (1908), 9–12.

Craig, Edward Gordon, 'The Actor and the Übermarionette', *The Mask*, 1:2 (April 1908), 3–15.

Craig, Edward Gordon, *Index to the Story of My Days* (London: Hulton, 1957).

Davis, Mary E., *Ballets Russes Style: Diaghilev's Dancers and Paris Fashion* (London: Reaktion, 2010).

Debusscher, Gilbert, 'Creative Rewriting: European and American Influences on the Dramas of Tennessee Williams', in *The Cambridge Companion to Tennessee*

Williams, ed. by Matthew Roudané (Cambridge: Cambridge University Press, 1997), pp.167–188.

Denison, Patricia D., ed., *John Osborne: A Casebook* (New York: Routledge, 2007).

Doherty, Gerald, *Oriental Lawrence* (New York: Peter Lang, 2001).

Dollimore, Jonathan, *Sexual Dissidence: Augustine to Wilde, Freud to Foucault* (Oxford: Oxford University Press, 1991).

Draper, R.P., ed., *D.H. Lawrence: The Critical Heritage* (London: Routledge, 1997).

Eagleton, Terry, *The English Novel: An Introduction* (Oxford: Blackwell, 2005).

Ekman, Hans-Göran, 'Strindberg and Comedy', *The Cambridge Companion to August Strindberg*, ed. by Michael Robinson (Cambridge: Cambridge University Press, 2009), pp.70–78.

Eliot, T.S., 'London Letter', *Dial*, 73 (1922), 329–331.

Ellis, David, *D.H. Lawrence: Dying Game 1922–1930* (Cambridge: Cambridge University Press, 1998).

Ellmann, Richard, *James Joyce*, rev. edn (Oxford: Oxford University Press, 1983).

Elvery, Beatrice, *Today We Will Gossip* (London: Constable, 1964).

Eyre, Richard, *Talking Theatre: Interviews with Theatre People* (London: Nick Hern, 2009).

Farjeon, Herbert, *Friends* (London: Samuel French, 1923).

Fedder, Norman, *The Influence of D.H. Lawrence on Tennessee Williams* (London: Mouton, 1966).

Fernihough, Anne, 'Introduction', in D.H. Lawrence, *The Rainbow*, ed. by Mark Kinkead-Weekes (Harmondsworth: Penguin, 1995), pp.xiii–xxxiv.

Frazier, Adrian, *Behind the Scenes: Yeats, Horniman, and the Struggle for the Abbey Theatre* (Berkeley: University of California Press, 1990).

French, Philip, 'A Major Miner Dramatist', *New Statesman*, 22 March 1968, p.390.

Gardner, Viv, 'No Flirting with Philistinism: Shakespearean Production at Miss Horniman's Gaiety Theatre', *New Theatre Quarterly*, 14 (1998), 220–233.

Garnett, David, *The Golden Echo* (London: Chatto and Windus, 1953).

Garnett, Edward, *A Censured Play: The Breaking Point* (London: Duckworth, 1907).

Garnett, Edward, *The Trial of Jeanne d'Arc and Other Plays* (London: Cape, 1931).

Garnett, Richard, *The International Library of Famous Literature*, 20 vols (London: E. Lloyd, [1900]).

Goldoni, Carlo, *The Good-Humoured Ladies*, trans. by Richard Aldington (London: Beaumont, 1922).

Goldring, Douglas [as 'An Englishman'], *A Stranger in Ireland* (Dublin: Talbot Press, 1918).

Goldring, Douglas, 'Introduction', in Goldring, *The Fight for Freedom: A Play in Four Acts* (New York: Thomas Seltzer, 1920), pp.5–11.

Goldring, Douglas, *Odd Man Out: The Autobiography of a 'Propaganda Novelist'* (London: Chapman and Hall, 1936).

Goldring, Douglas, *The Nineteen Twenties: A General Survey and Some Personal Memories* (London: Nicholson & Watson, 1945).

[Gomme, Andor], 'Drama', *Times Literary Supplement*, 6 March 1969, p.253.

Bibliography

Greiff, Louis K., *D.H. Lawrence: Fifty Years on Film* (Carbondale: Southern Illinois University Press, 2001).

Harris, Frank, *Bernard Shaw* (London: Victor Gollancz, 1931).

Harrison, Andrew, 'Meat Lust: An Unpublished Manuscript by D.H. Lawrence', *Times Literary Supplement*, 29 March 2013, p.15.

Harrison, Jane Ellen, *Ancient Art and Ritual* (London: Thornton Butterworth, 1913).

Hauptmann, Gerhart, *The Dramatic Works of Gerhart Hauptmann: Volume Three*, ed. by Ludwig Lewisohn (New York: Huebsch, 1914).

Heilbrun, Carolyn G., *The Garnett Family* (London: George Allen & Unwin, 1961).

Hills, S.J., 'Frieda Lawrence', *The Times Literary Supplement*, 6 September 1985, p.975.

Hoggart, Richard, *The Uses of Literacy* (Harmondsworth: Penguin, 1969 [1957]).

Hopkin Hilton, Enid, *More Than One Life: A Nottinghamshire Childhood with D.H. Lawrence* (Phoenix Mill: Alan Sutton, 1993).

Houghton, Stanley, *Hindle Wakes* (London: Sidgwick and Jackson, 1919).

Houssaye, Arsène, *Man About Paris*, trans. by Henry W. Knepler (London: Gollancz, 1972).

Hunt, Violet, *The Flurried Years* (London: Hurst & Blackett, [1926]).

Hyde, Virginia Crosswhite, 'Introduction', in Lawrence, *Mornings in Mexico and Other Essays* (Cambridge: Cambridge University Press, 2009), pp.xxv–lxxxi.

Ibsen, Henrik, *Three Major Plays*, trans. by David Rudkin (London: Oberon, 2006).

Innes, Christopher, *Modern British Drama: The Twentieth Century* (Cambridge: Cambridge University Press, 2002).

Isaacs, Edith J.R., 'Introduction', in Edith J.R. Isaacs, *Theatre: Essays on the Arts of the Theatre* (New York: Books for Libraries Press, 1927), pp.vii–xviii.

Jefferson, George, *Edward Garnett: A Life in Literature* (London: Cape, 1982).

Jones, Owen, *Chavs: The Demonization of the Working Class*, rev. 2nd edn (London: Verso, 2012).

Jones, Susan, *Literature, Modernism and Dance* (Oxford: Oxford University Press, 2013).

Joyce, James, *Letters of James Joyce: Volume II*, ed. by Richard Ellmann (London: Faber, 1966).

Kane, Sarah, *Complete Plays* (London: Methuen, 2001).

Karasick, Norman M. and Dorothy K. Karasick, *The Oilman's Daughter: A Biography of Alice Barnsdall* (Encino: Carleston, 1993).

Kaufman, Julian M., 'A.H. Woods, Producer: A Thrill a Minute, A Laugh a Second!', in Arthur Gewirtz and James J. Kolb, eds, *Art, Glitter, and Glitz: Mainstream Playwrights and Popular Theatre in 1920s America* (Westport: Praeger, 2004), pp.209–216.

Kennedy, Dennis, *Granville Barker and the Dream of Theatre* (Cambridge: Cambridge University Press, 1985).

Kennedy, Dennis, ed., *The Oxford Encyclopedia of Theatre & Performance: Volume 2: M–Z* (Oxford: Oxford University Press, 2003).

Kermode, Frank, *Lawrence* (London: Fontana/Collins, 1973).

Kinkead-Weekes, Mark, *D.H. Lawrence: Triumph to Exile* (Cambridge: Cambridge University Press, 1996).

Kimber, Gerri, 'The Night of the Zeppelin', *Times Literary Supplement*, 5 September 2014, pp.14–15.

Knowlson, James, *Damned to Fame* (New York: Touchstone, 1997).

Krasner, David, *A History of Modern Drama: Volume I* (Oxford: Wiley Blackwell, 2012).

Law, Jonathan et al., eds, *Brewster's Theatre* (London: Cassell, 1994).

Lawrence, Ada and G. Stuart Gelder, *Young Lorenzo: Early Life of D.H. Lawrence* (New York: Russell & Russell, 1966).

Lawrence, D.H., *Sons and Lovers* (London: Duckworth, 1913).

Lawrence, D.H., *The Complete Plays of D.H. Lawrence* (London: Heinemann, 1965).

Lawrence, D.H., *The Letters of D.H. Lawrence*, ed. by James Boulton et al., 8 vols (Cambridge: Cambridge University Press, 1979–2001).

Lawrence, D.H., *The Lost Girl*, ed. by John Worthen (Cambridge: Cambridge University Press, 1981).

Lawrence, D.H., *The White Peacock*, ed. by Andrew Robertson (Cambridge: Cambridge University Press, 1983 [1911]).

Lawrence, D.H., *Love Among the Haystacks and Other Stories*, ed. by John Worthen (Cambridge: Cambridge University Press, 1987).

Lawrence, D.H., *The Plumed Serpent*, ed. by L.D. Clark (Cambridge: Cambridge University Press, 1987).

Lawrence, D.H., *Women in Love*, ed. by David Farmer (Cambridge: Cambridge University Press, 1987).

Lawrence, D.H., *Aaron's Rod*, ed. by Maria Kalnins (Cambridge: Cambridge University Press, 1988).

Lawrence, D.H., *The Rainbow*, ed. by Mark Kinkead-Weekes (Cambridge: Cambridge University Press, 1989).

Lawrence, D.H., *England, My England* (Cambridge: Cambridge University Press, 1990).

Lawrence, D.H., *Sons and Lovers*, ed. by Helen Baron and Carl Baron (Cambridge: Cambridge University Press, 1992).

Lawrence, D.H., *The Fox, The Captain's Doll, The Ladybird*, ed. by Dieter Mehl (Cambridge: Cambridge University Press, 1992).

Lawrence, D.H., *D.H. Lawrence: Complete Poems*, ed. by Vivian de Sola Pinto and F. Warren Roberts (Harmondsworth: Penguin, 1993 [1964]).

Lawrence, D.H., *Kangaroo*, ed. by Bruce Steele (Cambridge: Cambridge University Press, 1994).

Lawrence, D.H., *Twilight in Italy and Other Essays*, ed. by Paul Eggert (Cambridge: Cambridge University Press, 1994).

Lawrence, D.H., *The Women who Rode Away and Other Stories*, ed. by Dieter Mehl and Christa Jansohn (Cambridge: Cambridge University Press, 1995).

Lawrence, D.H., *Sea and Sardinia*, ed. by Mara Kalnins (Cambridge: Cambridge University Press, 1997).

Lawrence, D.H., *The First 'Women in Love'*, ed. by John Worthen and Lindeth Vasey (Cambridge: Cambridge University Press, 1998).

Bibliography

Lawrence, D.H., *The First and Second Lady Chatterley Novels*, ed. by Dieter Mehl and Christa Jansohn (Cambridge: Cambridge University Press, 1999).

Lawrence, D.H., *The Plays*, ed. by Hans-Wilhelm Schwarze and John Worthen (Cambridge: Cambridge University Press, 1999).

Lawrence, D.H., *Lady Chatterley's Lover and A Propos of 'Lady Chatterley's Lover'*, ed. by Michael Squires (Cambridge: Cambridge University Press, 2002).

Lawrence, D.H., *Studies in Classic American Literature*, ed. by Ezra Greenspan, Lindeth Vasey and John Worthen (Cambridge: Cambridge University Press, 2003).

Lawrence, D.H., *Late Essays and Articles*, ed. by James Boulton (Cambridge: Cambridge University Press, 2004).

Lawrence, D.H., *'Psychoanalysis and the Unconscious' and 'Fantasia of the Unconscious'*, ed. by Bruce Steele (Cambridge: Cambridge University Press, 2004).

Lawrence, D.H., *The Virgin and the Gypsy and Other Stories*, ed. by Michael Herbert, Bethan Jones and Lindeth Vasey (Cambridge: Cambridge University Press, 2005).

Lawrence, D.H., *Mornings in Mexico and Other Essays*, ed. by Virginia Crosswhite Hyde (Cambridge: Cambridge University Press, 2009).

Lawrence, D.H., *The Poems*, ed. by Christopher Pollnitz, 2 vols (Cambridge: Cambridge University Press, 2012).

Lawrence, Frieda, *'Not I, But the Wind'* (London: Heinemann, 1935).

Lawrence, Frieda, 'A Note by Frieda Lawrence', in Tennessee Williams, *I Rise in Flame, Cried the Phoenix* (Norfolk, Conn.: New Directions, 1951), p.8.

Lawrence, Frieda, *Frieda Lawrence: The Memoirs and Correspondence*, ed. by E.W. Tedlock (London: Heinemann, 1961).

Lawrence, Frieda, 'Lunch with Mr and Mrs Bernard Shaw', in *Frieda Lawrence: The Memoirs and Correspondence*, ed. by E.W. Tedlock (London: Heinemann, 1961), pp.147-148.

Le Bon, Gustave, *The Crowd* (New Brunswick: Transaction Publishers, 1995).

Leavis, F.R., 'Mr. Eliot and Lawrence', *Scrutiny*, 18:1 (1951), 66-73.

Leavis, F.R., 'Shaw against Lawrence', *Spectator*, 1 April 1955, pp.397-399.

Leavis, F.R., *D.H. Lawrence: Novelist* (London: Chatto and Windus, 1962 [1955]).

Leavis, F.R., *Thought, Words and Creativity: Art and Thought in Lawrence* (London: Chatto and Windus, 1976).

Lewis, Pericles, *The Cambridge Introduction to Modernism* (Cambridge: Cambridge University Press, 2007).

Lodge, David, *Lives in Writing: Essays* (London: Harvill Secker, 2014).

Longenbach, James, *Stone Cottage: Pound, Yeats, and Modernism* (Oxford: Oxford University Press, 1991).

Lowell, Amy, 'A Voice in Our Wilderness: D.H. Lawrence's Unheeded Message "to Blind Reactionaries and Fussy, Discontented Agitators"', *New York Times Book Review*, 22 August 1920, Section 3, p.7, reprinted in Lowell, *Poetry and Poets: Essays* (Boston and New York: Houghton Mifflin, 1930), pp.175-186.

Luhan, Mabel Dodge, *Lorenzo in Taos* (Santa Fe: Sunstone, 2007 [1932]).

MacCarthy, Desmond, *The Court Theatre* (London: A.H. Bullen, 1907).

MacCarthy, Desmond, 'A Poet's Realism', *New Statesman*, 18 December 1926, p.310.

Mackenzie, Compton, *My Life and Times: Octave 5, 1915–1923* (London: Chatto and Windus, 1966).

Maddox, Brenda, *D.H. Lawrence: The Story of a Marriage* (New York: Simon and Schuster, 1994).

Malani, Hiran, *D.H. Lawrence: A Study of His Plays* (New Delhi: Arnold-Heinemann, 1982).

Mansfield, Elizabeth, 'Introduction', in Lawrence, *The Trespasser*, ed. by Elizabeth Mansfield (Cambridge: Cambridge University Press, 1981), pp.1–40.

Mao, Douglas and Rebecca L. Walkowitz, 'The New Modernist Studies', *PMLA*, 123:3 (2008), 737–748.

Marinetti, F.T., *I Poeti Futuristi* (Milan: Edizione Futuristi di 'Poesia', 1912).

Marland, Michael, 'Introduction', in D.H. Lawrence, *The Widowing of Mrs Holroyd and The Daughter-in-Law* (London: Heinemann, 1968), xi–xxxvi.

Marx, Karl, 'Critique of the Gotha Programme', in *The First International and After: Political Writings Volume 3*, ed. by David Fernbach (London: Verso, 2010), pp.339–359.

McDonald, Jan, *The 'New Drama' 1900–1914* (Houndmills: Macmillan, 1986).

McGuinness, Patrick, *Maurice Maeterlinck and the Making of Modern Theatre* (Oxford: Oxford University Press, 2000).

Merkin, Ros, *Liverpool Playhouse: A Theatre and its City* (Liverpool: Liverpool University Press, 2011).

Merrild, Knud, *A Poet and Two Painters: A Memoir of D.H. Lawrence* (London: Routledge, 1938).

Meyers, Jeffrey, *D.H. Lawrence: A Biography* (New York: Cooper Square, 2002).

Millett, Kate, *Sexual Politics* (London: Virago, 1993).

Modiano, Marko, 'An Early Swedish Stage Production of D.H. Lawrence's *The Daughter-in-Law*', *D.H. Lawrence Review*, 17 (1984), 49–59.

Moi, Toril, *Henrik Ibsen and the Birth of Modernism* (Oxford: Oxford University Press, 2006).

Moore, Harry T., *The Priest of Love: A Life of D.H. Lawrence* (London: Heinemann, 1974).

Moran, James, 'Pound, Yeats, and the Regional Repertory Theatres', in *Regional Modernisms*, ed. by Neal Alexander and James Moran (Edinburgh: Edinburgh University Press, 2013), pp.83–103.

Moran, James, *The Theatre of Seán O'Casey* (London: Bloomsbury, 2013).

Morash, Chris and Shaun Richards, *Mapping Irish Theatre* (Cambridge: Cambridge University Press, 2013).

Muggeridge, Malcolm and Helen Corke, 'The Dreaming Woman', *The Listener*, 25 July 1968, 104–107.

Murry, John Middleton, *Between Two Worlds* (London: Cape, 1935).

Nehls, Edward, *D.H. Lawrence: A Composite Biography*, 3 vols (Madison: University of Wisconsin Press, 1958).

Bibliography

Neville, George, *A Memoir of D.H. Lawrence (The Betrayal)*, ed. by Carl Baron (Cambridge: Cambridge University Press, 1981).

Nightingale, Benedict, *Great Moments in the Theatre* (London: Oberon, 2012).

Norris, Barney, *To Bodies Gone: The Theatre of Peter Gill* (Bridgend: Seren, 2014).

O'Casey, Seán, 'A Miner's Dream of Home', *New Statesman*, 28 July 1934, p.124.

Pasler, Jann, 'Music and Spectacle in *Petrushka* and *The Rite of Spring*', in *Confronting Stravinsky*, ed. by Jann Pasler (Berkeley: University of California Press, 1986).

Patmore, Derek, 'A Child's Memories of D.H. Lawrence', in *A D.H. Lawrence Miscellany*, ed. by Harry T. Moore (Carbondale: Southern Illinois University Press, 1959), pp.134–136.

Payne, Iden, *A Life in a Wooden O: Memoirs of the Theatre* (New Haven: Yale University Press, 1977).

Percy, Esmé, 'Bernard Shaw: A Personal Memory', *The Listener*, 26 May 1955, pp.929–931.

Pittock, Malcolm, 'D.H. Lawrence: Dramatist?', *The Cambridge Quarterly*, 43:3 (2014), 256–272.

Purdom, C.B., *Harley Granville Barker* (London: Rockliff, 1955).

Rahimi, Atiq, *The Patience Stone*, trans. by Polly McLean (London: Vintage, 2011).

Razili, Seyed Mostafa, 'A Discussion with Shirin Maghanloo: D. H. Lawrence in Ninety Minutes'. Available at: http://soodaroo.blogfa.com/post/42 [accessed 15 August 2014].

Read, Jack, *Empires, Hippodromes & Palaces* (London: Alderman, 1985).

Roberts, Warren and Paul Poplawski, *A Bibliography of D.H. Lawrence*, 3rd edn (Cambridge: Cambridge University Press, 2001).

Robinson, Joanna, 'The Performance of Anti-Theatrical Prejudice in a Provincial Victorian Town', *Nineteenth Century Theatre and Film*, 35:2 (2008), 10–28.

Rosenthal, Amy, 'Lawrence the Playwright', in *The Widowing of Mrs Holroyd* theatre programme (London: Orange Tree, 2014), pp.8–9.

Ruderman, Judith, *Race and Identity in D.H. Lawrence* (Houndmills: Palgrave, 2014).

Sagar, Keith, 'D.H. Lawrence: Dramatist', *D.H. Lawrence Review*, 4:2 (1971), 154–182.

Sagar, Keith, *D.H. Lawrence: Life into Art* (Harmondsworth: Penguin, 1985).

Said, Edward, 'Foreword', in Ranajit Guha and Gayatri Chakravorty Spivak, eds, *Selected Subaltern Studies* (Oxford: Oxford University Press, 1988), pp.vi–vii.

Sale, Roger, *Modern Heroism: Essays on D.H. Lawrence, William Empson, & J.R.R. Tolkien* (Berkeley: University of California Press, 1973).

Salgādo, Gāmini, *D.H. Lawrence: 'Sons and Lovers': A Casebook* (London: Macmillan, 1969).

Salmon, Eric, *Granville Barker: A Secret Life* (London: Heinemann, 1983).

Schwarze, Hans-Wilhelm and John Worthen, 'Introduction', in D.H. Lawrence, *The Plays* (Cambridge: Cambridge University Press, 1999), pp.xxiii–cxxiv.

Seabrook, Jeremy, *Pauperland: Poverty and the Poor in Britain* (London: Hurst, 2014).

Shakespeare, William, *William Shakespeare: The Complete Works*, ed. by Stanley Wells et al. (Oxford: Clarendon Press, 1988).

Shaw, G.B., *The Quintessence of Ibsenism* (London: W. Scott, 1891).

Shaw, G.B., 'Mr. Bernard Shaw on D.H. Lawrence and "The Savage Pilgrimage"', *Time and Tide*, 6 August 1932, p.863.

Shaw, G.B., *Saint Joan*, ed. by Dan H. Laurence (Harmondsworth: Penguin, 1957).

Shaw, G.B., *The Complete Plays of Bernard Shaw* (London: Hamlyn, 1965).

Shaw, Leroy R., *The Playwright & Historical Change* (Madison: University of Wisconsin Press, 1970).

Sitwell, Osbert, *Laughter in the Next Room* (Boston: Little, Brown and Co, 1948).

Sklar, Sylvia, *The Plays of D.H. Lawrence: A Biographical and Critical Study* (London: Vision, 1975).

Spurling, Hilary, 'Old Folk at Home', *Spectator*, 22 March 1968, pp.378–379.

Steele, Bruce, 'Introduction', in *England, My England* (Cambridge: Cambridge University Press, 1990), pp.xix–li.

Stern, Ernst, *My Life, My Stage*, trans. by Edward Fitzgerald (London: Gollancz, 1951).

Stevens, Hugh, 'From Genesis to the *Ring*: Richard Wagner and D.H. Lawrence's *Rainbow*', *Textual Practice*, 2013, 1–20.

Storer, Richard, *F.R. Leavis* (Abingdon: Routledge, 2009).

Strindberg, August, *Miss Julie and Other Plays*, trans. by Michael Robinson (Oxford, Oxford University Press, 1998).

Styan, J.L., *Max Reinhardt* (Cambridge: Cambridge University Press, 1982).

Synge, J.M., *The Playboy of the Western World and Other Plays*, ed. by Ann Saddlemyer (Oxford: Oxford University Press, 1995).

Szondi, Peter, *Theory of the Modern Drama*, ed. and trans. by Michael Hays (Cambridge: Polity, 1987 [1956]).

Thacker, Andrew, ' "that trouble": Regional Modernism and "little magazines"', in *Regional Modernisms*, ed. by Neal Alexander and James Moran (Edinburgh: Edinburgh University Press, 2013), pp.22–43.

Thamer, Hans-Ulrich, 'The Orchestration of the National Community: The Nuremberg Party Rallies of the NSDAP', in *Fascism and Theatre*, ed. by Günter Berghaus (Providence and Oxford: Berghahn, 1997), pp.172–190.

Thomas, Jacqueline, 'Happy Days: Beckett's Rescript of Lady Chatterley's Lover', *Modern Drama*, 41:4 (1998), 623–634.

Thompson, Doug, 'The Organisation, Fascistisation and Management of Theatre in Italy, 1925–1943', in *Fascism and Theatre*, ed. by Günter Berghaus (Providence: Berghahn, 1997), pp.94–112.

Wallis, Mick and Simon Shepherd, *Studying Plays*, 3rd edn (London: Bloomsbury, 2010).

Waterman, Arthur, 'The Plays of D.H. Lawrence', *Modern Drama*, 2:4 (1959), 349–357.

Williams, Raymond, 'Introduction', in Lawrence, *Three Plays* (Harmondsworth: Penguin, 1969) pp.7–14.

Williams, Tennessee, *I Rise in Flame, Cried the Phoenix* (Norfolk: Conn.: New Directions, 1951).

Bibliography

Williams, Tennessee, *The Collected Poems of Tennessee Williams*, ed. by David Roessel and Nicholas Moschovakis, rev. edn (New York: New Directions, 2002).

Williams, Tennessee, *Tennessee Williams: Notebooks*, ed. by Margaret Bradham Thornton (New Haven, Conn.: Yale University Press, 2006).

Woods, Ralph Louis, ed., *A Second Treasury of the Familiar* (New York: Macmillan, 1950).

Worthen, John, *D.H. Lawrence: The Early Years 1885–1912* (Cambridge: Cambridge University Press, 1991).

Worthen, John, 'Towards a New Version of D.H. Lawrence's "The Daughter-in-Law": Scholarly Edition or Play Text?', *The Yearbook of English Studies*, 29 (1999), 231–246.

Worthen, John, 'Lawrence as Dramatist', in *The Cambridge Companion to D.H. Lawrence* (Cambridge: Cambridge University Press, 2001), pp.137–153.

Worthen, John, *D.H. Lawrence: The Life of an Outsider* (London: Allen Lane, 2005).

Worthen, John and Lindeth Vasey, 'Introduction', in Lawrence, *The First 'Women in Love'*, ed. by John Worthen and Lindeth Vasey (Cambridge: Cambridge University Press, 1998), pp.xvii–lv.

Yeats, W.B., *The Collected Works of W.B. Yeats: Volume II, The Plays*, ed. by David R. Clark and Rosalind E. Clark (New York: Scribner, 2001).

Newspaper sources

Daily Telegraph
Eastwood and Kimberley Advertiser
Era
Evening Standard
[Manchester] Guardian
Independent
Irish Times
Los Angeles Times
New York Times
Nottingham Daily Express
Nottingham Evening News
Nottingham Evening Post
Nottingham Guardian
Nottingham Journal
Observer
Outlook
Stage
Sunday Times
The Times

INDEX

Index

Index

Index